A POETRY PEDAGOGY FOR TEACHERS

Also available from Bloomsbury

Making Poetry Happen, *edited by Sue Dymoke, Myra Barrs, Andrew Lambirth and Anthony Wilson*

Making Poetry Matter, *edited by Sue Dymoke, Andrew Lambirth and Anthony Wilson*

Using Graphic Novels in the English Language Arts Classroom, *William Boerman-Cornell and Jung Kim*

Process Drama for Second Language Teaching and Learning, *Patrice Baldwin and Alicja Galazka*

Using Literature in English Language Education, *edited by Janice Bland*

Secondary English Teacher Education in the United States, *Donna L. Pasternak, Samantha Caughlan, Heidi L. Hallman, Laura Renzi and Leslie S. Rush*

A POETRY PEDAGOGY FOR TEACHERS

REORIENTING CLASSROOM LITERACY PRACTICES

Maya Pindyck and Ruth Vinz with

Diana Liu and Ashlynn Wittchow

BLOOMSBURY ACADEMIC
LONDON • NEW YORK • OXFORD • NEW DELHI • SYDNEY

BLOOMSBURY ACADEMIC
Bloomsbury Publishing Plc
50 Bedford Square, London, WC1B 3DP, UK
1385 Broadway, New York, NY 10018, USA
29 Earlsfort Terrace, Dublin 2, Ireland

BLOOMSBURY, BLOOMSBURY ACADEMIC and the Diana logo are trademarks of
Bloomsbury Publishing Plc

First published in Great Britain 2022

Cover design: Charlotte James
Cover images © "Ticket Series," Mixed Media, 2020 by Maya Pindyck

A catalogue record for this book is available from the British Library.

A catalog record for this book is available from the Library of Congress.

ISBN: HB: 978-1-3502-8539-2
PB: 978-1-3502-8538-5
ePDF: 978-1-3502-8541-5
eBook: 978-1-3502-8540-8

Typeset by Deanta Global Publishing Services, Chennai, India
Printed and bound in Great Britain

To find out more about our authors and books visit www.bloomsbury.com and
sign up for our newsletters.

For the teachers

CONTENTS

Contents

CREDITS

PREFACE

Wallace Stevens (1940) wrote in a letter to a friend: "people ought to like poetry the way a child likes snow" (p. 349). There are many reasons to like snow—the feel of crunch underfoot, snow days away from school, spreading our wings to make angels, snowflakes falling through an illuminated sky. And, there are reasons not to like snow—too cold, too deep, or inconvenient for driving. Truth is: how each of us thinks about snow is likely the result of how we have *experienced* snow, how we have come *to encounter* snow. The same could be said of our attitudes toward poetry.

As Tony Hoagland (2013) suggests, school experiences have something to do with our feelings about poetry: "Somehow we blew it. We never quite got poetry inside the American school system, and thus, never quite inside the culture.... Let us blame instead the stuffed shirts who took an hour to explain that poem in their classrooms, who chose it because it would *need* an explainer; pretentious ponderous ponderosas of professional professors will always be drawn to poems that require a priest" (p. 2). Hoagland is half right. Some teachers ruin poetry for students by telling them what a poem means or by encouraging them to *talk about* a poem before there is time *to be in and with* a poem. Schooled practices often emphasize that poems have predetermined meanings and a student reader's role is to demonstrate *the* meaning with specific evidence *from* the poem. The poem becomes a specimen for examination under the microscope of interpretive practices. Such an encounter may lead to discoveries but more often dulls how readers experience a poem. Even with the best of intentions, those of us who teach poetry may actually be doing a disservice to our students and to poetry. We disagree with Hoagland's proposition that the teacher is to blame, but we do believe that a teacher has key influences in shaping students' attitudes and experiences. Poet Billy Collins (1988) emphasizes Hoagland's point in his poem "Introduction to Poetry," where he reminds us not to "tie the poem to a chair with rope/and torture a confession out of it" (p. 58).

Poetry is not some object to insert inside a culture by a presumably competent "we." Culture is not readymade, waiting for the "right" poems and interpretive practices to enter. Culture continuously constructs anew as should conceptions and forms of poetry. *How* we come to read and write any text (in)forms our sense of cultural constructs with very real imprints on our bodies, minds, reading practices, and hearts. Unlike what Hoagland suggests, poetry is not a nationalistic promise or a humanistic remedy. We cannot talk about poetry as some saving grace (even if it does save lives) or as some uniquely empowering form because it is impossibly difficult, abstract, elitist, and inaccessible. Approaches to poetry can be reimagined and in ways that will open new conversations about, feelings toward, and desires for how poetry circulates within to inform and shape culture. Maybe "we blew it" as Hoagland writes, or, maybe, we need to explore how to blow new winds of life into our encounters with poetry. And, like dandelion puffs, caught in currents of air, disseminate a radial openness to encounter and engage with what poems make possible. This is inevitably a political act. As Jahan Ramazani (2009) reminds us, "decolonization is not only a political and military process but also an imaginative one—an enunciation of new possibilities and collectives, new names and identities, new structures of thought and feeling" (p. 162). We must continuously challenge and contribute to productions of culture and recognize the political implications of how and what we imagine as possible.

Experiences with poetry do not consist only of using a range of strategies to infer and interpret poems by identifying and commenting on the poet's purposes and viewpoints. Readers can lose the present-ness of a poem through these practices. We have learned as teacher/poets and poet/teachers that emphasis on interpretation can lead to tedious readings and set up a relationship with poems that seems counterproductive. What is produced out of many classroom practices is the demand for unequivocal, correct responses.

We conceive of reading and writing poems differently. The terms "teacher/poet" or "poet/teacher" suggest to us an embodiment—to make poetry and language *move* in enticing and sometimes ungraspable ways. We ask of ourselves and those whom we teach to carry with them curiosity, imagination, and a healthy hedonism for *more*— more approaches, more angles, and more poems. Read one poem and then another. Write one line, one stanza, and another. Do not *teach* poems—do not tear them down through analysis and explication. Or, in the wise words of Deleuze and Guattari (1987): "Don't bring out the General in you! Don't have just ideas, just have an idea (Godard). Have short-term ideas. Make maps, not photos or drawings. Be the Pink Panther and your loves will be like the wasp and the orchid, the cat and the baboon" (p. 25). In short, allow poetry to guide the teacher/poet in you.

It is the attitude of the Pink Panther we need to employ to make the space and time to wander, wonder, and invent multiple perspectives that will shape dynamic encounters with poetry. Poems have the potential to live vibrantly in our minds and bodies, inviting mystery and an un-harnessed awareness that something remarkable happens when we read and write poems. These beliefs in poetry's far-reaching capacities motivated us to write this book. Throughout, we explore how poems, in subtle, yet powerful, ways, are textual practices for re-engaging with the world by reorienting a pedagogy that emphasizes how to confront, see again, pause in the unknown and the familiar, and come to understand that poems not only express the world but also enable and perform the world through aesthetic, cultural, and ethical imaginaries.

Poems are everywhere—on subway cars, in our blood, and through that little rhyme, line, or image that haunts our dreams. Poems are always there (except not so much in schools and we wonder why not). Poems are in the wind, the sounds of ice cracking from a glacier, the gleam of fish scales in a shrinking lake, or the hum of bird's eggs. Poems are where they must be, altering and deepening our understanding of people, ecological systems, ideas, objects, and feelings.

How often do we glance up to see the moon at night? "Look at that moon," you might say to the person with you. Or, there might be a poem in that moon:

> The moon spills
>   its red glow
> between stars and an inky
>   night sky.

Seeing the moon against the night sky—a frequent occurrence. Held for a moment as a poem, this night sky urges us to pay attention to what might have gone unnoticed or unfelt. Part of what we want to emphasize here is that reading this poem requires no special knowledge, but it does require focus, an attentive awareness of a moment captured as a poem that can bring us closer to the commonplace as well as the elusive. A central pedagogical principle in our approach is: Read the poem; linger in the moment; direct and redirect attention toward what you notice, feel, and see and what brought you to that place by examining the intra-workings of the poem.

With these thoughts in mind, it seems only fitting to take a moment and read a poem.

> Your absence has gone through me
> Like thread through a needle.
> Everything I do is stitched with its color.

Read aloud. What do you notice? What stays with you? Sounds? Images?

The title of this poem is "Separation" by W. S. Merwin. *Separation*—give the word space and time. Now, to the poem again.

Separation

> Your absence has gone through me
> Like thread through a needle.
> Everything I do is stitched with its color.

Give this poem time to seep into your cell work, bones, and brain. Let it inhabit and haunt. Where does this poem go after it moves from the page and into your mind and body? What are your reactions and feelings? Are there events in your life that surface in response to your reading? Poems teeter on a tipping point between the explainable and unexplainable—they vibrate and hover there on the edge, and sometimes leave us incapable of rendering meaning by anything other than by seeing, hearing, or feeling the poem again. Creating a repertoire of strategies for ourselves and our students to slow down and linger in poems and focusing on notices, questions, and points of attention are primary first steps in facilitating reading practices with poetry.

After taking time to articulate initial reactions, we shift focus to how a poem activates and consolidates forms of attention. What resources of language and poetic devices bring us to the edge of experience, on the verge of knowing or feeling? Additionally, we consider the purposes for poetry in our lives, education, and public discourses. How might poems draw us into examinations of the world, exacting us into different forms of attention and awareness whether or not we are considering fog or frog, faces rigid or hands trembling, the smell of grief, or a fallen fruit inflecting a drought's persistence? In each chapter, we describe and exemplify modes of poetic attention that we hope you find generative for your personal encounters with poems and to inform your teaching practices. Together, these chapters articulate a geometries of attention that has the potential to reorient classroom literacy practices in order to encourage more imaginative and expansive encounters with poetry and foster a love for poetry.

Though most of our thinking in this book occurs through the medium of writing, we occasionally think with visual images: mixed-media works that Maya created from found sources. These visuals are not illustrative of any particular point, nor are they firmly attached to any singular concept. Instead, each visual is intended to invite a moment of pause and to open up loose forms of thinking, questioning, and connecting. Perhaps the visual works are a less namable geometry and a more visual form of attention—an angle through which a newly seen idea can be moved in ways that make thoughts possible.

ACKNOWLEDGMENTS

Our gratitude runs deep and wild, like a river—and, river-like, emerges from flows to pool and over-brim its banks.

Poems—you haunt us, walk with us, teach us, and chide us to keep learning and searching.

Poet-contributors: Ama Codjoe, Aracelis Girmay, Charles O. Hartman, Chloe Yelena Miller, Dan Chu, Geoff Babbitt, Hila Ratzabi, Jean Hartig, Jennie Panchy, Kamilah Aisha Moon (rest in love), Kaveh Bassiri, Melanie Maria Goodreaux, melissa christine goodrum, Rachel M. Simon, Rebecca Keith, Sarah Riggs, Suzanne Gardinier, Taije Silverman, Victoria Restler, Yesenia Guerra—thank you for offering your poems, responding to writing prompts, and sharing your brilliance with our readers. To students past, whose poems lurk in the recesses of memory and file cabinets—Rebecca, Stephen, Natasha, Wang Shu, Rosa, Max, Rashida, Irene—your words from long ago surge back, and we are reminded of your joy with poetry and bravery in your writing.

Maria Giovanna Brauzzi, believer in this book and wonderful editor, and your supportive team at Bloomsbury, including Anna Ellis and Nivethitha Tamilselvan: Thank you.

Diana Liu and Ashlynn Wittchow—keen readers, vital interlocutors, cite sleuths, and curators of a formidable wellspring of resources from which all of us will learn. You are teachers extraordinaire and your shared perspective and solidarity in the importance of teaching poetry in meaningful ways powered our will to complete this project.

We are grateful that our shared love of poetry and teaching now reach fruition in this book and remind us that this collaboration began in conversations at Teachers College, entangled in powerful moments of contemplation with our colleagues and friends in the English Education program.

Our students and teachers who are too many to name, thank you for all you taught us—your questions and musings, part of the long tradition of muses necessary in all our lives.

And, you, Wallace Stevens, guided our book with your "Thirteen Ways." We cannot imagine this particular articulation of teaching poetry without your words nudging us forward.

Dear families, you surround us with love and laughter and patience. Noa and Alma. Tyler. Trace, Jason, Katie, Stacie. Samantha, Tobias, Aidan, and Helena. Warren. To you and to the world family, let poetry run deep and wild in all our lives, like a river.

INTRODUCTION
POEMS AS PROVOCATEURS

Like every act of teaching and every poem ever written, this book is an assemblage—an assemblage of theories, teaching experiences, poetry practices, poems, metaphors, and images among other things. In each act of making—whether a poem, an invitation, or a lesson plan—we choose what we need to make our work as impactful as possible for you, our readers. As educators, our teaching assemblages are made of everyday decisions and materials: how much time to offer for free-write activities, when to insert group or collaborative work, which readings to assign and which passages to foreground, sketchbooks and/or laptops available for writing, how to arrange the desks and chairs in our classrooms, or how to center what our students bring to the class. In this fundamental sense, a poem is exactly the same: an assemblage of preexisting elements—words, spaces, silences, breaks, punctuation marks, voices, and paper—animated by readers who transact with it.

With each assemblage we create as readers, writers, and teachers of poetry, the aim is to impact the person who encounters it. We hope our students or readers will be moved by how we curate particular experiences, whether emphasizing ways to read poems, congeal a community of poets toward a common good, reflect on one's own relationship with nature, or fall in love with poetry. We never have control that any of these things will happen. We do, however, have creative powers to make a lesson, a poem, a book that puts thought/feeling[1] into action. Making a poem and educating a student both require a creative, intuitive mind—or, more precisely, an awakening of a mind that each of us already has accessed at point(s) in our life as readers and writers—and an understanding that the student/reader/writer is always a part of the assemblage, energizing it with an irreproducible life force.

Within this particular assemblage, this book titled *A Poetry Pedagogy for Teachers*, you will find overlaps, echoes, repetitions of, and expansions on previous ideas and practices. Each chapter does not necessarily offer a "new" idea but rather a distinct way of framing ongoing literacy practices with connected invitations to reorient oneself in relation to that practice. Another lens. Another perspective. Another way of languaging. You may find some of the chapters recursive, referring to practices introduced in previous

---

[1]It seems useful to mention that when we speak about thoughts and feelings in this book, we are speaking about one and the same thing. Our minds and bodies are not disconnected realities, as Cartesian thinking and correlating mechanistic views of the universe would have us believe, but mutually shaping relations. There is, of course, much more to be said about this that exceeds the scope and purpose of this book; we bring it up to situate our language in a belief system that sees the mind and body as one entangled situation.

chapters and/or riffing on previously stated ideas. This is an intentional part of the book's movement: a staggering, stuttering human effort to articulate a poetry pedagogy rooted in classroom experiences and possibilities, dedicated to teachers.

Attention as Poetic Praxis

"Let me have your attention, please!"
"All eyes on me!"
"Look at the blazing color in the sunset."
"Notice Sarah's wry smile."

Each of these commands is a call to attend to someone or something and encourages focused attention. The first two are calls to attend to the person speaking. The third directs attention toward the intensity of color. We might see something quite different in Sarah's smile than what another person saw as wry, but the command directs our attention toward the characteristics of the smile. These examples highlight how attention can be directed through language. We also know that whether or not we attend as requested will depend on our interest, curiosity, and how capable we are at intervals of attention. Just how do poems garner attention, and, if we explore the resources of attention-getting and making, what might we learn about reading, writing, and teaching poems?

Perhaps the following definitions of attention are indicative of the impulses behind poetic devices used to capture attention: *applying the mind to something; a condition of readiness; consciousness; notice; awareness; ability to focus; sustaining focus and shifting it at will; interest; scrutiny; absorption; contemplation; deliberation; diligence; engrossment; immersion; intentness; enthrallment; musing; alertness; raptness; pondering; recognition; decorum.*

The word "attention" is a living contradiction, working in both symbiotic and disruptive relation to all its definitions and uses. "Attention" summons protocols, rules, order—a militaristic mandate, even, to be "at attention," alert, erect, and facing the teacher at the front of the classroom. The word purrs at the part of us clinging to politeness and civility. Concerning the reading and writing of poetry, attention might suggest a close reading in which all bodies face the same direction, with each reader positioned in similar ways toward a better interpretation. A shared reading, intact, orderly, and measurable thrives under a teacher's attention.

At the same time, focused attention might open deep contemplation as Rilke (1914/1982) urges: "Go now and do the heart-work on the images imprisoned inside you" (pp. 133–5). Something spurs the mind and heart to attend. This does not happen in isolation, though it often happens in solitude. Our distinct ways of attending are always in relation to other bodies: human and more-than-human, textual and sonic, or visual and verbal. In this sense, attention is a space to ponder with/in an encounter ripe with material. Attending causes us to linger and notice something more and differently:

- There is nothing romantic about attention.
- Attention makes space and time to ponder, reflect, and do the heart-work.
- When I give my full attention, I lose myself and find an image, a song, a texture.

Cultivating a geometries of attention, then, is a central premise of our pedagogy. Attention is also restless. Shifting. Not easily satisfied. Poems are provocateurs and attention seekers. Poems lean in and shift our attention.

Exercising Your Attention

If you learn that over 10,000 known types of mushrooms have been identified by mycologists, where is your attention drawn? What curiosities? What questions? If we suggest that mycologists suspect this is only a fraction of mushrooms that exist, does your attention become more focused, more complex, more or less localized? Further, if we suggest there are various species of mushrooms, how will this orient your attention? We could go on and name the species: saprotrophic, mycorrhizal, parasitic, and endophytic. What we want to emphasize here is not only different modes of attention but also the movement or shifts of attention that focus on an experience. Why do we each notice certain things and not others? If we begin to notice how our attention shapes and shifts as we read poems, this is a way of understanding what the poem provokes in us.

We have come to believe that there are habits of attention with which we grow so familiar that they are habitualized. We attend to people, pets, world events, and the weather often without thought. We pay attention to our car keys only when we cannot find them. It may take a poem-as-provocateur to remind us to pay attention to the skin of earth or ripples in the oceans, the rhythms of moon and sun, or clouds passing across continents. Poems nudge us to pay attention to possibilities that the schoolhouse of the world serves as a conduit for ideas, awakenings, imaginings, cultural practices, and generative futures. From this perch of restlessness and uncertainty, poems and poets seem equipped to serve as provocateurs rather than as conveyors of ideas and information.

Did your attention wane from mushrooms while you were reading the previous paragraph? You see the problem and the possibility with attention? It is now our responsibility to bring you back to mushrooms.

quick awakening
edible food or fatal
aroma of Earth

What holds, sustains, or shifts your attention when you encounter this haiku by teacher and poet Yesenia Guerra? Is there a place that peaks your attention? The experience of reading this poem, even one as simple as haiku, will undoubtedly differ for each of us. How and where does this haiku gather, orient, and shape your attention?

Let your attention nestle for a moment in the visual layout of this "mushroom" haiku: three lines of alternating lengths and surrounding blank space. Pay attention to how the length and break of a line create speed and/or slowness, and how the poem as a whole (perhaps the duration of a single, deep breath) affects movement in time. Notice that all our questions explore the dialogic between where your attention is drawn (where did you attend?) and our prompts to attend (visual layout, length and break, duration). We avoid asking what you think the poem *means*. We fear the hunt for meaning truncates the exploration and surprise that a poem activates through its drifting, associating, and linking various points of attention.

In a State of Perpetual Provocation

Wallace Stevens's (1954) poem "Thirteen Ways of Looking at a Blackbird" was our provocateur and became the spine and organizing force for this book. His thirteen-stanza poem is a metaphor on provocation and perspective. Our readings and rereadings of his poem, as we were grappling with the best ways to share our pedagogical beliefs about poetry and the importance of teachers' immersion into reading and writing of poetry themselves, challenged us to push beyond the boundaries of what we know, invited us to see further than we anticipated, and to invent for ourselves thirteen ways of attending to poems that provide the principles of our pedagogical beliefs. And, we are still basking in this poem's provocations.

We don't want to keep you any longer from reading—either coming to this poem for the first time or rereading it.

Thirteen Ways of Looking at a Blackbird

I
Among twenty snowy mountains,
The only moving thing
Was the eye of the blackbird.

II
I was of three minds,
Like a tree
In which there are three blackbirds.

III
The blackbird whirled in the autumn winds.
It was a small part of the pantomime.

IV
A man and a woman
Are one.

A man and a woman and a blackbird
Are one.

V
I do not know which to prefer,
The beauty of inflections
Or the beauty of innuendoes,
The blackbird whistling
Or just after.

VI
Icicles filled the long window
With barbaric glass.
The shadow of the blackbird
Crossed it, to and fro.
The mood
Traced in the shadow
An indecipherable cause.

VII
O thin men of Haddam,
Why do you imagine golden birds?
Do you not see how the blackbird
Walks around the feet
Of the women about you?

VIII
I know noble accents
And lucid, inescapable rhythms;
But I know, too,
That the blackbird is involved
In what I know.

IX
When the blackbird flew out of sight,
It marked the edge
Of one of many circles.

X
At the sight of blackbirds
Flying in a green light,
Even the bawds of euphony
Would cry out sharply.

XI
He rode over Connecticut
In a glass coach.
Once, a fear pierced him,
In that he mistook
The shadow of his equipage
For blackbirds.

XII
The river is moving.
The blackbird must be flying.

XIII
It was evening all afternoon.
It was snowing
And it was going to snow.
The blackbird sat
In the cedar-limbs.

Read the poem a second time. Let the words and images seep in. Take time to capture your mind's churnings—shifting images, vanishing points, words that linger. Questions? You might want to have a notebook where you record fragments, incomplete thoughts, questions, or visual notes as you continue to read this book as well as drafts of poems and ideas for teaching.

IF we continue with the principle of poems as provocateurs, where does Stevens's poem focus your attention? What resonates and stays with you? How does your attention move and shift as you read each stanza? What remains out of reach in your understanding? These questions might feel different from the commonsense approaches to poetry in classrooms where the intention is to search out answers to the question: What does this poem mean? We value time to articulate our minds' muddle and search out poems that take us into thoughts and emotions we might never fully understand or be able to explain. What if the poem is a moment created—to just let it "be" and to resonate with and within us? What if the poem moves with us, becoming anew each time we think of it or read it again?

Imagine that a poem is an invitation and invention, filled with the possibility for experiencing, sensing, feeling, and yes, welcoming you to play with *indeterminacy*. What are reading practices that might enliven and enable readings other than those we have most often learned in school? Reorienting practices that counter the current logics of interpretation lead readers to consider a kind of inquiry that requires their participation in and with the poem. We asked several colleagues to read Stevens's poems and here are a few of their responses. One reader told us: "I started thinking about the idea that perceptual experience is associated with an openness to look at one thing intently." Another said: "Each stanza carries me to a different place but the blackbird is the constant. That stays with me." A third moved into writing: "I decided to try to see the first hour of my day in thirteen ways." And a fourth reader questioned: "Have you ever had the feeling that you just skim the surface of things because of your habitual ways of seeing? I feel like my body moves into this poem. I'm inside something like a glass paperweight looking at life from the inside out." And a final reader noted: "I just don't see the associations in a logical way; it's like the logic is in my bones." As these readers demonstrate, the network of indeterminacies opens spaces for diverse responses. And the restless mind is provoked by the poem and by the types of questions, attentions, or activities that "frame" each response.

In her reflection titled "Theory Like Poetry," scholar Jen Weiss (2008) writes, "I do not expect an answer to a problem when I read a poem; but I hope to find a new way of looking at something that I have been staring at for a long time" (p. 76). Just as Stevens keeps the focus on a blackbird in order to see it in these various ways, we, too, view acts of looking at (or being with) a poem in multiple ways as an exercise in finding new perspectives. Reading slowly, rereading, returning to a word or a line or a stanza, mouthing a line aloud, feeling the words across the teeth, helps us to see—and to feel—a poem anew. This way of reading demands patience and alertness to whatever might unfold. Instead of following a school logic grounded in meaning and analysis, we invite you, our readers, to follow what Gilles Deleuze (1969/1990) calls "the logic of sense"—an attention to those sensations a poem triggers, impossible to pin down or ever fully know (p. 20). The challenge then is to enter the invention of a poem and not attempt to make it too familiar by overinterpretation. Stevens offers an example of the mind-in-motion in his poem, providing glimpses through each stanza of refracted spectral images, each stanza shifting, changing, recombining to change again and again. As readers, we move with Stevens's stanzas, circling in and out of a fragmented sense of "blackbird," and we are left changed, somehow. What we aim to do in this book mirrors what we think Stevens accomplishes in this poem—offering a pedagogy that continuously reorients our perspectives on how to experience poems through shifting modes of attention.

PART I

CHAPTER 1
LET THE POEM DO THE TEACHING

I
Among twenty snowy mountains,
The only moving thing
Was the eye of the blackbird.

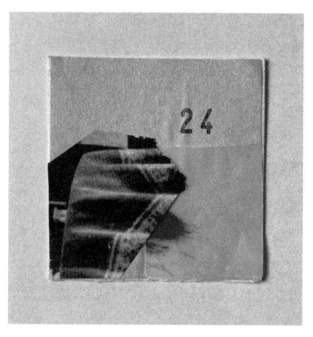

Stillness in proximity with movement; snowy mountains juxtaposed with a blackbird—how do these three lines work together to direct and shape attention?

To be *in* and *with* a poem requires some *lingering* through rereading, pausing, visualizing, gazing. Take a moment to read the stanza aloud. Let the sensations, words, images, and sounds travel through your body and find refuge there. Invite the stanza *in*. Hang on the edges of meaning—between what you understand and what seems just out of reach. Resist the temptation to speak *about* the stanza. Let it be *in* and *with* you.

Where do you find yourself? Maybe snowy mountains come into view. What stays with you, hovers in your mind's-eye? Note the surprise—the startling quick zoom to the eye of the blackbird. Is the eye the only moving thing?

A bird's eye is anatomically incapable of movement. Does it matter if we know this fact or not? Who would ever imagine we could literally capture the eye of the blackbird against the vastness of twenty mountains? We will each come to the scene differently—maybe in puzzlement, perhaps in surprise, or momentarily caught in an image or memory, or ready to go on to the next stanza. For now, pause and read this stanza again:

> Among twenty snowy mountains,
> The only moving thing
> Was the eye of the blackbird.

Let the stanza *in, in-side* you. Let the stanza just "be" for a moment. The stanza isn't going anywhere. Observe where your attention is directed and how it moves or shifts. *Slow* the reading.

As we suggested earlier, various theories of reading and subsequent pedagogies have led to interpretive practices that inform the ways we have not only been taught to read poetry but also how these conventions have informed how poems are produced. Such interpretive practices, we argue, influence social attitudes toward poetry and shape critical taste. These practices may get in the way of our encounters with a poem's generative spaces, and our intention is to demonstrate ways to decrease or dissolve the distances between reader and poem.

Let the Force of the Poem Speak

Various practices of literary textual study and criticism have taught us *to direct* our attention in particular ways. Consider your own experiences with reading poetry in school. You might have been asked to look for images, figurative language, symbols, or to notice rhythm or rhyme schemes. If you focused on these particulars often enough, you likely developed habitual ways of attending. What experiences with a poem may be lost with these approaches as we carry these interpretive practices with us as reading habits? If the end goal of reading a poem is to be able to state what it means or to write an interpretation of its meaning (justifying, of course, with quotes *to prove* how it does so) then we must ask: What is the purpose of reading a poem? Interpretation is *one form* of response. What is lost when schooled practices become our habitual way of reading and interfere with how we might understand and experience the creative possibilities of poetry to help us live our lives with fuller awareness?

Let the poem do its work *with* you. What does it mean to read a poem, to let it *whisper-teach* you to attend to aspects of the world in new and different ways? Is it possible to linger to *give into* the poem?

> Among twenty snowy mountains,
> The only moving thing
> Was the eye of the blackbird.

What might it mean to follow a poem's moves/moving, allowing the poem itself to have authority in holding your attention in a time-space field of its own? Poems may startle us awake or make us feel alive in memory, image, or idea. Do we always care to know why? Sometimes it is just enough *to be* with the poem.

Principles of Attention-Making *with* Poem as Guide

The *obvious and ordinary* are hardly noticeable in the stream of stimuli we encounter in our everyday lives. And, then, suddenly an image, sound, or voice demands our attention. *What do poems teach us about the principles and practices of poetic attention?* Begin with the simple idea of receptivity—a poem *is* both a medium and a material of attention-making. Once there is receptivity to reading a poem or writing one, attention must be paid. How the poem gathers attention is an intricate dance between reader, writer, and the shaping tools, materials, and structures of language that compose a *poem-as-text* into a spatial-temporal presence of attention. The poem itself, like the eye of the blackbird in Stevens's first stanza, moves the mind and the body to attention just beyond the edge of meaning, shimmering to stay dynamic even as the words fall away from the page. Notice how a poem is breathing, sighing, laughing, pulsing, tuning—all together to orient attention, which, of course, leads us back to the poem itself.

Resist the Expert Conjecture: Let the POEM Be with You

Poet Bill Stafford (1998) believed that ordinary language has a secret code, an unspoken tongue beneath words (p. 29). If we accept Stafford's conjecture, it makes it nearly impossible to reduce a poem into an explication, summarize its constituent parts, or find it necessary to track down and sniff out *meaning*. The experience of reading a poem may generate feelings of incompleteness or discontent as we wrestle with the desire to "solve" what we do not understand. Some of this results from schooled practices where we are taught that the purpose of reading poems was to figure out what the poem or poet means. But, if a poem lurks on unspoken edges—more than is evident in the grammars of image, rhythm, figurative language, or any other crafting architectures—then we might suggest that the poem leads us *back to the poem itself.*

We realize it is easier to talk about these ideas than to demonstrate them through an encounter with a poem. Let's take a moment to think this through with James Wright's (1992) poem:

The Jewel

There is this cave
In the air behind my body
That nobody is going to touch:
A cloister, a silence

> Closing around a blossom of fire.
> When I stand upright in the wind,
> My bones turn to dark emeralds.

Take time to notice, question, reread in ways that are satisfying to you. Any images, lines that linger? What do you experience in reading this poem? We find it helpful to share how others respond, so here is Ruth's commentary on reading this poem for the first time, trying to follow our own advice of letting the poem *be with* her as reader:

> I read the poem silently, then aloud. I lingered on the last two lines. The temptation was strong to turn my mind to puzzling out meaning, but I wanted to feel its unspoken-ness. I needed to keep the poem in my mind and body, vibrating off my tongue. Wright sets my mind awhirl with places to attend—cave, air, cloister, blossom of fire, dark emeralds. One of the ways I hold a poem close is to say a line or lines over and over until they are deep in my body, in the very cellwork. For me, the last two lines have staying power: "When I stand upright in the wind,/My bones turn to dark emeralds." For someone else it is probably other lines. I read Wright's final lines over and again and felt an urgency to write. Here is the result: *A cheerful thunder begins and then rain. The rain deepens. It rolls off the porch roof. The black earth turns blacker, absorbs the needles of rain without a groan. The sky is low and bones turn to coal or diamonds. The hum of sky and birds' eggs.*

And I am reminded that a simple line of a poem has the potential—to what? Set the mind awhirl—to remove us from isolation as we reach toward others. And then, I move into writing again. And, just now, on the edge of these words and images and sounds I found *with* Wright, I start a poem of my own.

> Black earth turns blacker
>
> absorbing needles of rain
>
> without a groan and ink deepens
> the sky against a moan of thunder.
>
> Poppies fall to their knees
> in a swerve of wind. Floating
> above, every gathered song of birds
> hums the trees awake

You see the idea? We travel in the company of poems and poets and learn with and from them ways to prompt our own seeing and saying in the world. A poem is more than a text to be explicated, to be tamed into a stated meaning. The poem *is* its meaning and experience for each reader. Poems are one way we explore together, as Tess Gallagher (1986) writes, the feelings, imaginings, and experiences we have in ways that work "against the taxidermy of logic" (p. 83). We emphasize in our teaching this communion with poems and encourage our students to write poems in response to poems as a way of reorienting interpretive practices focused on explication of poems.

Emphasize Connectedness and Intimacy with a Poem

Poems bring to light unexpected revelations, intimacies, and awarenesses toward life. We believe the purpose of poetry education is to engage students in creative possibilities, encounters with the imagined, and peak their curiosities about the world in which they live. This requires us to risk opening our hearts and bodies to the intimate relationship between poems and ourselves. How might this relationship be encouraged for our students as well? We believe that finding ways to bring readers *closer* to poems is the starting point.

Let's take haiku as an example. Haiku is a traditional Japanese form often taught in schools. An introduction to haiku usually includes a definition of form first: three lines with five syllables in the first line, seven in the second, and five in the third. A typical teaching sequence might follow by naming the subject matter of haikus; that is, a haiku is most often written about nature in its seasonal expression. Next, try writing one. Yes, try one. Where to start? Something in nature? Now, describe a tree branch in three lines and in words that meet the syllabic count?

The problem here is that we are working first from the logic of *definition and form*. What happened to the branch, to its relationship to what surrounds or is part of it, or to what the viewer/poet notices or feels? Why this branch or a branch at all?

Let's begin again. This time let's start by reading a haiku by Matsuo Basho (1688) rather than providing a definition of haiku by form and content.

[I come weary]

I come weary,
In search of an inn—
Ah! These wisteria flowers!

Be with the poem and the poet in this moment. Feel with and through the words, ideas, and images. What feelings or experiences linger? Ask yourself this question: What is the effect of brevity in three lines? This focus on three lines may remind us of the first stanza of Stevens's poem. How does the brevity affect each, both?

To answer the question on the effect of brevity, move from reading to writing. Take a moment to look away from this page to your surroundings. Scan. Gaze. What draws your attention? Write down a phrase to describe what you see.

Clouds blow the moon dark

Now, close your eyes. Let your mind's eye make the next move. Try to capture where your mind moves in another phrase.

Fireflies glimmer like lanterns

Once more. Close your eyes. Where does your mind take you?

Steady and clear

An Invitation

For a few days, commit to a daily practice of making time to pause, paying attention to what surrounds you. Record in three brief phrases, one built on the other, as demonstrated earlier. At the same time read haiku. Find traditional ones from Basho, Issa, Buson, and Shiki. See how these migrate and mutate over time and place. Ezra Pound's "In a Station of the Metro" or Richard Brautigan's "Haiku Ambulance" suggests how individual poets have participated in derivations of haiku that contribute to their practices in attuning and attending to the world around them.

After this preliminary preparation in reading and writing, take a closer look at the effects of how haiku reaches for the "ah-ha-ness." Consider how brevity, form, and language work together to create this compressed encounter. Choose parts of the week's writing and from your jottings create haikus. Only then might you better understand how the form shapes thought and controls language. By observing, reading haikus, and writing them, you will find it much easier to answer this question than if you were working from definition: What is the effect of a haiku? Writing haiku may be the most poignant way to learn about the form and effect of haiku.

We recommend reading Kwame Dawes's essay "And What of the Haiku?" (2007) published on the *Poetry Foundation*'s website and reflecting on his claim that, as an American devoted to the writing of haiku, "I will always come to haiku as a stranger—as a tourist hanging out with the form and constantly aware that I must come to these forms with reverence and with the posture of one who is a guest, eating at someone else's table." Dawes embraces the collaborative renga form, or writing haiku with other poets, as a way "to really study the insides of western poetry largely because there is something about the haiku that runs counter to the typical western instinct in poetry." Consider how studying and being with a non-Western form can influence our literary instincts as (Western) readers and writers. How might the posture of arriving as a guest at someone else's table orient our relationship to a poetic form? What forms of care and respect might that approach cultivate? For Dawes, this recognition does not prevent him from continuing to write haiku. Quite the opposite, he is dedicated to trying out, studying, and working the form to the best of his ability.

If we only read poems through a limited range of strategies—to identify a poet's purposes and viewpoints—what intimate and experiential connections to the poems and the poets might be lost? Our Invitation was intended to involve you intimately in reading and writing haiku as a way of understanding haiku. There are not five strategies, a checklist of figures of speech, or ways to explicate a poem that will lead to effective reading any more than there is one way to experience a song, a sculpture or a photograph.

And yet, through a long history of schooled interpretive practices, we have come to a commonsense understanding of poetry that may limit our encounters and the ways we employ our attention to poems.

As Louise Rosenblatt's (1964) conception of the poem-as-event reminds us, an aesthetic stance enables us to have an in-the-moment experience and intimacy. Poems are written out of some deep need, intuition, and intention to wonder, notice, console, or point to the unusual and the difficult. How do we come to feel a poem, viscerally, as we write or read one? The poem does the teaching. Hold on to this moment.

Avoid the HUNT for Literary Devices. Let Them Find YOU

This discussion and the work of dwelling with haiku lead us to make this point directly, and we hope persuasively. Let literary devices and forms find you. Let them seep into the meaning as you read without assuming these are the keys to unlock some puzzle that is supposed to be the meaning of a poem either in reading or in writing. If we allow figures of speech and other devices to work indirectly, becoming part of *a way of* expressing rather than being identified for the sake of finding and naming them, then what? Consider this question: To what effect is a literary device employed?

Take a few minutes to read Robert Frost's (1920) "Fire and Ice," and allow the poem *to be* with you:

Fire and Ice

Some say the world will end in fire,
Some say in ice.
From what I've tasted of desire
I hold with those who favor fire.
But if it had to perish twice,
I think I know enough of hate
To say that for destruction ice
Is also great
And would suffice.

Linger for a moment longer. Where is your attention concentrated? What stays with you? Words, sounds, an image, the beat of rhyme or what? Read the poem again. What lingers? Work *with* Frost. The poem influences what you notice, but you are a partner in the making. Suddenly, you *see:* not *things as they are* but the less obvious spaces of *what might be*? Here is a central question: How far do we push questions or explanations before we *lose* the impact of experiencing the poem?

Think of Poems as Voyages of Discovery

Imagine for a moment: What might it be like to go inside a stone? We suspect this might not be something you would ask or question often in your daily lives. But, the poet

Charles Simic (1971) considers this, draws us into a journey of us-in-stone through his poem "Stone."

Stone

Go inside a stone
That would be my way.
Let somebody else become a dove
Or gnash with a tiger's tooth.
I am happy to be a stone.

From the outside the stone is a riddle:
No one knows how to answer it.
Yet within, it must be cool and quiet
Even though a cow steps on it full weight,
Even though a child throws it in a river;
The stone sinks, slow, unperturbed
To the river bottom
Where the fishes come to knock on it
And listen.

I have seen sparks fly out
When two stones are rubbed,
So perhaps it is not dark inside after all;
Perhaps there is a moon shining
From somewhere, as though behind a hill—
Just enough light to make out
The strange writings, the star-charts
On the inner walls.

What would it be like to live inside a stone? How might you describe this? First graders were asked the same question. A series of quick responses from the imaginative six-year-olds:

Dark, oh, so dark you can't see your breath.
Cold like shivery.
Hard to crack out.
I'll need snacks inside?
It would always be dark.
Is there room for my Mom?

It seems everyone, including Simic, might have a version. You might want to create a version of your own.

After reading Simic's poem, I thought about taking an object and asking students to go inside that object, to wander its inner walls or its imagined middle. As with a six-year-olds, I wonder if there is a slant of light, the shiver of cold. Conjuring up questions, my imagination is set awhirl again. Suddenly I'm there in the stone, and I can feel the dew of morning on my porous outside. Or, maybe I start rolling down a steep hill, tumbling over and not feeling the thud as I hit one boulder after another in my free fall. And, because Simic led me on this little riff I carry strange writings, star-charts, and the mystery of caves and cave painting. Yes, and you, dear reader, are you now considering your own possibilities, tumbling in different directions?

Talk with the Poem Rather than about It

To be *in* and *with* a poem requires some *lingering* through rereading, pausing, visualizing, or gazing. Choose a poem either from these opening chapters or one you would like to read or reread. Take time to read and reread. Make notes on any changes in focused attention or questions, notices, or reactions through the multiple readings. If possible, locate a recording of the poet reading. Explore where a poem takes you by mapping or drawing your journey through it. What happens when you set the poem aside? Write an additional stanza to be in conversation with other stanzas in the poem. Write a poem to talk back to or be in conversation with the experience of a poem. In these ways, we, as readers, can center on what is drawing or demanding our attention. What a remarkable mystery it is—animated by how words and sounds and blank spaces work together through the crafting—that a poem can nurture our capacities to imagine, to care, to feel empathy, and, yes, again to set the imagination awhirl.

CHAPTER 2
SPEAKER, WRITER, AND READER AS MULTIPLICITIES

II
I was of three minds,
Like a tree
In which there are three blackbirds.

As Walt Whitman (1892) famously writes in the fifty-first section of his poem "Song of Myself," "I contain multitudes"—we feel this truth (p. 29). We *are* expansive beings, encompassing vibrant contradictions. Each "I" is filled with multiple, shifting experiences, beliefs, and possibilities. Today I am of at least three minds.

Since we do indeed contain multitudes, then what to make of the Enlightenment notion of an essential, rational *I* who possesses one authentic voice? This idea of a signature "I" persists in writing workshops, surfacing in the common assumption that each person possesses a singular written "voice": an emanating expression of the poet's "true" self. If I contain multitudes, why am I presumed to have just one voice? In other words, what is this authentic "voice" that I am thought to express and that I am told defines my writing?

Often when we make the suggestion to students, student teachers, or teachers to experiment with poetry (its craft, intentions, expressions) *by* writing poems, that wide-eyed, unblinking gaze comes back at us with comments like:

"It is so personal. SO private."
"I feel I'm exposed and stand naked."
"Sharing what I write is, well, so risky."

We see confidence leaking away and something slowly seeping into its place. If we provoke conversations about why students see writing poetry as exposing themselves, revealing the private or risking telling too much about themselves, it always leads to "voice." That's it. That's all. A poem exposes the *voice* of the poet.

"I'm not sure I've developed a strong voice."
"My voice sounds unsure and too emotional."

Even before starting to write, "voice" has won the battle of confidence.

We are coming to think that "voice" is a misplaced idea—voice as a spotlight placed on the poet/writer *as* speaker of the poem, and voice as what defines a writer's style. In response to the first idea, there can be some confusion between a poet and the speaker of the poem (persona). Remember the dictum: The poet is *not necessarily* the speaker/persona of the poem. Problem is: When we write a poem and then share it with others, that dictum fades and what is left is the poet and her/his/their voice joined together as a single representative of meaning and the emotional tenor of the poem. The aesthetic that drives poetry can get entangled with becoming conscious of common assumptions of self-representation.

We wonder: Who is the "I" speaking in or through a poem? Or, more precisely, what is a poem's relationship to this "I" who writes particular words using a particular voice? One widespread misconception prominent in classrooms is that poetry functions as a direct expression of some singular, "authentic" voice. Teachers often approach poetry as a conduit for self-expression or confession—a chance to access and "free" some signifying voice as a way to liberate or empower what has come to be accepted as a student's "true" voice. Through poetry, the student is imagined to somehow confess, or at least express, an authentic self.

However, as Cathy Park Hong (2006) shows in her essay "How Words Fail," this understanding of poetry is a crock of—well, a crockpot of well-intentioned, but narrow, visions of the speaking subject as a self-reflecting mirror:

"Finding your voice" is a familiar workshop trope, one that assumes poetry is an expression of an authentic self. I was asked to write in natural, plainspoken speech (none of which felt natural or plain to me), and this teacher mistook the result as me. He embraced the principle that a poem represents a person who is a unified whole, and that the syntax of the poem is a window to the person's, or writer's, mind. The professor's assumptions proved only that I was a damn good mimic.

–Cathy Park Hong, "How Words Fail," Poetry Foundation Online, 2006

Similarly, in a 2014 interview with *NEA Arts Magazine*, Toni Morrison reflects on her advice to her writing students to write about what they don't know. Morrison prompts her students to try out voices and perspectives of characters completely foreign to them: "I don't want to hear about your true love and your mama and your papa and your friends. Think of somebody you don't know. What about a Mexican waitress in the Rio Grande who can barely speak English? Or what about a Grande Madame in Paris? . . . Imagine it, create it." She expects her students to try on different voices, and to imitate imagined characters bravely and shamelessly. This approach to writing not only *suggests* but also *insists* that students leave the familiar confines of their diction, experiences, and knowledges.

The assumption that what a person is capable of writing is bound by their autobiographical experiences possesses a violence, too. Think of Ocean Vuong's essay "Surrendering" published in *The New Yorker* in 2016 where Vuong recalls being an "E.S.L. student from a family of illiterate rice farmers" who had recently immigrated to the United States from Vietnam. He didn't have anything close to "mastery" of the English language, and he managed to write a poem so beautiful that his teacher was convinced it was plagiarized and proceeded to humiliate Vuong in front of his peers. Vuong had crafted his poem from speeches and phrases he heard spoken—recordings of "Great American Speeches," particularly one by Dr. Martin Luther King, Jr.—words alive and curious that he would look up in the dictionary. He was not writing in "broken" English, as his teacher may have expected of a poor student of his age and background. He was breaking English apart to stardust by tuning into words spoken, and then creating his own poem from those words buzzing with mysterious meanings. Without grasping the words—perhaps *because* he could not grasp those words—he crafted an impossible poem, made of multiple sources and of an expansiveness that both exceeds and contains Vuong.

> I was a fraud in a field of language, which is to say, I was a writer. I have plagiarized my life to give you the best of me.
>
> —*Ocean Vuong (2016, para 11).*

We do not see in many English classrooms calls for students to abandon what they know or have experienced. In fact, an opposite approach seems to dominate the teaching of poetry in many schools; teachers often use poetry as a way to draw out "personal" experiences that already have an important meaning in the student's life. It is from these prior-determined, personally relevant experiences that poetry is anticipated to emerge. Our personal experiences provide some of the richest material to engage in and through poetry; the problem has nothing to do with the content or inspiration of one's writing, but with the assumption that one must be writing from that experience, or that there is a single way to understand that experience, or that the poem is a window into the poet's "true self" instead of a fusion of existing languages, alive and ripe for assembling.

Unteaching "Voice"

So, we have been thinking of ways to un-teach the idea of "voice" and to engage, instead, the multiplicities we each contain—multiple voices, stories, imaginings, experiences, and the multiple resources we draw from and *with which* we always write.

To explore these multiplicities, we have taken Morrison's advice to demonstrate versions that create new persona, different "voices" out of poems. Take, for example, this recent poem by the poet, professor, and jazz musician Charles O. Hartman, author of seven books of poetry and, most recently, *Verse: An Introduction to Prosody* (2015):

The Pianos

> *All graceful instruments are known*
> —The Grateful Dead

Amid so much sleep,
we remember the waking phrases:
iterations bored or rapturous,
resounding hours, rehearsals
of the opulent impromptu, the melody
sketched by a right hand
once and let drop.

We almost remember the hundred hands'
thousands of operations
fashioning us for the sleek
showroom, the dim loft,
the highly favored dorm,
the not-quite-defunct
club: solarium, atrium.

Among us we have taught
some children what they are.

Whether we're Grand (the satin
titan with mammoth underbite)
or Upright (but *spinet* is an ugly name),
everyone has a fallboard eyelid.

We all need work. My felts
haven't been pricked for years.
The sostenuto's flabby.
A long life can be ghastly, last
decades in an untunable basement:
peeling, untouched
even into noise.

Once on a loading dock
Steinway CD 318 and I
passed back to back:
Gould's own, on loan to Evans.
This was before the fall.
Another I knew stroked Tatum's fingers,
then Peterson's—a junker by then,
with a fresh coat of paint.

When Monk's burned, everyone
went dumb for a day.

When I first came home
under the round window—
even as I heard the truck's

pads and dollies tucked back in
while guys flexed shoulders for the next—
on that still first morning
I answered Bach with Bach, and when at last
she stood and away from me
to speak to some others,
I knew her heart was mine.

Based on the "voices" of the pianos in this poem, how do you imagine them? How might a guitar speak differently? Hartman's poem generates further prompts—a fire quickens: What if you were asked to figure out at least three other "voices" that could belong to this poem? Who might they be? How would you describe the perspective of each? First might be the Steinway CD 318. Or, the children taught by the pianos. Or, the "her" one piano seems to have fallen in love with. Or, the hundred hands mentioned.

Hartman's poem inhabits multiple piano personas and other poems may take on human personas very unlike the writer. Sometimes we need to take on personas to wrestle with challenging personalities we might encounter in real life, which may or may not be the case in this poem that makes us laugh, by poet and teaching artist Melanie Maria Goodreaux, author of the book *Black Jelly*, 2019.

The Appetizers that Ate Us

Our eyes will not meet and our glasses of pink wine will not clink,
and each toast you make towards our friendship will go unheard.
I am too busy for you today.
There's a phone call plastered to my ear that means business.
This party is very exclusive and you will pay for it.

The amount of the bill will make you cry and add up to a whole day's work.

The cost will debit an entire relationship from the docks.

I won't remember who we were before the picked-over cold calamari left at the
table

I complained about.

I won't know that you ate most of the fries I coveted

because you were hungry after your day job at the morgue.

These shoestring potatoes will mean more to me than any memory we ever
shared.

When the waiter takes away that final knob of chicken and the last three frigid
fries hiding at the bottom of a fancy vase (pronounced vaz),

I will sum you up and scratch you off the list.

You were a friend that ate too much at my table.

I was a friend that left our visit for something more important.

Stingy love will sink its teeth into our hearts.

The selfies will report their selfishness.

And none of this fried cauliflower,

devastated by ketchup, will really be us.

Shifting perspective can enable us to imaginatively enter another body without claiming to speak "for" or "represent" that body. Our ability to shift perspective foregrounds the question of how a scene is visualized. It also emphasizes the situatedness of our familiar, habitual lenses. As Donna Haraway (1988) asks, "With whose blood were my eyes crafted?" (p. 585). How does a person come to be seen? Through what histories and ideas do we see another person, or group of people, or place? We see the work of poetry as a deep engagement with sight—one that cannot be reduced to gender, race, class, or sexuality but that is always marked in some way or another by gendered, raced, and classed realities. And all those intersecting markings shift in discordant concert with the transnational routes a poem, and a person, takes.

Attention to multiplicities can also be a way of attending to our multiple influences, autobiographical or not. We contain multiple histories, journeys, languages, loves—and poetry can tap into those intimate tracks and traces. We might not be able to explain why we are drawn to the Arabic language, to hip-hop, to folk songs, and to klezmer music. We do know, though, that there is a place for our hybrid mashups in poetry. Take this poem we love by LaTasha N. Nevada Diggs (2013):

the originator

here's the remedy for your chronic whiplash—

    coming to you via triple ones on a mission—

        pop a wheelie for originators of the flash.

            check ya dial, emboss the rock b4 a fella dip dash.

                grand to slam a party—peep two needles in collision:

        here's the remedy for your chronic whiplash

        flare your dome w/ a pinch of cheeba succotash—

got my avenue peaking rapid circumcision—
pop a wheelie for originators of the flash.
ululate the call; gods never caught tongue-lash—
tweak an EQ. my hash sparks double vision:
here's the remedy for your chronic whiplash.
got my tambourine for ya partner. pass the calabash.
smile for the DJ when the cut spits—peep the precision.
pop a wheelie for originators of the flash—
never fret what the beat can establish in the trash.
master meter on Orion, starship blast w/ supervision:
here's the remedy for your chronic whiplash—
pop a wheelie for originators of the flash—

If you can, find a way to listen to Diggs reading the poem or any poem she's written. Her voice brings these already electric words to new life. Note how this poem's multiple languages cascade and flood any "standard" notion of English. I want to feel this poem in my mouth, read it aloud, and remember how much I love language—that wild, changing thing made up of multiple wild, changing other things.

The problem of an essential voice is also a problem of style. When we attempt to define ourselves by style, we narrow the possibilities of our writing. I don't usually write hybrid poems like Diggs, and I definitely don't perform them with the kind of musical intelligence and straightforward power that she embodies. To learn from Diggs, I don't just read her work, I try to enter her poem's rapid movement and sonic dance party in my own way. I already know it won't be one tenth as good as her poem, so I just relax and enjoy the process:

take this chicken soup w/ shkedim for memory.
soothe your neurotic esophagus w/ backwash & bone, shtetl-real—
the flower blooming red-fast in the bowl's bottom's been here forever—
sababa—still, you kvetch all the way home
—amod dom! yeah, you know
what savta's chicken soup can do; she spoons it
& you're good for forty days & nights. burn
this nation's tongue w/ memory
faster than the headless chicken sliced for shabbat—

We encourage our own students to exercise as many voices and styles as possible—to get out of their signature comfort zones. As Mary Oliver (1994) writes in her wonderful *A Poetry Handbook*, "I think if imitation were encouraged much would be learned well that is now learned partially and haphazardly. Before we can be poets, we must practice; imitation is a very good way of investigating the real thing" (p. 13). Maybe we ought to suspend our desires for originality and "authentic voice" and focus instead on imitation. Practicing poetry is certainly recording observations, writing and revising poem after poem, but it is also a matter of copying down, of imitating a voice or style or line that you have fallen in love with, just as you might take on the joke or the laugh of a loved one that you have lived with long enough to begin to merge into a twosome singularity.

When we read poems that we love, we might be satisfied with a moment's recognition, share poems with friends, or have the urge to imitate—borrow from the poets we admire, or take the energy or craft of the lines into the making of our own poems. A good poet knows how to spot a poem's fire and try, earnestly, to make her own fire out of words, images, silences, linguistic speeds, and slownesses. A good poet knows s/he/they always live(s)—and needs to live—in the company of other poets.

Tending Our Multiplicities

Tending to our multiplicities through poetry is also a way of telling multiple stories about, and versions of, ourselves. As author Chimamanda Adichie (2009) emphasizes in her viral TED Talk "The Danger of a Single Story," the assumption that a person's life can fit into a singular narrative (and usually a dominant, Eurocentric one) is oppressive and stifling. All of us have many stories to tell and ways of telling them. We contain multitudes, and I have yet to see a box built that can neatly contain all the experiences and stories that make a person.

An Invitation

Write a poem titled "Me/Not Me." Don't censor yourself and don't think you have to show this to anyone. Record your stream of consciousness in list form, making and unmaking your declarations of identity, until the carpal tunnel sets in.

Multitudes

"i poem *multitudes multitudes multitudes*"
—Danez Smith (from their poem "Two Poems," published in
The Offing, December 18, 2019).

I return to Stevens, reading this second stanza three times, feeling frustrated, intrigued, and confused. I want to know more about the specific number three. I also want to know why a mind is like a tree and not like, as the philosophers Gilles Deleuze and Felix Guattari (1987) offer, a rhizome that grows laterally, sprouting unexpected offshoots. But maybe a tree can act like that too. There are so many different kinds of trees in this world. I've probably only seen a handful where I've lived for the most part of my life. And what are those three blackbirds doing in the tree? Talking to each other? Meditating? Tweeting? If I have three minds how do I—or can I—think? How are these minds connected and how do they enable us to contemplate blackbird? What curiosities does this stanza spark for you?

Just as we might be of three (or more) minds in which three (or more) blackbirds live, startle, flutter, and nest, we read a poem crisscrossing our experiences, feelings, images in the poem, and the weight of certain words or lines. We are at once reader, writer, producer, and speaker. While the role of reader is most often understood as that of interpreter or critic, we try to nurture in ourselves and our students the idea that there are multiple roles of readers. In what follows, we explore these three, often overlapping, roles: Reader as Explorer Who Carries a Makeshift Trident for Splitting Open Poems; Reader as Maker of Formidable Encounters; and Reader as Thief.

Reader as Explorer

In an interview for the Louisiana Channel's series "Advice to the Young," Laurie Anderson (2016) urges young artists to "be loose." She warns against pigeonholing or branding the self as one thing, and she talks back to the prevalent idea of art as personal expression. Anderson suggests that artists can be most free when they follow a curiosity, engage materials, and approach subjects as multiple. She laughs that she calls herself a "multimedia artist"—a meaningless term, she says, that gives her the freedom to work across multiple materials and multiple ideas. For Anderson, this means getting away from the idea that art is about personal expression and, instead, thinking about art as an act of curiosity and exploration—an act that could take you in any possible direction.

There's something in this sense of following a curiosity that makes us think of "splitting open"—the image of a seedpod or blossom or maybe a dandelion. We're thinking about the fragments that erupt and settle from acts of splitting open. If peeling back is akin to personal expression (stripping layers to arrive at an authentic voice), splitting open might be the startle of the bird's chirp—its vibrations echoing and dispersing into air opening something un/familiar within the listener or reader.

No scheme of explanation or interpretation can peel back and reveal, layer by layer, some inner core of meaning of a poem. Energy resides within poems to keep the pressure on, to create a near force field, a moment to *be within* the experience as if at any moment the poem would split open and blossom a thousand fragments of meaning. This tension often resides in the spaces between how a poem is tempted to "speak" and a competing desire to "un-speak" or leave spaces of silence where it is clear we cannot know or articulate how the poem means. Recognizing this felt tension leads us to wonder at the logic of working from the *outside to inside* of the poems in some of the practices of interpretation.

Questions that position us *outside* a poem might be: "What does the poem mean? What is the poet (or the persona) trying to say? How did the poet craft the poem to accomplish this feeling? What were the poet's intentions?" These questions put distance between the poem and its reader, encouraging the reader to puzzle a path to the inside in order to find meaning. But a poem may not be a container of meaning with an answer to be found.

Let's flip the logic and ask: "Where am I *within* the poem? What am I experiencing and where am I located? What can I make of a poem from inside its body?" *If* we allow the poem to encase us, just "to be," for us to live within its skin for a moment, we may not be able or desire *to speak* meaning. Rather, we might be able to explore a poem by *being with it* rather than treating it as material for conquest. Within Stevens's stanza, I am inside the tree, with three blackbirds perched on me. In a second reading I am one of the three minds, or all three—and now I am a blackbird, burrowing my beak in my feathers with my two sisters by my side. I stand still inside this stanza. The tree that may be me is moving, but imperceptibly. Why do I feel strangely at home in this stanza, having never seen an actual blackbird?

We may feel the edges of meaning, pregnant with multiple possibilities, emotions, and beyond a "truth" near to splitting open. A force field of energy of how we might describe experiencing a poem rather than interpreting it. Or, in the words of Adrienne Rich (1993), "Someone is writing a poem. Words are being set down in a force field. It's as if the words themselves have magnetic charges; they veer together or in polarity, they swerve against each other" (pp. 86–7). A poem is made of words and structures set into motion as an energy field of perception and arousal.

Only by accepting the uncertainty, the inability to articulate meaning—that is, the silences filled with experiencing—some *feeling* that we can grasp but not explain arises. Poems don't mean. They aren't about communicating information. We have the freedom to un-speak their meaning if we understand this. When focusing on the spaces to walk around in a poem, we see poems not as a discourse of logical exposition but as a field of multiple relations and energies.

As teachers, we ask: How is that in practice? What ways of reading and writing poems enact that "splitting open" movement and leave behind multiple fragments to pick up, reinterpret, and rewrite? Let's read Rita Dove's provocative poem to play out some of these questions:

Adolescence-II

Although it is night, I sit in the bathroom, waiting.
Sweat prickles behind my knees, the baby-breasts are alert.
Venetian blinds slice up the moon; the tiles quiver in pale strips.

Then they come, the three seal men with eyes as round
As dinner plates and eyelashes like sharpened tines.
They bring the scent of licorice. One sits in the washbowl,

One on the bathtub edge; one leans against the door.
"Can you feel it yet?" they whisper.
I don't know what to say, again. They chuckle,

Patting their sleek bodies with their hands.
"Well, maybe next time." And they rise,
Glittering like pools of ink under moonlight,

And vanish. I clutch at the ragged holes
They leave behind, here at the edge of darkness.
Night rests like a ball of fur on my tongue.

From inside this poem, we ask questions: *Who do you imagine these men to be? What feeling does this poem leave in you? From what perspective do you see the speaker of this poem? Where are you in the room? What are the ragged holes you clutch in your own life? Who or what has made them? Where does the scent of licorice take you?*

Imagine you are an object in this bathroom (maybe the bathtub edge, its tiles, its blinds, or an object unnamed in this poem). As that object inside this bathroom, who do you see and how? From what position? What is happening in this scene from this perspective?

An Invitation

Try a few lines of a poem from one of these vantage points. Then, choose a line in Dove's poem that speaks to you (a line you find resonant) and read it multiple times. Does that repeated reading change the line? Begin your own poem with that line. On what voyage toward a new poem will that line take you? What are thirteen different ways of reading that line or thirteen different places that line might take you?

Now do that same exercise with a group of peers if possible. Multiply your readings, encounters, and movements with these lines together.

Reader as Maker of Formidable Encounters

We rest for a moment at the foot of an imagined tree, envisioning its deep root system. That system reminds us of the company of other poets, dead and alive, that we carry with us as we continue to change as readers and writers. The trunk, the branches, the leaves are all the different parts of the tree and all capable of becoming different forms (paper, table, shutters). And yet, despite the different forms, they all belong to the same system, working together with a mysterious and shared intelligence.

Stevens's second stanza captures an image of the multiplicity and dimensionality of almost any poem or experience we might encounter. Like a tree with a complex root system, we cannot see on the surface of a poem the places from which it draws nourishment and inspiration. And, another mind is at work here, too: that of the reader with a complex root system of experience and imagination.

We suggest an expanded role for the reader from interpreter, commentator, critic to that of co-traveler, investigator, imaginer, capillary. The reader is always a part of the body of a text—not some separate entity that approaches the text from outside. Through acts of reading we become entangled in a text, find ourselves as its extensions, mired in a text's nervous system, its blood flow.

The purpose of the poem is not for a reader/listener to exclaim: "So, there it is: this is what this poem is about." We hope, rather, to become decidedly "less" sure. Newly inhabiting a poem involves *bravely* not capturing "what is" but opening *elsewhere than where we are in the moment.* That is the promise. We do not *yet know* as we read a poem and it *suspends* and *immerses* us into moments of the world's rhythms, mysteries, obstinacies, and emotions. As readers, we are makers of unforeseen encounters and able to work with poems to create new spaces and new questions. We are making the poem as we encounter it in the space of the not quite yet made, in its *in-between-ness*.

This vision of the reader propels the following questions: What response-ability do we have as readers if we see ourselves as integral parts of a text's body? What changes in our encounter with a poem if we envision ourselves as readers entering from an already inside, vibrant place nestled in the force field we call text? In what ways have we become habituated to read with meaning-making in mind? How can we inhabit a poem without the conquering impulse to claim understanding?

If we were moving from Reader as Explorer to Reader as Maker, we might ask our students to create their own poems in response to "Adolescence-II" and articulate their own experiences of this time in their lives. Here are some invitations that might lead them in that direction:

(1)   Write a poem to Rita Dove where you present to her your view of, or experience with, adolescence. What would you say in relation to her poem?

(2)   Think up four concrete nouns that, for you, describe your experience of adolescence. What if those four nouns become the first word in each line in a four-line poem? (Play with this creative constraint or create another.)

(3)   Collaborate with another person and create a dialogue poem on adolescence, stanza by stanza.

(4)   Curate a constellation of poems around Dove's "Adolescence-II." What other poems would you join in relation? Multiply its friends and neighbors.

Sometimes it is enough to just wander and wonder with the words. Other times, reading a poem moves us into writing a poem or playing with language, an image, or a rhythm left pounding through the heart. We call attention to our multiple ways of reading poems because each of us probably has proclivities for how we come to, attend to, and come away from poems. It might be helpful to recognize those ways of working and think about how expanded notions of reading, responding, and acting on our readings might nurture our student readers of poetry. Maybe it takes growing accustomed to poetry as play to begin to understand, too, that poetry always exceeds our understanding and invites multiple encounters, even as it (and maybe because it) calls to us in singular and precise ways.

Reader as Thief

We leave the tree momentarily for the rhizome: the ginger root, the potato moving laterally underground, sprouting unexpected offshoots. We offer "reader as thief" as a playful movement (what Ruth has called play-giarism) in the spirit of repurposing and remaking in ways that break away from initial use or meaning. Reader as thief also suggests an evasion of identity. We are reminded of Ocean Vuong's beautiful essay "Surrendering" where he describes his experiences as an ESL student struggling to write in English and finding his way as a poet by plucking words he heard in recorded speeches by Dr. Martin Luther King, Jr. from a cassette tape titled "Great American Speeches." Vuong's resulting poem was so good his teacher was convinced it was plagiarized. He concludes his essay: "I had pressed my world onto paper. As such, I was a fraud in a field of language, which is to say, I was a writer. I have plagiarized my life to give you the best of me." It is this spirit of "thief" that we embrace—not the intentional stealing of material to claim as one's own property, but as the freedom to take what's needed toward a creative way onto paper. What writers do.

As readers, writers, and teachers of poems we ask: How to break away from the source to form new routes and voices?

What triggers this theft and play, and why might it be important to learn more about the resources available to us in poetry's multi-architectures of affect and meaning? We offer the following student poem from Natasha, a tenth grader, who is an avid reader of poetry. In this case, Ruth asked students to choose a poem that was of interest to them and reread that poem, several times a day, for a week. She also invited students to memorize parts of the poem if that seemed useful. The final part of the rereading sequence was to learn from the poem and poet by, as Ruth phrases it, "talking with, through, or back to" a poem by writing a poem in conversation with the original. Natasha wrote the following poem:

Grandmother

Late October, a first frost
changes leaves to golden
coins, At first, just one,
stains the green tree yellow,
others, seeking to be like
their friends, take on yellow, then red,
then gold before an unknown hand picks
them from the tree. Then the drying.
No dying. That's it. Dying,
like you, grandmother. Your blackberry
skin sprinkled now with yellowing. You
want to follow your friends. You linger
like the last leaf—ready for picking. We fold
you in, holding on to you a little
longer. It's not fair how you try
to fall away. Each day, a little more. Each day
we hope not now. Not now. Not ripe
for picking.

Take a moment to "be" with Natasha's poem—to see, feel, or hear it again. What lines, phrases, or images stay with you? Is there a central nervous system of the poem—that is, a particular energy in content, form, tone? What current flows through the lines?

Now, we invite you to search out a copy of the poem that inspired Natasha. Seamus Heaney's "Blackberry Picking" begins with late August blackberry picking. Heaney (1999) ends his poem with the line: "Each year I hoped they'd keep, knew they would not" (p. 7). We suspect this gives evidence of what Natasha learned from Heaney, but read the two poems side by side for the fullness of how Natasha learned from and spoke back to Heaney's poem.

Natasha provides this insight:

> The only blackberries I've ever tasted come from a plastic carton from the Acme Market down our block. Until I read this poem, I just didn't think about where they came from. But what caught me in Heaney's poem was the loss of sweetness and I couldn't help think of my Gran who died a couple of months ago. One strong memory is of her beautiful dark skin and the smell of sweetness. Nothing tastes so sweet as those memories right now. Heaney sort of helped me speak to that.

The poems, Natasha's and Heaney's, are inextricably linked. What are the influences we see from the invitation to read, reread, and talk "with and through" the poem of another? In writing and reading poems, something transpires between writer and reader, and we want to make certain we acknowledge and encourage these transactions as teachers, writers, and readers. It is this collaborative act, this process of engaging, that has the potential of involving us in reading poems differently.

We see this link particularly in Natasha's lines: "The drying./No dying. /That's it, dying"; there's a vague sense that rhythm and sound from Heaney speaks in Natasha's poem. Read both aloud, side by side, if you haven't. There are subtle and not so subtle conjunctions of images, some working more below the surface, some rising up to astonish us. In Natasha's poem there is a strength, a confidence, but also the undervoice where Natasha is nudged and coached to give voice to something important, in a way she might not be able to without Seamus Heaney in her company.

In what ways, then, can others' poems help us find the words, the enthusiasms, the imagery, the sound, and sense to help us speak? After Natasha read this poem to her classmates, she said, "I hadn't written about my grandmother but by staying with that one poem of Heaney's I think that if I study poems long enough, I can find out HOW they work."

Thank you, poems: you mysterious, non-mechanistic machines we multitudes enter again and again—multiplying encounters with you, splitting you open to generate new curiosities, following your fruits like good thieves, and making fresh senses of you.

CHAPTER 3
SMALLNESS WITHIN THE *ALL*

III
The blackbird whirled in the autumn winds.
It was a small part of the pantomime.

In his poem "Fuck Time" (POETRY, May 2020), Inua Ellams writes, "We are small as moth wing fall" (p. 121). Through these words, we can feel the shimmering truth of our carbon constitution shared with other species. We *are* small, and it is easy to forget just how small in relation to the vastness of the world that continues to thrive (at least the parts that we have not already destroyed), unconcerned with us. Our smallness can feel humbling, disorienting, connecting, and energizing: we are a part of something—of all things—and our bodies are far from solid, certain, and bounded.

Attending to Smallness

Alongside these words by Ellams, we turn our attention to that smallness that we are and that we often overlook when reading texts in school-stained ways: searching for big themes, grand messages, impersonal interpretations, and overarching truths. Poetry is made of smallnesses—of moth's wing, a certain slant of light, a fly's buzz, rain hitting a wheelbarrow, starshine, and clay. Poetry invites us to tend to smallness as a way of noticing and caring for all the things that make the pantomime, or the images we grow to believe in and name *the world*.

What *is* worthy of a poet's or reader's attention? Who gets to say? Attentiveness and scrutiny of the small might be a needed alternative to what may seem mundane, unseen, or trivial in our time of ever-expanding forms of information. Might it be that the smallest detail has attention-stretching possibilities unlike the most expansive lanes of internet traffic or the constant churn of visual images that flash across the screens of our daily lives? Do we hear the small creak of a branch against a window or the sound of a blackbird "whirled in the autumn wind"? Do we notice the computer cursor's mechanical heartbeat appearing and disappearing between words as we type? How might hearing the world "small" nearly matter?

Attention to smallness is one of our pedagogical propositions, to put it as clearly as possible, to pay attention to smallness within the vastness of possibilities of the *all*. And what is the importance of this attention? This may be an archeological way of being—paying attention to even the smallest artifact that informs us of our world, nature, cultures, and the unseen or ignored. Sensing small is a way of taking notice and has the potential of being released through a poem for readers to receive and writers to share.

One way we practice sensing small is by reading and writing odes. We think of Pablo Neruda's (1990) odes to his socks, to broken things, to an artichoke, and of Aracelis Girmay's (2011) ode to the little "r" in her name, and of Ross Gay's (2013) ode to drinking water from [his] hands. Standing in a crowded New York City subway train a few summers ago, I noticed a beautiful smear of scratches on the aluminum doors. I decided to write an ode to the subway door's scratches, which was eventually published in *Seneca Review*'s May 2020 issue. It begins:

O thin swerves left
by bodies I'll never know. O

curves kissing the "n" of "not"—
[as in: "do not" / as in: "do not

lean on door"]—before
plunging in haphazard matte

glory skimming the metal shine
of silver panels erect with capacity.

An ode is a song of praise, a letter of gratitude, a seeing, and a tending to a specific *you*: subway door, sock, onion, spider, dust ball, cockroach. (Yes, I have written an ode to a cockroach, and it actually helped me come a smidgen closer to loving them—I admit I'm not there yet, but I'm trying!) An ode can be a way of subverting what matters in our neoliberal, capitalist world. It is a way of re-mattering what matters. In the writing—in the language we use—we remake our imaginations and therefore our worlds.

> *The blackbird whirled in the autumn winds.*
> *It was a small part of the pantomime.*

What is the tiniest thing you notice in these two lines? What feels quietest? What is barely there, in the pantomime, its smallest part? Maybe it's the blackbird itself, whirling in the winds. I imagine it as a speck glimpsed from the periphery as I plow through those winds after work, trying to get home to my daughters as quickly as possible. I read these lines again and think of how a whirling bird in the wind can feel more a part of the wind than its own thing. Did Stevens see such a scene or imagine it? And what is the pantomime he meant of which the winds and whirling bird are a part?

I cannot say what Stevens intended to communicate in this stanza, but I can move with these lines, read alongside them, and consider the parts of the pantomime I experience. I can tune into what whirls, visibly or not, in the winds when I step outside. The stanza opens its hand to me: *Come closer to this thing you don't know. Take another look.* I pause. I try seeing without my eyes, to see what I might sense when I don't look at the words in my habitual ways—how fine can my sensing become?

An Invitation

Zoom into one word in that stanza. Try speaking to it. What might you say to the winds? To the autumn? To the little "e" in our taken-for-granted "the" that often stays silent while linking so many letters together into words, making with those words lines, poems? Write a poem to this stanza.

> *The blackbird whirled in the autumn winds.*
> *It was a small part of the pantomime.*

Alongside classroom practices of "close reading," we wonder what a "too close" reading of a text might look like—so close your nose touches the page. The word "small" in these two lines—and how the small seems a necessary part of a larger scene, vision, or imaginary—reminds us of the value in noticing elements in a text that haven't already been deemed significant, thematic, or even formal by a teacher. To our teacher readers: How do/can we work with our students to notice those elements of a text that we ourselves have not yet noticed?

Sensing Small

Part of our examination of smallness involves turning our attention to the silences that make a poem. In her book *Minor Feelings*, poet Cathy Park Hong (2020) recalls a writing workshop where the visiting professor, Myung Mi Kim, taught her that "[t]he poem is a net that catches the stutters, the hesitations, rather than the perfectly formed phrase" (p. 139). The poem's energy comes from what the writer withholds more than from what the writer says. We focus on the necessity of silence in poetry later in this book, but that silence is a subject belonging to this chapter, too, as we engage the powers of sensing small. Slowing our bodies down can help us catch the nuances of a phrase—its breath, its pause, its stutter—and better tune into the intricacies of making a poem.

Our focus on smallness also enables us to reimagine the English classroom. Instead of a place to assert big themes, main ideas, and clear conclusions, perhaps the classroom can become one that renders visible what often seems invisible or unremarkable and that makes the familiar unfamiliar. "Sensing small" can help us notice and foreground those elements of literature that have affective force and belong to a broader set of relationships—not just to other people but to all things: rainforests, trees, chairs, moths, blackbirds, and blackboards. Such elements sometimes exceed our linguistic capacities, and we find that makes our work all the more exciting as readers and writers of poetry, and also as teachers. By sensing small, we can come a little closer to what lives on the margins of a text, beneath a text, behind or below a word, the slant of a line or letter, in a dream about the text or sprung from the text or foreshadowing a text, haunting a text, living in a river's deep memory of a text.

> *The blackbird whirled in the autumn winds.*
> *It was a small part of the pantomime.*

Free from the burden of any grand or special status *and* living in active resistance to that burden, poetry asks us to pay attention to the small, everyday things that we sometimes step over or fail to notice. "Come closer to this thing you think you know," whispers poetry. "Take another look." We make poems out of the stuff we live with, stumble open, and/or dream up. It is precisely the power of poetry to remake the everyday "more truly and more strange" (Stevens, 1923, p. 111) that makes it accessible to anyone at any moment. Whether an ode or not an ode, a poem depends on how we see. Poetry asks us to sense small, to linger a little longer at the lump of mashed potatoes on the plate, to see the browning leaf on the street, hear the honking horns' symphony, the scar on the left arm, or the psychic imprint of a microaggression. As each of us knows when we reach for a poem at a time of intense grief or joy, there is nothing grand, difficult, or special about poetry. And yet this act of sensing small may be one of our most critical tasks as readers, writers, students, and teachers. We see poetry's call to sense small as a way of sensitizing readers and writers, expanding our capacities to love and care for each other, and also as an invitation to follow something without knowing where it will go. Sensing small could be seen as a trust exercise in committing yourself to something in the world that you—or some public—deems unworthy of poetry.

There is an exercise that we love (among many) in Robin Behn and Chase Twichell's *The Practice of Poetry* (1992): "Translations: Idea to Image (for a group)" by Carol Muske (p. 8). The exercise asks students to "translate" an abstract idea like love, self, death, or soul into a tangible image. Once students generate an image, they then "track" their image into more images and enlarge the scene of the image, bringing it to cinematic life. When students do this exercise, the "large" abstractions collapse into small, concrete moments. Love becomes burning my mouth on hot cocoa with my grandmother by my side; the self, a browning banana peel; and death is the fireplace we never light but stare into, night after night. Part of what we love about this exercise is that it exposes abstract concepts as useless when it comes to poetry. What matters isn't the theme or idea of "love" but how love becomes embodied in irreproducible specificity through and by language.

The blackbird whirled in the autumn winds.
It was a small part of the pantomime.

I return to the subway train where I wrote that ode to the subway door's scratches. I have been angry and exhausted on so many commutes, focusing on the earphones plugging the ears of commuters, on our cramped shoulders and rigid claims to our seats. Usually, I fail to see the abstract dances of smudges and lines on the silver metal of the subway doors. What prompted this noticing? I snapped a picture and took out my notebook to jot down what became my poem. In writing that poem, those crowded bodies that once irritated me became sources of awe and wonder. Where are they coming from and where are they going? What other marks do our everyday, collective movements leave behind? If our acts of co-commuting can create such beautiful residues, what else might we be able to do together?

Feeling more awake and curious about the world's marks, I wanted to write a poem. And as I started writing, I began to notice other vibrancies around me: someone's initials carved onto a seat, a woman's animated hands as she spoke with her friend, the floor that looked like an explosion of confetti in the night sky. I could feel myself waking up through, with, and because of the act of writing. Sensing small may have everything to do with that reciprocity. We become more attuned to our world by sensing small and thus better able to receive those moments in writing. At the same time, our writing of those "small" moments or things can generate broader thoughts and questions about our world.

The poet Fanny Howe (2003) writes about bewilderment and Tony Hiss (2010) writes about wonder. Both of those ideas feel relevant to the poetic practice of attention to the smallness within the *all*. As countless others have pointed out, we all have wonder as children and that wonder seems to fade with age. We need to actively restore it, to allow ourselves to become again bewildered and surprised by the world. When we are able to see the familiar as suddenly unfamiliar, our scope changes, and our position to the thing we are seeing shifts. Smallness humbles. Attention to smallness sparks newly intimate relationships to things and opens up possibilities for what those things might become, undoing habitual modes of sight.

The blackbird whirled in the autumn winds.
It was a small part of the pantomime.

An Invitation

Erase lines in a poem you've written. Reassemble what's left—to make the language differently awake, to reactivate the language.

> *the autumn*
> > *was small*

Or maybe

> > *blackbird pantomine*

Smallness whirls in a part of that gap.

CHAPTER 4
WE ARE ALL IN THIS TOGETHER

IV
A man and a woman
Are one.
A man and a woman and a blackbird
Are one.

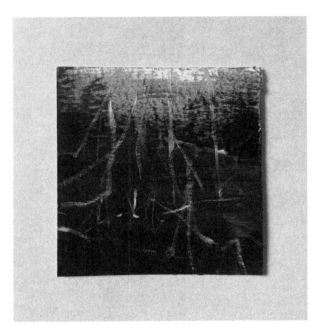

In what seems ordinary—man, woman, blackbird—the coming together of three, the "are one" changes everything into something more complex, rare, and extraordinary. One word—"one." Two words—"are one." How does the ordinary become extraordinary when the multiples become one? Or, when one becomes multiples? Imagination requires no fixed boundaries or geographies between self and other or between man and woman and blackbird. *Collectivities* may expand our notions of the familiar and of our sense of self in relation to otherness and release the potential for seeing, feeling, and imagining differently. By considering poems as landscapes that offer topographies of culture and community, we enter, create anew and gain access to spaces for exploration and response *with* others. Whether in a poem itself or in a collective reading, writing, or performance of poems, isolation slips away.

Where and how have poets and poems created, taken on, or become part of collectivities? In every culture and time period, poets have gestured to cultural commentary and imaginings often with ceremonial considerations. Awareness and attention to the power of collective poetry-making have found occasion for poetry almost everywhere. As listeners or witnesses of collective stories, we dip into the waters of archetypal broodings and bondings that call us to attend with and through others to our histories, commemorations, and witnessing. Where are opportunities to form unlikely alliances through poetry? How might collaboration offer possibilities for engaging in something larger with poetry than our individual poetry-making sensibilities and possibilities? If we approach poems as landscapes for exchanges across culture, difference, and community, how might we perform interconnectedness through collective poetry-making or poetry-as-action?

We Are in This Together

A man and a woman
Are one.
A man and a woman and a blackbird
Are one.

What is at the heart of this stanza for you? *Intent* seems in contention with some *illusive logic*. An assemblage of *three-as-one* weaves together collective identity and individual performativity. Stevens's stanza relies on a poetic assemblage of images to challenge a rational or relational version of self to other selves. This leads us to a question: When does one become part of the ONE of a collective? When do we find ourselves in sync with that phrase we hear but may not pause to reflect on: *We are in this together.*

What does the phrase mean, and what are occasions when we readers participate in experiences that reflect more than our individual interests in ways that testify to being "in this together"? The Black Lives Matter protests come to mind and the feeling of walking collectively in rage and in refusal to live in a world in which all lives do not matter equally. A friend described the protest as walking together as one organism, and I can feel that in the cacophony of bodies and sounds and signs of which I am a part when I walk with everyone. People hand out water bottles and apples to protesters. A woman shouts from a bullhorn to please move to the side. Two men spread out a cloth printed with images of George Floyd's face. A woman holds a sign: "All lives can't matter until black lives matter." The collective swells—we need each other. We need poets, too, to provoke, witness, and cast an ethical gaze.

Read this poem "Some Manhattan Rivers" by the poet Suzanne Gardinier, who often works poetic forms in her writing (and then check out her books, including *Today: 101 Ghazals* and *Iridium & Selected Poems*):

Some Manhattan Rivers

summer of 2020, George Floyd 1973-2020,
Breonna Taylor 1993-2020, ashé

to those who defied the curfew, June 2020

Holding the orphan island, two rivers:
two currents: one salt, one sweet.
The river of plague pouring through, making silence,
the plague summer river of fire in the streets:

fire in the trash cans of keep-it-like-this,
in the police cars of face-down & obey,
in the eyes of the skinny kids learning power,
out after curfew to make the new day,

the east river salt, capillary of vastness,
mothering the place whose parents they took,
the west river both ways, dissolving the ravage,
unforgetting holy book—

If you step outside the law you can smell them,
when you're supposed to be asleep,
& hear them patiently deciding
what to leave & what to keep,

salt for the tears of centuries,
for the theft on the scale of the sky,
sweet for who's beside you helping
rinse murder from the island's old eyes:

Two currents: all the rivers' wisdoms
against the law's old thefts arrayed,
salt & sweet, in your body, your city,
to be loved, honored, & obeyed

all night, the rivers teaching the voices
to pour through the feudal catacombs,
outside, where you can smell smoke & salt water
& something you can't place yet, is it home.

We read the rivers in this poem as both guide and action: what the speaker asks us to
follow/listen to ("all the rivers' wisdoms/against the law's old thefts arrayed") and the

pouring of human action in resistance ("river of fire in the streets") the sweeping floods of hope and change. The poem's rhyme scheme holds a steady rhythm, evoking for us a kind of pulse or working beneath the words, the heartbeat of the Collective as One. This memorializing poem whirls around rivers and finds its way by way of rivers. Sometimes it takes another thing—a river, a blackbird, a tree—to say what we need to say about injustices of human experience.

An Invitation

Take a few minutes to think about a cause or situation in which you participated with others. Is there an image, photograph, or slogan that speaks to you and provides perspective on this moment that would assist you in writing a brief description of what you feel, see, hear, and sense? Now, write the first few lines of a poem where you *bring your reader into the middle of the collective*—we are in this *together*—standing right in the swell of the One of this experience. Imagine your students taking up this Invitation for the collectives in which they participate.

In moments of collective grief and social unrest, poetry does its necessary work to pump blood back into our hearts, to remind us of our interconnectedness, and to create a movement inside what is happening. *The New York Times* recently asked a selection of poets which poems they turn to in times of strife. Names appear and reappear. Websites and anthologies bloom. Collections gather. Books are reprinted for a hungry public. Poems speak through us, asking to be written and shared.

There seems to be a congregate need to "come together as one," to feel a part of a community witnessing, mourning, and feeling the need to share and be a part of the sharing in moments of unusual isolation and loneliness. *The Poetry Society of New York* and *Pandemic Poems Project* (2020) created a joint effort through a call to poets globally: "m'aider, come help me." On May Day 2020, PSNY along with Kate Belew's *Pandemic Poems Project* paired poets up from all over the world to collaborate on *Pandemic Poems*. Poets were partnered, given a first and last line. Then, each pair collaborated, line by line, to write a sonnet in the twenty-four-hour collaborative poetry experiment. Throughout the day, the poem-in-progress traveled back and forth between partners. PSNY and *Pandemic Poems* strung these separate sonnets together to create a sonnet crown (or "corona"—ironic, yes?) of magnificent proportions. This is one example in a long list of diverse platforms and invitations that have attempted to keep communities of poets connected. Each of these projects gives us ideas for ways to invite our students to participate in collaborative poetry-making over shared situations and concerns and inviting classmates or the community to share in collective events.

Events of Commemoration

Collectivities merge across the everyday landscapes of our lives, and they live in our body politic. How do such relationships evidence diverse questions and beliefs about the role of poetry in the public good? As we learn through Adorno's (1983) writings about art and the Holocaust, there are no easy ways to understand poetry's purposes and effect on the public as a collective. In Adorno's initial reflections, he considered artistic representations as complicit in diminishing human action and suffering. Later, he changed his mind to consider the potential of art, poetry in this case, to serve as an ethical witness. We are reminded of Carolyn Forché's (1993) sense of poetry as witness and her description of her own poems as "documentary poems" invested in her version of truth telling. Just how might poems and poets serve as intrinsically civic and collective? There is an impulse and need toward the collective, particularly in times of difficulty and at moments when we lose our bearings, or move toward celebration.

We are also reminded of 9/11 and the collective responses that swarmed through poetry in that moment. If we look at the Library of Congress website, there are thousands of individual poems that form a collective commemoration. It's astonishing to note that within the first five months, 25,000 poems had been published that in one way or another spoke to events of 9/11. Add to this, numerous edited collections that provide another type of collectivity, a bringing together of individual poems into intertextual and dialogic conversation, ripe for whispering and speaking in and across pages in an imagined conversation. A very different type of collective is achieved in *People's Poetry Gathering—Poem Towers* (2001). Two 110-line poem towers (each line contributed by a different poet) attest to a need for a collective commemoration, for *all-as-one* voices to speak. Billy Collins's (2002) poem "Names" is an example of collective grief evidenced in our conjoined oneness. The poem ends with this haunting line:

"So many names, there is barely room on the walls of the heart."

An Invitation: A Collaboration of Your Own

Think of a name, place, event, or action, along with a relevant date, that commemorates a moment that is important to you (or continue with the event/situation in your earlier poem). It might be a personal, national, or global event that has resonance and meaning for you—Hurricane Maria in Puerto Rico, the 2021 earthquake in Haiti, a personal moment with a friend at the Grand Canyon, the Women's March in January 2017 with your Mom or sister. Your moment might be as simple as a morning run. *As you determine the particular moment to commemorate in a poem, stop to think about a person or persons with whom you might share this moment and might ask to collaborate a bit later in writing a poem together, drafting companion, or letter poems to each other.* Take a few minutes to write down the name, place, event, action, and date. Use the name and date as the title or first line of your poem and write a few lines from there. About the time you think you have nothing more to say, write the name and date of the event again. Then, don't hesitate; just keep writing whatever comes from the corners of your mind or behind your conscious thoughts. Keep writing—complicate, connect, or contaminate with random thoughts. It's compost to go back to later, rich with fertile soil for composing a poem.

In Dialogue with Another

Now, reach out to that person (or persons) who might join in a shared writing experience. You might simply send the title of the poem with its description and date. Or, send your poem as an early draft and invite this person to write a separate poem, write into your draft, or write a poem in response, in dialogue with, or one that talks back to your rendering.

Here is an example of an exchange that grew from this Invitation. In January of 2018, Ruth and Wang Shu visited Tiananmen Square after the two had finished teaching a course together in Beijing. Ruth wrote this seed of a poem and sent it to Wang Shu via email.

Tiananmen Square, Beijing, January 19, 2018

Do you remember the biting freeze on our
fingertips? Cold contesting our hot breath
until our glasses fogged through mouth-masked
covers? Do you remember the wind's howl,
fourteen below zero and the guards standing
firm against tortuous blades of ice stabbing
their exposed cheeks and eyes?

Do you remember me asking how Tian'anmen
Square, translated as Gate of Heavenly Peace, holds
back from weeping its history? Tiananmen Square,
1989, one million gathered. Hunger strikes, death,
the howl of a different wind. And we walk on, you
holding my arm as we step over a threshold into
the Forbidden City. You tell me that for five centuries
outside visitors were forbidden here. Do you remember
the look on your face as you whispered: "The isolation
was demanded to assure no foreign ideas would corrupt."

The wind howls. I think I see a tear of ice form on your
cheek. "It is bad luck, you tell me, to share secrets here."

Wang Shu wrote back:

Tiananmen Square, January 19, 2018

Do you remember against the wind and cold how
the ancient city stands proud? The thresholds we crossed
have endured since 1420. Imagine the one million workers
each meticulous, one will caress even the smallest of cracks

on the Meridian Gate. Such care. Such pride. Do you
remember crossing the Golden Stream Bridge to the Hall
of Supreme Harmony? The animal protectors cast in bronze.
Do you remember I told you the Phoenix brings happiness
and luck, the unicorn, Haetae, justice? And of the cold,
the biting wind, it departed, was dampened with stories
of justice where harmony and power are in balance. Do
you remember I said: "Notice in the corner there Huabiaos,
the squatting lion, a reminder to Emperors to go to the people.
Learn their grievances. That's how a Forbidden City will
survive the cold for 600 years.

While we might think of poems as written by individual poets, we find these invitations into formal and informal collaborations are made easier by rapid technologies. Imagine the collaborative poem that might form from these two separate poems, although one has already prompted the other. Without the interactive and multiple viewpoints and tensions these create, the separate poems may not have the same richness as a combined effort. And, in many ways, Wang Shu's poem, even as these are placed side by side, *talks back* to Ruth's understanding in poignant ways—the two forming a contesting one poem—*together.*

With our growing attention to the role of collectives in poetry reading and writing, we are continuously finding a variety of ways to engage ourselves, our writing groups, our students in collaborations that help us imagine the possibilities of the many as one. Surprisingly, we have found this engagement distinctly possible in the atmosphere brought on by our current pandemic, where "social distance" is necessary to ensure our own safety and the safety of others. Our physical distance in quarantine has enabled the space to nurture and meditate on the events, people, places, and relationships that are important. It has also opened up fresh ways of connecting with others from that place of solitude.

Voicing Together

Take a look at examples of recent collaborative poetry writing that you can find online. For example, Kwame Dawes and John Kinsella write, "A Coda to History," copyrighted on June 11, 2020 in the Academy of American Poets' Poem-a-Day collection. A collaborative poem by Yusef Komunyakka and Laren McClung, "Trading Riffs to Slay Monsters" was Poem-a-Day on June 12, 2020, also copyrighted to the Academy of American Poets. Both are accessible on the Academy's website. These are two examples of a growing body of collaborations that represent the possibilities of voicing together through poetry. These examples of a dialogic created through shared creation present more collective and plural viewpoints. We learn *with* each other through these joint creations.

We have created a variety of invitations for our students to create multivoiced poems as a way of performing collectivities. In one version, students come together to write a multivoiced poem around a topic of interest. If we take the concept of "Freedom" or "Citizen," for example, and three poets write and perform a collaborative poem, there are numerous choices available for structuring the polyvocal poem. We have found it helpful in either writing or facilitating others' writing of multivoiced poems to have the group set ground rules, *creative constraints*. For example, the three poets in this hypothetical three-person group might decide that each will write a five-line poem. Then, they might perform these by reading their three different versions in unison. It might be that they decide to collaborate in writing another five-line stanza together, thus creating a unison reading to complete their collective version of "Freedom" or "Citizen." Another *creative constraint* might include writing alternative lines—potentially each person writes the first line and passes that to the second person who writes the second line and the third person writes a third line to finish the stanza. The possibilities are endless. As an alternative, the three writers could write a collaborative poem. Each way of working will show unique aspects of the individual and collective ways of thinking through and putting ideas into language and craft. Hopefully, you start to see how varied the choices are. Imagine an animal rights poem or one on the extinction of the white rhino. A poem about Justice? Joy? A Hummingbird?

We have also facilitated numerous collective ways of reading poems in our classes. One favorite is to ask students to read a poem aloud, at their own pace as if they were the only person reading for the entire class. Catch is: everyone in the room is reading at their own pace—a cacophony of voices much like the night sounds of crickets chirping and frogs croaking. The overlapping sounds of these spoken encounters, vocalized at once, create a different experience for the speaker/listener. We often record these collective readings and play them back to the group. The poem, in the initial reading with other voices around nearly echoing each other, is quite different from the one we heard coming through our individual bodies and voices. All voices join together, different accents, different emphasis, different pacing. It can feel awkward to read a poem aloud alone before twenty classmates, but together, as part of a cacophony, a different encounter with the poem emerges—messy but exciting in the voicing together.

Imagine for a moment how Octavio Paz's (1979) "Wind, Water, Stone" might sound if you and several others read it simultaneously. If you have the opportunity to try this with your students or with colleagues, try several versions—all reading at the same time, one taking each stanza, if a four-person group, one reads each line in the stanza, and other variations. Consider the differences in readings depending on the constraints set on the voicing together. How does each variation change your experience with the poem and your relationship to the group?

Wind, Water, Stone

for Roger Caillois

Water hollows stone,
wind scatters water,

stone stops the wind.
Water, wind, stone.

Wind carves stone,
stone's a cup of water,
water escapes and is wind.
Stone, wind, water.

Wind sings in its whirling,
water murmurs going by,
unmoving stone keeps still.
Wind, water, stone.

Each is another and no other:
crossing and vanishing
through their empty names:
water, stone, wind.

How might this poem be experienced if the collective readings come back to you through a recording where your voice is barely distinguishable from all the others? What questions and ideas might spring from this collective reading? How is the experience of the poem, your attention to the poem in sound, meaning, idea potentially different as a result of these readings? Consider engaging your students in voicing together. The possibilities are endless and the collaborations generate interest and energy in poetry study that provides a different dimension to what is often solitary activity.

The Air We Breathe

A familiar phrase—*the air we breathe*. Say it aloud: *the air we breathe*. Once more: *the air we breathe*. Saying it over and again may either engage your attention to question its meaning or numb you through the repetition until the phrase does not *mean*. Do we have a collective understanding of this phrase: *the air we breathe*? This seems simple enough to say we do, but a little look around the multiples might suggest otherwise.

Of what is the air we breathe composed? Can we name the collective that is our air? Oxygen, nitrogen, water, carbon dioxide, ozone, and other trace elements? In what proportions and how do our lungs process *air*—that is, we humans, an elephant, koi, the basil in the garden? How does our view of the simple phrase, *the air we breathe* take on new meaning, raise new questions and perspectives? We might move to the *qualities* of the air we breathe which takes us to perspective on allergies, toward pollutants, in a pandemic, to the environment, or global warming.

Do we have a collective understanding of what it means when we say "that something is as natural as the air we breathe?" The way a feeling of "natural" is akin to our necessary, taken-for-granted air. And, yet, we find the "natural" is not natural when we take a more collective view. We live in a world where the "natural" feeling of living cannot be separated from the ongoing violence of whiteness that keeps taking air, breath, and life away from Black men and women. *I can't breathe.* As white authors committed to poetry—which has always been and always will be a political act invested in our shared humanity—we cannot look away, cannot see ourselves as separate from this violence. Poetry becomes for many people a way of giving breath to one's life and to others' lives on the page and through a poem. Especially in moments of terror, fear, rage, anxiety, and uncertainty, we tangle ourselves together toward understanding.

As Audre Lorde (2000) reminds us, "poetry is not a luxury" (p. 364). It is a matter of survival. Poetry enables us to better sense the air we breathe and to respond to lives lost as a result of white people literally taking breath from BIPOC people. We turn to this haunting and tender poem by Ross Gay (2015) which lives in Split This Rock's poetry database:

A Small Needful Fact

Is that Eric Garner worked
for some time for the Parks and Rec.
Horticultural Department, which means,
perhaps, that with his very large hands,
perhaps, in all likelihood,
he put gently into the earth
some plants which, most likely,
some of them, in all likelihood,
continue to grow, continue
to do what such plants do, like house
and feed small and necessary creatures,
like being pleasant to touch and smell,
like converting sunlight
into food, like making it easier
for us to breathe.

Poetry has the potential to awaken a more collective consciousness that can transport us into an altered awareness from our own experiences and understanding. A poem may jolt us to reconsider a statement or idea as seemingly simple as "the air we breathe."

A man and a woman
Are one.
A man and a woman and a blackbird
Are one.

At times, we learn these things for ourselves. At other times, it takes a poet to orient our attention into new ways of thinking, seeing, or articulating. With Stevens, in a moment of recognition, man and woman and blackbird are one, breathing the same air. The primal workings of metaphor appear on a horizon of possibilities. We are not sure about you, but we still delight in the vagueness of what this stanza means. And, we feel slippage into some inscrutable realm, *nearer myth*.

Myth: Veined within Collective-Creating Imaginings

Slippage—back and forth from object to objects, story to stories, story to allegory to metaphor—built upon twisting pathways that form, cross and (re)cross, intersect in human imaginings. Myth. We turn our attention toward myth as we move this exploration of collectives further into shared multicultural memories. The roots of explanation, the performances of ritual and vestiges of image and spectacle—myth is an animation of questions and explorations. Through thickets and dreams of poems, we chase and explore over and again these mythic visions. When reality becomes unexplainable or unbearable, myth has the potential to assist in articulation, drawing from its currents and streams of metaphor to assist in finding voice and means to explain. In his essay "A Poet's Boyhood at the Burning Crossroads," the poet Saeed Jones (2015) discusses turning to myth in order to write. Myth provided a safe distance from his anxieties as a Black, gay boy remembering the brutal murder of James Byrd Jr. in Jasper, Texas. Jones reflects on his attraction to myth as a world far from his own struggles and fears. Taking on the voices of characters rather than writing in his "own voice" enabled Jones to write the poems he needed to write.

Finding voice through and with the myths we carry from the past, extending textual or cultural iterations of myth into the present, and creating anew in the future occupy the imagination of poets who use the collective memory of myth to exceed meaning and logic. Myths might be read as portals into ourselves, remade into our own stories and dreams, but myths also enable us to enter a collectively known body and momentarily claim that body *with* others. It provides a temporary haven to be who we wish and need to be in a collective space where many bodies carry the resonances of passed-along stories. And myths, like the myth of Icarus, get remade into other stories like Christopher Myers's (1974) *Wings*, which tells the story of Ikarus Jackson, a boy with wings scorned by his peers and his teacher. In the end, with a friend beside him, affirming his beauty and power, he continues to fly.

Myth offers opportunities for meditation and for attention to be drawn to the proverbial stories, explanations, and questions as myth is like a "charged" air that we breathe collectively. Not to make any assumption that we all live by and know the same myths, but these circulate, transmigrate, mutate, and shift through currents of the air that are culture-making. Individual poets draw on or transform stories, images, and metaphors from available myths. In doing so, they nurture a collective agenda that brings together their individual imaginings and wonderments with those stories, metaphors, or allegories that have gone before. A poem often feels like a living moment tangled in currents between an individual and the collective. Poems may speak of the past and to the present but also send messages to a collective future that may be unknown or unimagined. Myths speak through those who came before us and to those who will follow.

An Invitation

"In the Beginning. . ."

What words might follow? What does this phrase open in your reservoir and repertoire of connection to experience and myth? Take a moment to repeat this phrase and then write it down. Keep writing. What comes next? This may be the start of your own poem drawing on myth either explicitly or implicitly. Take a moment to write the first lines of that poem.

In the Beginning

"In the Beginning"—for the Greeks the story centers on Gaia creating Uranus and thus the Titans are born. In the Jewish *Torah* and Christian *Bible*, God commands, "Let there be light." And this is the beginning of layers of very complicated stories. In Hindu, Purusha, of a thousand heads, births the universe, and in Japan the Divine Siblings Izanagi and Izanami create the Islands from mud having themselves been created by a god spawned as the one green shoot from mud. In China, the Cosmic Egg creates the opposing forces of yin and yang while in Babylonia, Apsu (fresh water) and Tianat (salt water) spawn generations of gods. This small list of shaping influences into complex cultural myths is not intended to do anything more than remind us that myths circulate in the air we breathe. After these beginnings, stories of life, death, floods, heroes, returns, generosity, and stinginess—all these are taken up in poems. In our attempts to understand, stories breed other stories and stories lead to poems, and poems nurture other stories. The collective experience continuously shapes through this dialogic of poems speaking to and through other poems and stories/myths.

"In the Beginning" seems simple enough. As simple as is the phrase "the air we breathe"—until we pause and pay attention. Both phrases are the stuff of poetry and of myth. The poet Mathias Svalina's (2010) first book of poems *Destruction Myth* is a collection of forty-five creation myths. All forty-four myths open with "In the Beginning." The final longer poem begins, "In the End" and is future tense. Each poem presents its cycle of creation/destruction, which, of course, leads back to a new "In the Beginning." As readers we are led through a maze of taking on, re-creating, and making anew the cycle of beginning again, always. Within each beginning are the seeds of our destruction, and Svalina's collection of poems illuminates one exploration within a wellspring of myth—sites, stories, images, metaphors to think through this continuous cycle of birth and death, the creating and destroying forces ever moving, ever present, ever on our individual and collective memories and questions. But, there are twists in the proverbial stories. "In the beginning I was a thesaurus" (p. 38). "In the beginning I met a girl with red hair" (p. 39). ATMs, Kool-Aid, Larry Bird, heavy metal bands, and Chris Farley are just potential figures that form a pop-cultural iconography replacing the iconography of creation myths with their lush gardens of Paradise, apples as a fruit of knowledge, Purusha of a thousand heads, or the Cosmic Egg. To what ends? In its humor, reliance on the absurd, and repetition, Svalina calls into question our collective myths that, in many ways, evidence our efforts to explain how we came to be, who we are, and what we might become.

"In the Beginning"—just imagine for a moment collecting every creation myth ever told, retold, re-membered across time, space, and culture. Why this story, why these stories as part of our collective consciousness, and why are these important enough to continue to recreate and circulate as poems in our cultural conversations?

Classroom Contagions toward Collective Joy

In her beautiful book *To Be the Poet*, Maxine Hong Kingston (2002) reflects on her fourth-grade teacher, Mrs. Garner, who referred to poems as "gems." Kingston writes lovingly about this early encounter with poetry and how Mrs. Garner's offering of poetry became, for Kingston, a way to own the music of language: words rhyming and springing into and through the body. Teaching can be a form of contagion and a collective one. As educators we have an opportunity to build classrooms for collective practices that make possible joy and playful experimentation and possibility. What can a collective mind/heart, made from and in relation to individual minds/hearts, create from a collective *oneness*? What sense of purpose might a poem yield when written collectively, poems written in response to the poem of another, or poems written as the communication link between two people or a group? Retallack (2004), in *The Poethical Wager*, writes: "I believe we learn the most about what it can mean to be human from border-transgressive conversations" (p. 2).

We invite you to try out some of these collective practices that we have found generative and make them your own. Compile a class anthology of student poems or their favorite poems; create collaborative form poems, like the Renga, or pool student's poems and make centos out of them; draft a class poem, written in response to an event, a poem or novel studied in class; memorize a few lines from a poem and have a class conversation using only those lines; create collaborative exquisite corpses, double-voiced poems, random joining of published poets: What happens when John Keats meets June Jordan by using lines within their poems to create a new poem (or the same with two students in class)? Whew. The possibilities are endless. Enjoy the contagious possibilities. Our work has just begun.

CHAPTER 5
THE QUIET AND NOT-SO-QUIET IN POEMS

V
I do not know which to prefer,
The beauty of inflections
Or the beauty of innuendoes,
The blackbird whistling
Or just after.

Which do you prefer—"The blackbird whistling/Or just after"? With this question mark left hanging, you *might be* caught in the space of between-ness at the end of the "whistling/Or just after."

What *sounds* in the spaces between? Read the stanza, preferably aloud, once more. Notice, the eyes glance over space after "whistling" before they land on "Or," in a brief moment of quietness. The resources of silence—blank spaces, punctuation, line breaks, figures of speech, innuendo, inflection—all have the power to hold us in spaces of between-ness.

Innuendo or inflection? Which do you prefer? Both are named as beautiful. How might we consider the uses of innuendo and inflection as resources of sound and silence in poems? Innuendo, from the Latin word *innuere*, "to nod or point at," like a question mark leaves us with the not-quite-said/voice while inflection, from the Latin word *inflectere*, "to bend or curve" (a change in pitch, tone, tempo), allows for emphasis and meaning conveyed through sound, exacting a reader to *hear meaning*. In this stanza in Stevens's poem, consider its blend of sound, silence, innuendo, and inflection. What do you experience in sensation, experience, or affect? There is a humble energy in poetry when language is just beyond our reach, when we are on the exhilarating edge of near language where silences echo.

Writing poetry often feels like a beautiful wrestling match between what we want to say and what seems almost impossible to put into words. Poems might be testaments to the ways in which language fails us and the ways in which we still insist on using language to convey what we do not fully understand or to express those felt senses that hover just beyond and through what cannot quite be said. This ongoing effort to speak the unspeakable is a reminder of Kant's attempt to understand an aesthetic of the *sublime*—of the agitation that comes with trying to make comprehensible a feeling "incommensurate with our power of exhibition" (1790; 1987, p. 99). Putting into language an image or experience, let alone a feeling (especially an uncanny one), is as difficult as trying to tell someone about a dream. That does not stop us from trying.

This *trying* seems to have nothing to do with attaining "success." Rather, *trying* is an act of discovery and, as Wallace Stevens writes, we find "what will suffice" (1942, pp. 105–6). Through poetry, we can sense relationships between words and silences and thereby more carefully tend to what pulses between, beneath, and through words. Silence has power without direct coercion. As Stevens wrote: "to find, / Not to impose" (Stevens, 1982, p. 404). His speaker in the seventh canto asserts, "But to impose is not / To discover" (Stevens, p. 403). A poem may be a way of making time and space for erased voices and histories to be heard in more powerful or intimate ways than historical biography or narrative might convey. The resources of silence from blank space on the page to a simple question mark remind us of the power of and risk in expressing the not-quite-say-able and the need *to say*, or the acknowledgment of *the impossibility of being able to say*.

Attuning to Presences of Silence

I don't know which to prefer, the sounds or the silences, or, the spaces of in-between-ness. I don't know which to prefer, the surprise of the blackbird's whistle or the trace of the whistle left in the air. I don't know which to prefer, what I can say or what I can't say, what lives comfortably on my tongue or what belongs outside of the sayable, the words or the cadences, the beauty of language or where it fails. I don't know which to prefer and do not feel a choice is necessary—the exploration reveals the resources that convey silences.

Attending to *how* silence is present or made absent from a poem, we find it important to attune by exploring the presence of silence in poems. e. e. cummings's experiments with silence are instructive.

silence

is
a
looking

bird:the

turn
ing;edge, of
life

(inquiry before snow)

What do you notice in your first reading? Consider surrounding space, punctuation, and cummings's metaphors for silence. Look to the end line. What aspects of silence are captured in even the smallest of gestures, the open-ended parenthetical of the last line? What presences of silence linger as you read this poem once more? The idea of *reverberation* comes to mind—silences that vibrate in the surrounding spaces, single word lines, placement of a punctuation mark, or enjambment of lines. Taken together, what is emphasized for you in *how* cummings attunes himself and potentially you, his reader, to silence?

An Invitation

Linger on the word *silence* for a moment. How might you write silence? Silence. What is present when the word falls away? Try to capture a silence in words on a page by thinking of moments of silence in your day. Hear, see, smell, feel the silences. Write a few lines.

Here's a snapshot of the early part of my day in silences:

- The blank screen before I find the words to start writing this example.
- The moment between one drip from the faucet . . . and . . . the next, reminding me to call the plumber!
- Just as my daughter's lips part as she lifts her morning coffee from the counter.

The examples I wrote locate silence within a subject—the screen, the moment between drips, my daughter's lips parting to speak, a wind. This seems to follow how cummings locates silence in things, but he uses the resources of punctuation, enjambment, and the open end of the parenthetical to create the presence of silence.

I experimented with other ways, too, with how a verb might express these silences:

- Silence whispers through the white space on my blank screen.
- Silence consumes the ping of water against porcelain.
- Silence pierces the air after her comment.

Too direct? Not enough space for silence to reverberate, to linger, to vibrate? If I want to achieve the presence of silence, I need to make space for *reverberation*, for the reader to hold in the moments of silence rather than be told about silence.

I try again:

This is what my morning
Is . . . a screen
blank   before
the hermit thrush awakes
before dawn   before   the drip

drip   of water   before
this day   begins   before
my daughter's lips part   with
words   I write   these words

before I wake   (from dreams)

My morning *Is*

Experimenting in this way begins to focus attention on important questions: What are the resources available to create the *presence of silence*? How do sound and silence, the said and unsaid, the heard and not heard, work toward creating an experience or meaning in a poem?

Take lines you wrote from the silences in your day and experiment with ways to bring those together into a poem, using resources that emphasize silences. Try to articulate the effect of each resource you use.

As a final invitation, take any combination of what you have written and create a two-line poem. This constraint will emphasize the effect of the resources you use to nod toward silence. Ezra Pound's "In a Station of the Metro" offers us an example of this very tight control:

The apparition of these faces in the crowd;
Petals on a wet, black bough.

Read this poem aloud. What do you see and hear? Pound describes writing this poem in 1912 to capture a moment in Paris Metro's Concorde station. "In a poem of this sort," Pound (1916; 1960) notes, "one is trying to record the precise instant when a thing outward and objective transforms itself, or darts into a thing inward and subjective" (p. 89). A moment very much in contrast to what we may experience in the bustle, movement, sounds of wheels on track, brakes on metal in any underground subway system.

Divested of a narrative line or thread, a quietness suspends into the *now* of this poem's image. Feel the presence of silence—brevity, image, eighteen syllables. How might you describe a feeling or meaning that is held at this moment? Silence in image— contemplative, the feeling of near solitude, and yet, all this in a Metro bustling with movement and energy. Haiku-like with all the influence of his study of Japanese art forms, Pound chooses a variation. To what effect the two lines, the longer first line, the extra syllable of the second line? There are no right answers here, but in noticing and questioning, we *experience* the poem again and the power of holding a moment silent.

Why might we pay attention to the presence of silence in poems? How do the silences in poems orient us to experience silence and its import in our lives?

Reading Habits: Making Space for Silence

It is not an exaggeration to state that we can satiate ourselves easily with the sounds and noises of the world. Harder perhaps to seek out silence. While it is true that we come face-to-face with silences in life and nature, these sometimes go unnoticed in our over committed lives and "to do" lists. We have found that poetry deepens our experiences and understandings of these silences in nuanced and diverse ways. Poets escort us into the rich terrains of silence through their experiences and imaginings if we are willing to lean in and to learn ways to negotiate the spaces of silence they share with us. They take us into spaces of candor, ambivalence, and sadness and, perhaps, help us learn to maneuver our way in and around silences.

Pace Yourself

Probably one of the most important reading habits is *to slow* our reading as a way to make space for silence. This may seem an obvious point, but we have found that in school practices, as in life, the fast reader is honored, the person who can read, respond, and have an opinion about what is being read quickly. Fast-paced reading is associated with expertise. How, then, might we practice slowing down and to what effect?

To begin, we make space for silence by slowing the reading pace—read once, read twice, read aloud, pause after a line, a word, a punctuation mark, or a stanza. Breathe into the quiet spaces, the silences between and around what is making noise on the page. Feel the silences move in and allow words to linger and reverberate. Cultivate a reading practice of being in the spaces in-between. Trust dwelling in the spaces that are not conveying information or image.

Turn to the first line of Alison Croggon's (2002) poem "Silence broke my mouth":
Silence broke my mouth:

Fight the urge to skitter ahead to the next line. Lucky for you it isn't here anyway.

Silence broke my mouth:

Take a moment to write a few lines of response. What comes to mind? An image, an idea? What holds just there—in the space after "mouth"? A colon demands something more, yet, in this moment of a first reading, only silence follows.

What is the something more, *for you in this moment*, after the end of the line, the colon? It's not to guess what the poet's next line might be. It's yours to decide. Write the next line that follows this one and maybe the next. You may be thinking: "But I just want to read the poem," but experience the exhilaration of imagining and creating *with* the poet, *as you read*.

Try writing the second and maybe a third line. See where it takes you.

I lingered in the spaces after the colon and wrote:

Silence broke my mouth:

dangled between glass shards
and mouthed words, rolled up
and shut down beyond where
dark air moves, across the window,
my gathered breath . . .

Through this practice, I enter into a *conversation* with the poem I am about to read. In some ways this reminds me of a conversation where someone says something, pauses, and in *the silence of that moment*, we pick up and continue on with our thinking out of what has been said. The point is: we take in an idea and experience it by giving back not what was said but by continuing what we have made of what was given.

It may not be possible to name the ways this practice changes readings specifically, but we have found it focuses our attention on those spaces of silence that invite us to pause and hear the silence speaking into it. Only you can answer in what ways this practice influences your reading of a poem, but we hope you find it worthy of trying.

Now, meet Australian poet Alison Croggon. Slow your reading. Pause where it makes sense.

Silence Broke My Mouth

Silence broke my mouth:
the crumbs flew out the window
like paper butterflies or those magnolias
nonchalantly shattered on the grass.
These mirrors are confusing,
so cold and expensive, they ripple out
noiselessly like the sweet curve
of water from a cliff
where I am looking down, seeing further out

that blue point beyond
any voice.

After the declaration in her first line, what are the ideas and perceptions of silence you experienced? How do those compare with where you took the idea in your writing? Did you find yourself pausing at any point in the poem to take in what was there before reading further? If so, take a minute now to read those phrases or lines again. Take a breath and hold an image or word that resonates or reverberates.

As you read again, emphasize a moment of pause at the end of each line before you read on. Attend to the line breaks. Then, take a minute to look at the placement of punctuation marks. How do these affect where you pause and where you find silences? And what about that colon where we began? Consider how the lack of stanzas may work in tension with the punctuation and line breaks and these change the pace of your reading and where you locate your attention. And, finally, consider your experience with the poem and what stays and reverberates from your reading?

Negotiating with Messengers of Silence

Adrienne Rich declared that "Every poem breaks a silence that had to be overcome" (p. 84). Rich's idea has profound implications for a way of reading or listening. If the poem is a messenger, intended to break some form of silence, we have a starting point for attuning. We can ask: Into what silence does this poem speak? What silence is this poem intending to break, overcome, or gesture toward?

Read the following poem by Chloe Yelena Miller, author of the chapbook *Viable* (2021), with Rich's idea in mind:

His Short Story

No one saw the bomb.
Roadside trash explodes.
Our blood leaks into enemy blood puddles.
We die without knowing how.
The dead no longer miss the children.

He does not describe
leaving Mexico City,
studying inglés in New Jersey,
brushing Baghdad's sand off his skin.
He speaks
and does not speak
with care.

His daughter turns two on Sunday.
He misses her when he goes to work.

What are your first thoughts after reading the poem? Any images or lines stay with you? How might you describe what silences this poem is overcoming? What isn't said? Take a moment to reread.

We noticed the absence of information about the "he." The speaker seems to intentionally not name "him" but to focus on "his story," providing only the information about his life needed to convey the poem's intended emotional impact. The poem speaks to and with the silences that seem to be at the heart of the speaker's encounter with this man. He is both present and not present. Something appears to be missing (or silenced). There is a tension between the first stanza and the last couplet, prompting a question that we can barely ask: *Is his daughter alive?* We are met with silence.

Rich's words continue to haunt: "Every poem breaks a silence that had to be overcome." If poems are messengers and breakers of silence, our resources of language live beyond our words—line breaks, punctuation marks, stanza separations. The feeling of a closing couplet, the only couplet in the poem, communicates pain without direct acknowledgment.

We want to emphasize, however, and not miss the idea that poems, as with other art forms, are by their very nature attempts to speak into and beyond the silences in our everyday lives. It takes a poet/poem, the resources of language, and a reader/listener working together—all are messengers of the silences we are exploring.

And, just how might a poem be an attempt to penetrate silence, to understand its power as well? In many ways the speaker of a poem involves both self and reader in the exploration of the mysteries of silence, how it bends and twists and is present and is not in the same moment, the same breath or comma or open space of the page. We can see the silence, hear declarations about silence in the following poem by Rudy Francisco (2017):

Silence

I'm learning
that I don't always
have to make noise
to be seen,
that even my silence
has a spine, a rumble
and says, I'm here
in its native tongue.

This speaker declares self-recognition and acceptance of silence. In this way, we add the speaker of the poem as another of the potential messengers of silence: the poem itself, the speaker within the poem, the reader/listener lifting "it from grains/ of sand," and the resources of language and craft with attention to sounds, curves of syntax, line breaks, surrounding spaces, and punctuation. Every modulation is crafting the language toward the recognition of silences as tools, as messengers of silence.

Read Francisco's poem once more and attend to the resources that emphasize silences. What resources are employed in this poem? Pay attention to the title, the line breaks, the punctuation, the one sentence. To what effect on meaning and emphasis?

For me, the last comma gives us just a moment of silence before the final reveal, filled with the immensity of implication. Implication is also a messenger of silence. I cannot quite explain, "I'm here/in its native tongue," but I experience the silence of implication and breathe it in. I do not feel the need to explain. The moment is enough.

Working from Within

Rather than positioning ourselves *outside* the poem as an interpreter or observer, what if we reorient the logic and ask: "Where am I *within* the poem?" *If* we allow the poem to encase us and if we live within its skin and life for a moment, we might be better able to articulate what is being experienced rather than to state an intended meaning. Take a minute to explore this idea through a very simple image. Rebecca wrote this haiku as a tenth grader:

Catalpa swords hang
dying, splitting their bellies
scattering their seeds.

Where are you within the poem? Where are you held at this moment? A poem is a force field of energy—enter it. And despite the urge to explain it, just take a moment to linger inside the poem.

We return to Rilke's words: "The work of the eyes is done. Go now and do the heart-work on the images imprisoned within you" (p. 135). The heart-work requires working from within, surfacing the silences but letting them remain *in silence*. Rilke invites us (intentionally or not) to consider how a poem may be a way of unsilencing what has been imprisoned and not consciously available within us.

Take a closer look at Rebecca's haiku. She wrote this in response to an invitation in Ruth's class: "Focus attention out the window, take a few minutes to study what you see, then, create a frame around an object or a scene of focus—large or small. Write what you see and then describe WITHOUT stating your feelings about the subject."

Rebecca focused on a small stand of three catalpa trees, each loaded with seed pods. First, she wrote a detailed description, and, then, as she moved to the heart-work, that is, the silences that touched her *within* the scene, she indicated that she felt the need to "leave breaths of silence everywhere. Haiku allows the beauty to live in the moment, the birth that is to come just hangs in the air."

An Invitation

Try the same exercise.

Look around the room you are in or an outside view if you have one. Take a few minutes to scan. Then, focus narrowly on an object or a scene. Stay close in and write what you see followed by an expression of the sensations, emotions, or questions about what you are seeing. Read through what you wrote and choose a starting point. Make that your first line. Or, if you prefer, turn to a work of art that you love and try what follows.

Ekphrasis: "The work of the eyes is done . . ."

Find a visual artwork that you love. Look closely. What do you notice? Where does your eye hold for even a moment? What do you recognize? What story comes to mind? Where are you located in this image? Take a few minutes to write.

The Greek use of *ekphrasis—ek*, "out of," and *phrasis*, "speech" or "expression"— resulted in poems that conveyed visual information and allowed spaces to unspeak the passions and nuances through poems. Can words alone express emotional nuances? If words are intermediaries of more than what is said, the use of photographs, paintings, or sketches prompts ekphrasis poetry. The result is not to provide a verbal replica of the visual, but to create a grounded instance of *feeling through the seeing.*

We invite you to take what you wrote as description and the sensations and feelings that resulted and try a short ekphrasis poem. If helpful, one of the most famous ekphrasis poems is Keats's (1820; 1958). Here is the opening stanza:

Ode to a Grecian Urn

Thou still unravish'd bride of quietness,
   Thou foster-child of Silence and slow Time,
Sylvan historian, who canst thus express
   A flowery tale more sweetly than our rhyme:
What leaf-fring'd legend haunts about thy shape
   Of deities or mortals, or of both,
     In Tempe or the dales of Arcady?
What men or gods are these? What maidens loth?
   What mad pursuit? What struggle to escape?
     What pipes and timbrels? What wild ecstasy?

Consider the silences addressed within the descriptions. If you gaze at the urn, how is it a "foster-child or Silence and slow Time"? Keats takes on gaps in knowing through a series of questions, which is a reminder of how questions themselves and a question mark create spaces of silence.

Rilke's words return: "Go now and do the heart-work on the images imprisoned within you." We leave you with one more Invitation: *Sleep with the poems you just started to write. Let them enter your dreams. Come back tomorrow to keep writing again* into whatever spaces and silences you wish to speak.

Unspeakabilities

Someone is writing a poem. Words are being set down in a force field. It's as if the words themselves have magnetic charges; they veer together or in polarity, they swerve against each other.

(Adrienne Rich, What is Found There, "Someone is Writing a Poem," pp. 86–7)

Someone is writing a poem. What is the force field to which she alludes? The words have magnetic charges, but how they veer together or establish polarities may be largely due to the ways in which the spaces "between the words" are constructed and constructing. Rich's words tell us nothing of identities of the someone's writing—only of force and movement in this force field. Someone is charging a field, playing with energies, and selecting words and silences out of language's chaos. Like any event, the poem is "a doing, a making, a combustion fed both by a particular personality and a particular text" (Rosenblatt, 1964, p. 128). *The poem is not a universal; it is a universe—a multiverse*—made by and belonging to the poet, the someone, who is attempting to speak and unspeak, and to a reader/listener who is in negotiation and transaction with the poem.

Possibly a force field could not be more magnetically charged with sounds and silences than when a poet attempts to speak the unspeakable. Poets speak into taboos and undo silences of the often unnoticed or forgotten. They offer readers moments to question and fracture complacencies or reorient perspectives. Countless poems talk about things rarely talked about, often because of stigma or social disagreements surrounding the subject. We are thinking of hot, controversial, restless poems by June Jordan, Ijeoma Umebinyuo, Sharon Olds, Fatimah Asghar, and Aime Cesaire. To say that to speak of these subjects is exceptionally political is a misunderstanding of the political. The "aesthetic regime" (Rancière, 2004, p. 13) to which poetry belongs is inherently political. Poetry fights against the dominant logic of the sensible when what is deemed unspeakable or stigmatized gets addressed. In this sense, speaking unspeakable *content* contributes in a strongly felt, direct way to a political project of which all poetry—whether or not it gets self-consciously named "political poetry"—is a part of undoing silences and silencing.

Perhaps more than any other literary genre, poetry asks us to come close to what we don't know. As Camille Paglia (2006) writes, poetry points to something "*out there*, however dimly we can know it" (p. xv). The affective intensities sought and brought through poetry relate to this sense of unspeakability. How many people speak of *feeling moved* to write poetry or of how reading a particular poem caused them to *feel moved* in ways they had not before? This desire or need to read and write poems is a powerful testament to explaining the purposes of poetry in our lives. If we come to poetry with this idea of desire and need, we might more fully understand how a poem is an invitation to explore experiences, speculations, and, yes, silences—overwhelming, every day, particular, and, oftentimes, impossible to put in words.

There are moments when I come upon a poem that is a gift of illumination, a pulling across the silences, to witness for others who have not, could not, or have not been allowed to speak for themselves. Witnessing takes many forms—reaching out across time, place, circumstance, or, simply, across the table, to notice others, to witness *for* others. One simple and powerful moment that speaks to poets as a witness is when Anna Akhmatova, living through the worst of times in Stalinist Russia, writes in her poem "Requiem" of a woman who asks her "And can you describe this?"—meaning, the horror of Stalin's actions against political prisoners, including Akhmatova and her sons. Here are the first two sections of her poem, translated by New Zealand–born poet John Gallas (2014):

63

Requiem

Not some other country's sky,
Not some other's housing wings—
I was there, with them, my them,
my own misfortunates.

An Other Introduction

In the ghastly years of the Yezhov Terror, I passed seventeen months standing, waiting in line outside a Leningrad prison. One day, somehow, someone "identified" me. And a woman behind me, her mouth blue with cold, who, of course, had never heard of me, started out of her numb and shared distraction, and said to me, quite close (we all whispered, there):

Ah, can you write this?

And I said, Yes.

And something nearly a smile slipped across her face, and made it one again.

"Yes, I can," Akhmatova replies in her poem. And "Requiem" answers the question by blurring the lines of art and life to offer up not only the life situations that seem beyond our capacity to imagine but also a sense of responsibility and urgency in witnessing the depth of human suffering that travel with us in this world.

In such witnessing, there seems a sense of responsibility that poets feel to bring these experiences to the center. And yet, the poem must be open to a reader, filled with entry points and spaces and gaps to move through and feel the experience being witnessed. And, a poet might leave traces that encourage a sense of urgency for what we cannot always recognize for ourselves without the poet's vision to move beyond silence.

A contemporary poet, melissa christine goodrum, high school teacher and author of the poetry collections *something sweet & filled with blood* (Great weather for MEDIA, 2019) and *definitions uprising* (NYQ Books, 2013), wrote this poem of witness in 2015 in response to a death caused by police brutality:

Lament for a Son of the Oyate

before Devil Lake became Devil,
when the Sun lived laughter wild
among the long dancing trees,
and before the spirits, our ancestors'
warm spirits eased their lights
and left out . . .
over the livid-blue,

plentiful and many-pointed waters
then the wise-tall Great Elder
The Hollow Horn Bear say:
"The Mdewakanton are the grandfathers of us all."
Oyate   Oyate   Oyate
Oh, Spirit Lake Nation
tiyošpaye*

young Joe Charboneau is now our sun
his flames breathe into Ft. Totten's
long & winding memory
wakan, wakan—his greatest mystery
now this Joe, he breathes between the trees
Oyate   Oyate   Oyate
Oh, Spirit Lake Nation
tiyošpaye*

we: one large family & we welcome him home
a gentle soul recently Joe died, Joe came
back home, come home Joe Charboneau
Joe's transformation
Joe is now our missing son
this yellow sun breathing sentient
between the trees, the yellow flame
leaping higher . . . please allow us to see
to know the way
on our long and gathered journey
Oyate   Oyate,   Oyate
Oh, Spirit Lake Nation
tiyošpaye[1]

This poem by goodrum laments the dead man without any sense of pity. Its silences give the reader space *to feel*. This poem expresses a joy for whom this man was, his community of belonging, the Spirit Lake Nation, family, that recognizes his transformation, and sings him, dances with his spirit—the poem's roots in the Oyate's language also give the poem its energy. The use of "tiyošpaye" carries an unstated silence, the potential loss of a language and with it of a culture and potentially a history. We read this lament also as a declaration of love and persistence.

---

[1] All linguistic prompts adapted from Scott Richard Lyons's *Roots* entry on pro-boards, 6/18/07.

"Lament for a son of the Oyate" offers another gift. We imagine asking our students to write a poem where they integrate a voice and language—previously unspeakable to them—into a poem.

Ending here, with goodrum's words in the air, we leave you with an invitation to practice the art of unspeakability in poetry—or the art of saying the unsayable, honoring what isn't said, witnessing oppressive silences and breaking them, tending to affective intensities that lose language, resisting through speech, and trying with all your heart to work the silences you experience in your life.

CHAPTER 6
TENSIONS AND CONSTRAINTS

VI
Icicles filled the long window
With barbaric glass.
The shadow of the blackbird
Crossed it, to and fro.
The mood
Traced in the shadow
An indecipherable cause.

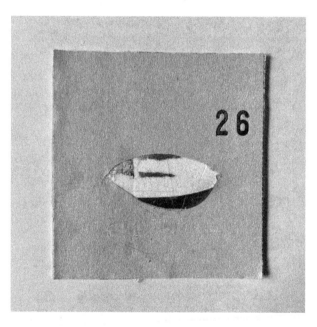

Reading this stanza spurs thoughts of poetic tensions and constraints. I imagine the long window as a kind of frame that contains the icicles—making them visible and also possible. After all, the icicles need a surface to hang from. Without the window's structure, the cold water would simply be ice, not icicle; we would lose that sense of "barbaric glass" crossed to and fro by the blackbird. Similarly, a poem's power often comes from its relationship to form. Like an icicle, the subject and the structure work together to create the poem, often manifesting an awkward beauty because of the subject's necessary tension with the closed window we might call poetic form.

Working Form

Poetic forms may be as common and diverse to poetry as wildflowers to a forest. Forms originate in particular times and places, but they travel across oceans and shift in their travels, creating "unexpected affinities" (Ramazani, 2009, p. 32). Forms—like the sonnet, the haiku, and the ghazal, to name a few—invite us to tune into a structure and learn what our words are capable of doing within the constraints instructed by a form. Forms are meant to cross boundaries, raise questions, and regenerate with each use; forms, in their transnational crossings and uses, are revitalized by the fact of their ongoing cultural displacement and in-between-ness, never belonging to a nation state (Ramazani, 2009).

Without tension or struggle, however, form can deaden poetic spirit. In Adrienne Rich's *What Is Found There: Notebooks on Poetry and Politics* (1995), Rich notes the difference between form and format. She warns that poetic forms can slip into format when "the dynamics of experience and desire are forced to fit a pattern to which they have no organic relationship" (p. 218). The key to writing in poetic form, Rich emphasizes, is to enable the form to change based on its relationship to the subject matter that lives in the poet's heart, and for the poet to embrace the tensions between poetic form and personally meaningful content. As Rich puts it, "It's a struggle not to let the form take over, lapse into format, assimilate the poetry; and that very struggle can produce a movement, a music, of its own" (pp. 218–19). In other words, form contributes to the life force of a poem when an active dynamism happens between the form and the poet's subject. However, when the form overwhelms the subject and the "lifeblood" of the poem is diminished for the sake of sitting inside a predetermined structure, form quickly becomes format. A poetic form needs, to quote Rich's quoting the poet Richard Hugo (1979), a "triggering subject" to animate and energize the form (p. 4). Often the word "trigger," in classroom contexts, signals trauma. We want to clarify that for our purposes, via Hugo, "triggering" means energizing—a topic that jolts you to action, to making a poem. There can be no poem without that triggering subject, no matter the form.

A commonplace classroom practice is to teach students the rules of a form and then write a poem following that form. For example, it would not be unusual for a teacher to note that a Shakespearean sonnet is fourteen lines, follows an a/b/a/b/c/d/c/d/e/f/e/g/g rhyme scheme, and uses iambic pentameter. Maybe the students learn the history of sonnets, they might read different types of sonnets or identify the sonnet rules in sample sonnets, showing evidence of their understanding. Then, they are off to write their own sonnets. The poem is evaluated based on the students' faithfulness to the sonnet form.

Rich explains that schools often mistake poetic forms with the vitality of poetry. Though she does not explicitly name formalism, it seems clear that Rich criticizes an approach to poetry that centers form above all else and demands adherence to form, turning form into formula. As Rich suggests, in many classrooms form dominates and the poem's subject becomes secondary matter instead of a necessary ingredient for an active wrestling with form, making it something new. (The image of the restless blackbird moving to and fro comes to mind as we write about this process of wrestling with form.) We could speak to the problem of a "standard style" of any form extending far beyond the teaching of poetry to the "five-paragraph essay," or, any instructional assignment where structure dominates and "the triggering subject" becomes squashed, if not dead, inside the formulaic. Given the all-too-frequent standardization—from its uses of language to its respectability politics—there is much more to be said about the violence of format/formula. As it relates to creativity, Rich writes, "Format has no literary power, and finally it destroys literary power" (p. 218). The life force of any poem, then, depends on keeping alive an organic, animate relationship to its structure.

When form meets its "triggering subject" and the necessary struggle ensues, we can feel the poem's pulsing. Teaching form in relation to the poet's vital subject matter enables generative tensions and openings that may not otherwise be possible if the writer remains in her/their/his usual (and usually free verse) comfort zone.

I turn to some recent poems I've written in free verse and see what form might make of my continued writings about the Israeli-Palestinian conflict, the dictating power of national identity, and the displacement of Palestinian people. I select the most recent poem I've drafted, "Belief." It begins:

Belief

My country lies to me.

It tells me what I love is national belonging
and not its native bird's singing,
how our throat's throttle when speaking
the words *mustard* and *friend*—
the sea's salt & memory.

Once, I believed my country,
thinking the children dead by its hands
an unfortunate necessity
for the preservation of our bodies.

I don't believe my country anymore.

I stop and consider folding it into a haiku. I am drawn to the haiku's essential qualities, including its economy of language to convey an image, its call for a dissolved boundary between self and what is seen, its subtle syllabic pattern, and its small shape. The haiku's basic form is easy to remember: three lines alternating 5/7/5 syllables. And there's the emphasis on nature and being in the present moment. I step outside for a few minutes. It's boiling, and even though I see plant leaves rustling, I can't feel any breeze. I go back to my studio and sit at my desk to reorient myself. Begin again.

"Belief"

Not its native bird
singing, how our throats—I don't
believe my country.

"Belief"

Sea's salt: memory:
children dead by my country's
hands. Dead by country.

"Belief"

Mustard, friend, the sea's
salt & memory refuse
the bombs & bodies.

"To my Country"

Once I believed you
and wanted to be you, now
my throat throttles salt.

Mary Oliver's *A Poetry Handbook* (1994) provides an accessible and inspiring discussion of poetic forms and their uses, urging readers to try out various forms and imitate different ways of writing poetry. She argues that "a poem requires a design—a sense of orderliness" and points out that the pleasure a poem generates in its readers cannot be separated from its form; the poem "gives pleasure through the authority and sweetness of the language *used in the way that it is used*" (p. 58, her italics). Exploring different forms can become a way of determining ways that language can be used. How we mobilize forms contributes to the shifting of those forms. Forms are not static and should not be taught as static things; they move, and, through their movement, take on new life (Ramazani, 2009).

I like to think of using poetic forms as a type of shape-shifting with the bones intact and the shadows of the form's history touching the present moment in which one sits to write a particular poem. Perhaps it makes possible "the mood/ traced in the shadow" of a poetic history rooted in, but untethered to, a particular context. Perhaps forms let us come closer to a place and time not our own and find an unexpected belonging.

Ghazal: A Form of Introduction

What poetic forms were you introduced to as a student in your K-12 English classrooms? How do you feel about poetic forms? What memories spring to mind and/or stay calcified in a feeling about form? Take a few minutes to reflect on your own experiences with poetic form.

It seems to us, though we may be wrong, that the most popular forms taught in US ELA classrooms tend to be the haiku and sonnet. Haiku frequently gets taught because it is deemed an "easy" and short form. The sonnet form, as presented in many English classrooms, often carries an onerous gravitas connected to the importance of Shakespeare. In occasional English Language Arts classrooms, a wider variety of poetic forms may appear, often introduced by a teaching artist, if not the classroom teacher.

The tensions generated by formal constraints extend, we believe, to a reorientation of our positionalities as Western subjects studying in the United States where "free verse" poetry tends to reign. For these reasons, I like to begin my poetry classes with the ghazal form. I teach at a small art and design college in Philadelphia to students who, for the most part, grew up in the surrounding Pennsylvania and New Jersey area and many of whom have never traveled outside the United States. Each fall I learn that the majority of my students have never studied poetry and consider themselves "new" to the subject. When asked to name poems they love, many reference the last poets they read: Dr. Seuss, Shel Silverstein, or that one Edgar Allan Poe poem they read in high school—usually "The Raven" or "Annabelle Lee." Needless to say, when I introduce the ghazal form at the start of the semester, most, if not all, of my students have no idea what I'm talking about. "The *what* form?"

Poet and professor Taije Silverman (author of the poetry collection *Houses Are Fields* 2009) offers us this beautiful ghazal that she recently wrote:

Season's Ghazal

Spring has come back with its full moon again.
Moonlight pummels my window, again and again.

Of that childhood I fabled, no graveyard remains.
Its keepsakes float up from mossed shipwrecks again.

My mother once promised that love doesn't end.
Loom, loop the yarn on your one skein again.

Are these lonely bone branches just cloaks for clear veins?
Crabapple, linden, bloom freely again.

Stunned mourners feel warmth through black coats in the sun.
Forgetful, they vow not to beg God again.

The dead are dandelion seeds, floating pollen.
Through breath that blows wishes, they find us again.

Without child or lover, I'm cut free from claims.
What abundance of nest pulls the air in again?

Days abandon our promises, longings, our names.
The sound *Taije* soughs a stream into silence again.

Based on Silverman's poem, what do you infer about the form's rules? Make a moment to read it again, noting form.

From the *Poetry Foundation*'s online Glossary of Poetic Terms:

Ghazal: (Pronounciation: "guzzle"), is an Arabic verse form dealing with loss and romantic love. Medieval Persian poets embraced the ghazal, eventually making it their own. Consisting of syntactically and grammatically complete couplets, the form also has an intricate rhyme scheme. Each couplet ends on the same word or phrase (the *radif*), and is preceded by the couplet's rhyming word (the *qafia,* which appears twice in the first couplet). The last couplet includes a proper name, often of the poet's. In the Persian tradition, each couplet was of the same meter and length, and the subject matter included both erotic longing and religious belief or mysticism.

I like to begin with the ghazal for several reasons: (1) Born in seventh-century Arabia and prominent in Iran, India, and Pakistan (despite its transnational routes/roots, which it shares with most poetic forms) as a lyric form of poetry historically accompanied by music, the ghazal could be considered a non-Western form that made its way west while still carrying echoes of its native Arabic and Urdu. I find that beginning with the ghazal reorients us as US-based writers, who, often it seems, feel most comfortable in free verse. Something dis- and re-orienting occurs when starting with an unfamiliar form born and living outside of dominant Western frames and purposes. Beginning with the ghazal can expose our own expectations of poetry and enable us to grow intimate with a form that feels new or unfamiliar. (2) The lyric nature of the ghazal form invites a tuning into the musicality of a poem, sharpening how we hear the poem spoken or sung. In a way, beginning with the ghazal is a choice to begin with music or sound. The ghazal asks us to listen, anticipate, and become carried away by its refrain. (3) The ghazal's rules are clear, simple, and ambitious. It is not easy to write a good ghazal, but a good ghazal can easily come through attunement to its form as it rubs up against one's subject matter. (4) The themes of love, loss, and suffering familiar to the ghazal propel us to write our own passionate poems, and I find that beginning from that place of experience can prompt a tight sense of classroom community. That said, approaches to those themes need not be serious! Students can obviously write ghazals about anything, including candy bars and YouTube videos of cats.

We invite you to pause and find some contemporary ghazals written in English, including those by Agha Shahid Ali, Patricia Smith, Aimee Nezhukumatathil, Angel Nafis, and Suzanne Gardinier. Consider the relationships between the ghazal form and the poet's subject matter—sometimes love, longing, politics, joy, pain—and revel in the various meanings and associations of the word "ghazal": young gazelle, the sound a wounded gazelle makes, conversations with women. Consider what these definitions surface for you and what kinds of poems you might make via the ghazal form.

An Invitation

Now, write down five words you love for whatever reason. Maybe it's simply for their sound, for their meaning, for the memories they bring up in you, any reason at all, and you don't need to share why.

If we were in a class together, maybe we would compile our words into a collective class list of beloved words and from those words, each select one for our own ghazal's refrain. It could be a word or phrase offered by a peer, or one that you wrote down. Go back to your list. Pick a word or a short phrase that lingers with you. Think of Silverman's choice of word, "again." Once you have your word, write two ghazals with the same word—one repeating the word, as is traditionally done in ghazals, like in Silverman's, and the second ghazal introducing the word but then using a rhyme to echo that word in each of the following couplets, as Aimee Nezhukumatathil does in her "Red Ghazal," which you can find online on the *Poetry Foundation's* website.

Nurturing Collaboration

After you've written your ghazals, think about how you might create a collaborative ghazal with a community of people—maybe your students, family members, friends scattered across the country or across the world. Consider various structures for this collaboration. Will one person write the first couplet and the next person write the second couplet and so on? Will you write parallel ghazals using the same refrain and then exchange couplets, reassembling them into poems? Will you agree on a refrain and then send each other sound or video recordings of a couplet read aloud, eventually threading the recordings into a chain? Will you all write into the same Google Doc for ten minutes at the same time and see what ghazal emerges in that short span of time?

During the pandemic in the spring of 2021, I team-taught a course called *Poetry & Time-Based Media* with a professor of animation and game arts. Inspired by the Bowery Poetry Club's "Poetry Like Bread" ghazal project, "a collaborative poem created by a world of poets to nourish us all through the Pandemic and to envision the world After" (bowerypoetry.com/bread), we asked students to each write one couplet of a ghazal centered on the refrain "space" and to create a video of their voice speaking their ghazal couplet ending with "space" (a word we all agreed spoke evocatively to the realities of the pandemic and that we collectively decided to use for our class poem). Some students filmed themselves speaking the couplet, as the poets on the Bowery's video project do, and others created animations or film montages to accompany their voices. We then weaved the MP4 files into a collective ghazal video. The class's collaborative video ghazal opens with the following lines:

I never thought the pandemic would make me take things for granted
with living back at home affecting my mental health and personal space.

I chat with friends alone in my room
and I'm sick of all this empty space.

School may become overwhelming from the constant assignments,
and sometimes we just need to break away for some space.

I wonder what astronauts dream of? Maybe they dream of nature
or the vast and unexplored ocean. But probably not space.

A whole year of wandering these cold, empty streets without their usual throng
of smiling strangers, and I think to myself: I've never not wanted space.

Creative Constraints in Response to Our Times

Thus far, we have discussed and practiced the generative uses of engaging existing poetic forms and working their tensions. The previous part of this chapter could be reiterated in the following questions: What happens to our subject matters inside an existing form— or bursting within that form? How can moving through and with a closed form open up new sensory understandings of our subjects? We see poetic form not as a corset but as a body we slip into to know and feel ourselves and our subjects differently. Writing within poetic forms enables us to work conventions shared by our poetry ancestors and unexpected kin. When we don't allow the form to overpower the vital force of our subjects, we can work existing forms to become new bodies.

In addition to studying and experimenting with existing poetic forms, like the ghazal, sonnet, villanelle, haiku, pantoum, we also have the power to make our own closed forms or creative constraints, like today's insta-poetry, pop sonnets, Twitter poems, and mashups with various media and genres. After exploring some current forms, including Jericho Brown's invented "duplex" form, I ask my students to come up with their own invented forms for us to try out as a class community. Here are a few ideas that students in my fall 2021 poetry class came up with: (1) Write a body of text so that a string of rhyming words appears in the text in the shape of a circle. (2) Write two lines describing an object/experience (similar in length). Then, sum up what you said in one word not used previously. Repeat step 1 but with three lines. Repeat step 1 to end the poem. Each stanza should encapsulate a different emotion. (3) Set an intention for your words to ebb and flow like a river. The water can move as slow and as fast as you wish. You can also change the trajectory any time.

I attended a workshop led by Evie Shockley at the Community of Writers at Squaw Valley in 2008 or 2009 where she introduced us to the "prisoner's constraint" form, asking us to imagine the constraints a prisoner may have when writing a poem, including the physical and psychic realities of constraint and the limited amount of lined paper on which to write. The prisoner's constraint form limits the letters included in a poem to those that do not go above or below a narrowly lined sheet of paper; for example, letters like *b, d, f, g, h, j,* and *y* each have at least one long limb that travels above or below the contained space between the two lines. Only letters that visually fit inside the lines, without crossing it, are allowed: *a, c, e, i, m, n, o,* for instance. Working the constraints attuned me to a prisoner's reality and highlighted my own taken-for-granted approach to my supply of pencils and paper, not to mention the freedom I have to write whenever and wherever I wish. The exercise also demanded a kind of struggle with language and an attention to the confining realities of space that I had not previously considered.

Writing a poem in the "prisoner's constraint" form generates for us the following pedagogical questions:

What poetic forms do our social, cultural, and/or political contexts summon, and how can we make the links between form and context explicit for our students?

What forms of writing (and writing materials) have we come to take for granted based on our own particular positions and privileges?

How can poetic form become a response to an oppressive structure and enable a kind of poetry that might not otherwise be possible?

Poetic constraints, then, can be responsive structures to the time and place we live, the limitations that delineate our points of access and connection to others, and the care that inspires poetry across times and places.

An Invitation

Consider a social, cultural, political, and/or environmental issue that you feel passionate about. Think about how this issue intersects with poetry. Jot down some ideas. How might you form a constraint—or rules—that reference that particular issue? As I write this invitation, I am thinking of a fact that I recently read: There are 192 endangered or extinct languages in the United States, most of them Native American. What could it mean to write a poem in English that is exactly 192 words, pointing to the absence of those languages? Or a collaborative poem made up of 192 autonomous lines that, together, cannot be understood and remain illegible to dominant literacies and common logic?

Once you've written your socially responsive constraints, try writing a poem that follows the rules you created. After writing the poem, consider what pedagogical questions emerge. How do the rules you created and followed affect your understanding of form and subject?

Writer, artist, and translator Sarah Riggs plays with form, including her sequence of textos (French for "text message"), telegrams, Post-its, and blackberries in her book *The 60 Textos* (Ugly Duckling Presse, 2010) as forms of reaching out to others. Her recent collection, *The Nerve Epistle* (Roof Books, 2021), is a book of intimate letters to other poets, artists, activists, and friends that continues this practice, especially across places and languages (France and Morocco, for Riggs). As Riggs reflects,

> The foreign connections require reach and they require play, because so often you get things wrong, you have to try things and without exactly knowing the codes. So I think I was finding ways of playing with distance and cultural difference, initially with those technologies when living in France, and then I "graduated" to the letter form during my current U.S. period while visiting back in France. (Personal communication, August 22, 2021)

For Riggs, the letter form was also a way "to reclaim connection and the imagination, the playing field for human bonds" in the context of Trump's presidency in the United States and what she describes as the "daily terror of address" that punctuated this time.

Two of her poems from *The Nerve Epistle* appear on the *Poetry Project*'s website:

Dear Ashraf,
I heard you were there
not being able to imagine it
we are writing you this song
how to send love to someone
never met. Heard you there.
Habib imprisoned this week.
In or out. A penetrating
Dialogue. A wish to send
owl's wings. Caught and
imported. For that hour,
second you there. Between
the films, sliver of an eye.
Sent you a rope to pull you
back into this place.

May 23, 2018

Dear Etel,
Those thoughts circle back
We had heard through the ocean
The creatures in troubled waters
We creatures turning about
Merely muse and a wonder
For the cavity: in there a coffee
Running alongside some questions
And you answered in green

You always answer in colors
The torrential thoughts in a window
or a cloud

Who is somebody in your own life you might invite to enter in correspondence through poem-letters? Have you ever corresponded, or communicated, with your students this way? Is there a person you know, personally or from afar, who you feel a need to reach out to? Perhaps these examples move you to consider your own ways of communicating with people in your life and how this form of address interfaces with your current sociopolitical context and beliefs.

The letter-as poem can also be a way of communicating with a person or people we don't know personally, living or no longer living, as in this poem by Taije Silverman (2021):

Orphan Letter

Dear bad dreams my sister has dreamed since she was a child

Dear left eye of my sister's
          after they take out most of the tumor, I would
          recognize you now she says when I stand in front of her, but

Dear but
Dear closed hospital, huge hospital
          and stranger at the desk saying anything you need

Dear elevators, up up up, and down, down,
Dear painting of a windowsill in Tuscany at reception
Dear nurses' aides who say I'm prayin' for y'all
          shut the lights off, close the door, she's sleeping, she's

Dear bird sounds for the blind
          who must cross this street from the hotel to the hospital,
Dear terrible birds, crazy birds, invented, unappeasable

Dear what's invented, dear death

Do you remember
My sister dreams the scariest dreams, you have to be
          so quiet when she's sleeping
          because if she wakes she'll wake suddenly and in terror

Dear what is safe, where do you go when you go
Dear question

There is something curious and inspiring about orienting one's writing toward a quickly shifting subject, letting the address move with the winds of the poem as it's written and trusting the form to take you where you need to go.

As teachers, we might also consider the letter form as a way of sharing with others the writers we love. In Ruth's "Poetic Imaginaries" class in 2012, she asked each of us to write a letter to a poet we love as an introduction to that poet. We were encouraged to reference writings by the poet, anything to give our reader a personal sense of the poet, and to write our letters however we wished. This letter was a form of introduction to share with our peers. I picked Jean Valentine. My letter to her began as follows:

Dear Jean,

I chose you and your poems because they are wise, old friends. *Shouldn't I have chosen a new poet for this assignment? Am I too comfortable in your words?* I keep returning to them out of hunger and sometimes out of guilt for abandoning my dreams. I return because I feel like I need your poems, maybe now more than ever. *Always, it seems, now more than ever!* They remind me of a part of myself that I don't know but do trust, fully, to be a poem—careful absence, mystery, animal, star. Nothing feels unnecessary in your poems. They feel to me intense & spare moments of need, love, loss, care. . .

Recently, I have tried to write more "narratively" to appeal to the people I share my poems with. My ego tells me to know my story. Wants my audience to "get" it. Something shook in me this morning when I arrived at the last line of your poem "My Mother's Body, My Professor, My Bower": "there is nothing to get." Jean, I couldn't stop crying. And then I heard you speak in an interview about trusting a friend who gets your poems—when she says "I don't get that," you know what to take out. (No absolutes!)

Dear Jean,

I remember my first introduction to you in Kate Knapp Johnson's office. Kate: "Jean Valentine writes poems that people either fall in love with or throw across the room in frustration." It's that question of "getting it," isn't it? Maybe people want to "get" you—to under-stand, to stand under or above your poems, to "grasp" you, squeeze your poems like a lemon, be able to explain (kill) what is felt. It's strange how vulnerable and completely at ease I feel with your poems (my sisters).

I continued to write the letter in starts and re-starts, circling back to the introduction *Dear Jean*. As I reread the letter now, I wish I'd sent it to her before she passed away, even though my letter to her was really a letter for my peers, a form of introduction that I hoped would draw them to her writing and spread love for her work. I am grateful for Ruth's invitation to write it. I recognize in it now some fundamental principles that Ruth and I share, anchoring some of this book's pedagogical moves. The invitation to write a letter to a beloved poet shifted me away from speaking *about* a poet to speaking directly *to* a poet, creating an intimate proximity and accessibility to their work.

Consider the letter, too, as a basic unit of language—a fundamental element to the making of words, of poems. Our shared alphabet. Go back to the letter in its double life: intimate address and elemental material for communication. Where does this thinking guide your teaching, your writing? What new forms will your words, made of letters, concoct?

Experimental Constraints

Consider for a moment your writing rituals, conscious or subconscious. When you begin to write, do you brew yourself a cup of coffee first? Do you sit with a notebook or at a computer? Do you type, write with pencil, or have a favorite pen? Do you need a quiet room or are you most productive when sitting in a public park? Record the rituals that seem connected to your writing practice, even if they change.

Now think about an experimental ritual you might want to try that could shake up your usual writing process. What ritual might take you out of your comfort zone, one that breaks away from habit, and/or that interrupts the routine of writing? It can be as quirky, elaborate, or as straightforward as you like. Maybe it involves interacting with other people, with plants, writing in a particular environment, or performing actions you don't usually take when writing. Think how elements of chance play into your experimental ritual. What controls have you loosened? Try out your experimental ritual and see what writing it generates.

Just as there is value in creating constraints in response to our sociocultural environments and predicaments, there is also something pedagogically powerful in creating for ourselves (and asking our students to create for themselves) arbitrary constraints in the spirit of experimentation. Experimental writing constraints enable us to loosen controls over "style" and "voice" and see where the method takes them. John Cage's famous chance operations are vibrant examples. Based on a Zen Buddhist philosophical standpoint, Cage believed in detaching from one's control or style in order to make the work—a poem, a painting, a musical composition—alive. The principle relies on chance to create the work. Cage created "chance operations," perhaps most famously his silent musical composition 4'33" for which he sat quietly at a piano in an auditorium filled with people expecting to hear "music." For Cage, the sounds that decision provoked (shuffling in seats, coughs, perplexed murmurs) and the tension between what was happening in the moment and the audience's preconceptions of "music" created the composition.

In a YouTube video titled "John Cage about silence" (July 14 2007), Cage reflects,

> when I hear traffic, the sound of traffic, here on 6th avenue for instance, I don't have the feeling that anyone is talking. . . . I have the feeling that sound is acting. And I love the activity of sound. What it does is it gets louder and quieter, and it gets higher and lower, and it gets longer and shorter.

His thoughts on the sound of traffic outside the window of his New York City apartment orient us toward the material of our everyday lives as potential frames, or constraints, for our work. Lucille Clifton's point springs to mind: the best place to write poetry is not in a "room of one's own" but at the kitchen table with six children running around (2010). We all have some form of constraints in our daily lives, and there is beauty, we believe, in turning those constraints into playful structures for writing.

Considering Cage's work and philosophy in the context of the English Language Arts classroom, we wonder about the ways creative constraints can open up new relationships to language. If I tell myself, for example, to open the first book I see on my desk to page 55 and make a poem of the first line or fragment of line, I see on that page, what happens?

I pick up Adrienne Rich's (2009) book of essays *A Human Eye: Essays on Art in Society, 1997-2008*, and at the top of page 55 encounter a fragment of James Baldwin's (1998) words, which she began quoting on the previous page: "has created cowboys and Indians, good guys and bad"

What poem might I make of this line? I could have been more specific with my constraints, designating that line as the first in my poem or deciding that whatever fragment/sentence I see at the top of page 55 will serve as the title of a poem.

Never have I written a poem with the words "cowboys and Indians" in it before this chance experiment. I'll try my best, giving myself an additional constraint: set the timer for ten minutes and see what poem comes from this line:

This Country

has created cowboys and Indians, good guys and bad
boys, milked our imaginations into hard eyes that see
the same story screen after screen—who you are
and what you play in our American dream—gun in one
hand, arrow in another—the same movie keeps
casting the same hero whose weapon sits inside
a cowhide pocket, and whose boots click to the sound
of his own standing on another man's land.

The thrill of chance moves me to open the next book I see to the same page and, again, record the first line I see on page 55. Gay Watson's (2014) "A Philosophy of Emptiness."

"way of acting in which human actions become as spontaneous"

Reader, what would you make of/with this line? I invite you to open up the first book you notice on your own bookshelf, or on your desk, to page 55 and write down the first line. What poem will you make of those found words?

Constraints open up fresh approaches to language and unexpected swerves away from how or what we "usually write." CAConrad's (2014) somatic rituals, which we discuss in a later chapter, could fit here as another example of experimental constraints created to be fully in the present moment, a practice which for Conrad came from a need to heal from a traumatic event. Inspired by Conrad's somatic rituals and to inspire my students to enter what Conrad calls "an extreme present," I ask my students to create their own weekly rituals (p. xi). They must do the ritual and write from/with it each week. They can choose whether or not to share the writing that comes from that ritual, but we never comment on what is shared. We allow our ritual writing to live as a quiet record of whatever writing came from our own carefully crafted constraints.

Some student weekly ritual instructions have included the following: (1) Place a stone in the middle of a circle and write from inside that circle with the stone in hand or on your lap. (2) Offer someone an apple. Write from whatever words were exchanged in that event. (3) Climb to the highest point of the room you are in (and change the room in which you write each week). Write from that height and perspective. (4) Pick a random song from one of your playlists and write something that follows the rhythm of that song.

What will be yours?

Tensions and Familiar Forms

Haiku

Think of the subject matter that you keep writing about—your grandmother, cultural belonging, gender identity, your children, immigration, bullying, your beloved dog that passed away—and how that "triggering subject," to return to Richard Hugo's phrase, might be written about as haiku. What happens to your subject when you try to tune into the essence of a moment and approach it using a familiar form that might at first seem disconnected from your subject? What might you say about immigration or by standing outside for thirty minutes beneath an oak tree, listening to the birds, then trying to distill that experience into a three-line poem alternating 5/7/5 syllabic lines? Work the tensions between subject and form and see where it takes you.

Often, we teach haiku as a means of creating an image or as an exercise in brevity and paying attention to the economy of language. There is value to these approaches, but there is much more a form like the haiku can offer us as readers and writers of poetry if we bring it into closer relationship with the subjects we obsess over. As Rich notes, tensions are generative when constraints move with meaningful subject matter. Read Etheridge Knight's series of haikus on poetryfoundation.org (from *The Essential Etheridge Knight*, 1986):

1
Eastern guard tower
glints in sunset; convicts rest
like lizards on rocks.

2
The piano man
is stingy, at 3 A.M.
his songs drop like plum.

3
Morning sun slants cell.
Drunks stagger like cripple flies
On jailhouse floor.

What do you notice about these haiku? What effect does the form have on the subject? Feel the length and shape of these haiku—the chiseled images they flash forth.

Conventions of form can allow us to enter new ways of engaging our subjects; the subject takes on a new body and reaches its readers differently than how we might write about it in more familiar ways. An unexpected music erupts when the scaffolds go up and one's voice can bounce and echo from wall to wall. In some ways, the form is a frame that enables us to better sense the images, the music, and the affective capacities of our language.

We can also find routes to our own subjects in other people's poems.

An Invitation

Borrow a peer's poem that you love and distill it to a new essence through haiku. How might you chisel the poem down to three lines, 5/7/5, making it say what you need it to say? The point is that you can make something you care about from anything and in a dynamic relation to any form. Subject matter can inform form and form can shed new light on subject matter.

We leave you with this funny and fresh haiku by poet Rachel M. Simon, author of the chapbook *Marginal Road* (2009).

Explaining the Offsides Rule

is easiest
with a tableful
of condiments

Sonnets

If I were to ask you to write a sonnet, what feelings does that "assignment" bring up for you? What have been your experiences with the sonnet form, if any, as a student? As a teacher?

When I teach poetry, I usually assign my students the task of writing sonnets—not because I believe there is something special or royal about the form and not because I think Shakespeare is king. I teach the sonnet form because I find myself compelled to undo student attitudes toward the form; many students come to class already hating sonnets because of how they were made to write them in high school—a grueling task amplified by the annoyingly pristine status of Shakespeare. Given their educational experiences, I make it a point to level the sonnet with other forms and approach it as what it is: just another form to come to know, maybe love, and awkwardly nestle, and/or struggle, within until some vitality we can call poetry ensues.

I like to assign Shakespeare's famous "Sonnet 130" and then follow up with Haryette Mullen's fantastic riff on it, "Dim Lady," from her book *Sleeping with the Dictionary* (2002). We explore the joy of repurposing, talking back to, and/or playing around with a well-known poem. For Shakespeare's speaker in "Sonnet 130," "My mistress' eyes are nothing like the sun" and for Mullen's speaker in "Dim Lady," "My honeybunch's peepers are nothing like neon." Mullen's parody of Shakespeare's sonnet makes from Shakespeare's original a new poem that feels fresh, real, and funny while carrying some of the rhythm offered by the sonnet's meter rules. Sometimes I assign Sherman Alexie's (2011) "Facebook Sonnet" and sonnets from Terrance Hayes's (2018) book *American Sonnet for My Past and Future Assassin* and ask my students to consider how their own pressing subjects (whether police brutality, systemic racism, sexual abuse, ecological devastation, or the nefarious characteristics of social media) matter anew when interfacing with the sonnet form. By taking up old forms, un-dusting them from their canonical containers, and using them as vessels through which to speak one's own truth, students both reclaim poetic forms, work their tensions, and connect with past poems, poets, times, places, and ways of writing. This nomadic approach to poetic forms gives teachers and students the power to make the form their own and to embrace the hybridity embedded in the crossing of any poetic form with one's own passions, voices, and minds.

An Invitation

If you were to take the subject matter that you carry in your heart and make of it a sonnet, what happens? Where do you struggle and where do you sing? What tensions arise for you? What sticky points? Move within the constraints of that form and see what it does to your subject. Use the form, however, you need to in order to say what you need to say. Embrace the relationship, and don't lose your "triggering subject" in the process— stay with the struggle and listen for what's happening as you follow the rhyme scheme and the rhythm within that fourteen-line frame.

Remember, too, that we need not "perfectly" follow any form; in fact, part of a poem's vitality may be in its loose approach to a form. Take, for example, this sonnet by poet, teacher, and musician Rebecca Keith (2021)—what she describes as a "shaky" sonnet. We see that shakiness as an important ingredient to this particular sonnet's force:

Miss Dishes' Dementia Goes Shopping

Shucked peas creamed corn honey,
butter for honey butter. C batteries

for the storm. See: batteries for storm.
A swarm of berries to preserve,
jam up and slather on toast, serve warm
to the guests who never show. What happened
when they moved across the river, left her
to shovel the snow. What was she expecting?
Nothing would grow inside her. So they pushed
their prams, a parade of pretty coos and squawks
while she threw pity tea parties, put her parts
in a box for the next life. Partyline for the lonely,
ambition pushed aside with the fat from the last fry.
A lifeline, anything besides a lie?

Traced in the Shadow

Returning to the icicles, their barbaric glass, and the agitated blackbird, feel anew the tensions that give a poem its breath. What is the blackbird's shadow without the glass? What mood might we trace in the sonnet's shadow? What does the long window enable us to see through its framing? Traced in the shadow lives the mood—what we cannot understand or decipher but know in our bodies. A poem, its own body, reminds us of the shapes our bodies can take in relation to what we read and write.

A reorientation of the teaching of poetic forms and constraints can bring about a clearer understanding of the nature of poetic forms—not as pure, immutable, and landlocked inside a particular cultural or historical context—but as transnational and always changing in relation to time, place, culture, use, and poet. This understanding of form can shift the direction of how we teach sonnets, haiku, ghazals, pantoums, villanelles, or bops to our students, emphasizing the relationship of structural rules to the writer's own bristling subject and the necessity of tension to cultivate a poem's life. Connectedly, such a reorientation brings us to rethink literacy practices bound by form to the point of format—practices that insist our students master an existing structure regardless of the writer's relationship to that structure. Writing practices that prize a writer's ability to grasp the rules of form without attention to how the writer's personally relevant subject matter and the form are moving together, miss poetry's point (or one of its many points shooting off into rays): the writer's passion for their/her subject matter and the conventional form must make an action together. There can be no blackbird's shadow moving in that particular way without the reflecting glass and the agitated blackbird. Constraints, we've argued, open up fresh writing practices and relationships to language, enabling us to recognize and mobilize our capacities to make a poem unlike one we've ever written "freely"—to re-sense everyday materials and actions as routes into writing. As poetry/art shows us, self-imposed limitations can become a practice of freedom: to enable another organizing principle to do its work and collaborate with our writing process. And to place one's trust in an indecipherable cause.

CHAPTER 7
ON SPACES OF WONDER AND BEWILDERMENT

VII

O thin men of Haddam,
Why do you imagine golden birds?
Do you not see how the blackbird
Walks around the feet
Of the women about you?

Why might a person be tempted to imagine golden birds and overlook the blackbirds that walk among us? What is the impulse to see things other than what is present—the impulse to create symbols, metaphors, or other figurative language that works from an aesthetic principle of seeing what *is not* rather than what *is*? You might have noticed this is the first stanza in Stevens's poem where a question is posed. You might question why. Quite simply, one question leads to others. If you scan the entirety of the poem, you will notice this is the only stanza that asks a question and, in fact, two. Another reason for wondering. Then, you might notice that these two questions are asked in Stanza VII, as close to mid-point of a thirteen-stanza poem as possible. Another question to ask; another reason for wondering.

The "What Ifs" of Wondering

Is the act of imagining itself a failure or is it our thin man of Haddam's failure in what is imagined? Why golden birds? Golden leads me to think of idolatry, of a gilded cover-up—a distortion, a glossing over of the actual. That leads to the question of why our man of Haddam is described as thin. Thin in physical stature? In mental perception? Thin as unable to perceive what is important? Why is the blackbird walking around at the women's feet? A tension overrides the stanza's questions. I notice the paradoxes—the relationship of the seen and unseen, of the imagined, and what is deemed real or the failure to see what is visible in the search for the invisible. Questions. Wonderings.

Stay close to what is around you, this stanza seems to suggest. *No need to imagine fancy birds that don't exist. Look at the ones you live with, blackbirds at the feet of those with whom you walk. Pay attention to those ordinary birds.* Is it possible that in the ordinary we have only to look to search out the extraordinary? Does a longing to desire the extraordinary obstruct both the noumena and the phenomena and the changing perception of both?

This stanza reminds me how our habits of seeing make the ordinary so "natural" that it goes unnoticed. Slipping into a kind of invisibility and leaving the imagination desiring something more—flashier—golden birds, or a prince, or maybe the fountain of youth. Poets often choose to reground, to bring the noumena back into the phenomena of living. Can we live both simultaneously?

Poems resist habits and habitual ways of seeing and (not) seeing by making, noticing, and pointing to the material of daily life: the blackbirds that stay close to the ground, the feet of women, the floor's wooden slats creaking, or the smell of the back of my daughter's neck. What else is there? What else do we imagine needs to be? The everyday parts that form a life ask to be seen, recognized, and acknowledged without necessarily being known or defined. And, how might answering these questions help us orient commonly taught interpretive practices to be more mindful of affective and experiential outcomes of reading and writing poems. Similar to the emphasis in Chapter 1 on poems as provocateurs, the focus here reiterates and extends these principles by rendering visible how the "felt senses" of wonderment and bewilderment are aroused through allusive, sonic, and textures of language and form.

Attending to the Ordinary

Let's begin by focusing attention on the material of daily life, recognizing that poems are not always operating in some separate or rarified dimensions apart from daily living. Yes, we see the blackbirds around us and sometimes these serve as the subject for poems. Turn for a moment to a different poem by Charles O. Hartman, titled "Same":

Same
Drying your back with a towel
for example: to do it while
remembering doing it
a thousand times in the past
three years, tens over decades,
holding the two in the one
thought, if thought is the word for what

being is like: this is not useful,
if use is what you want, but the feel
of terrycloth's rougher side
against skin you know
is naked, though you can't see it,
has the advantage of being

now. It's like practicing your daily
daily scales, and halfway down
letting one note sing
while you ask all the other fingers
what they think.

Consider this simple act of drying off a loved one's back with a towel, and how does this poem highlight that sensation, heightening how we, as readers, can feel that action done "a thousand times in the past/ three years, tens over decades. . ." We feel a sense of wonder at a familiar tenderness, especially in the last stanza.

That simple comparison of drying off a lover's back with a towel, "letting one note sing/ while you ask all the other fingers/ what they think," is so awkwardly precise it creates a feeling that lingers long after reading the poem. Sensation, which we will discuss more in Chapter 10, happens in poetry not just by way of sensory description but also from allowing a sense of wonder and bewilderment to enter a daily moment of connection.

Reading Hartman's poem, I remember bathing my children when they were babies— the simple ritual I engaged with love (and exhaustion). I wonder how the act of writing a poem about that daily tenderness may have affected my relationship to it. Perhaps it would have facilitated a more pleasurable sensory experience if I were not clouded with distractions. Reading Hartman's poem compels me to consider the relationship of bewilderment to our daily work and what happens when we pause to notice, appreciate, and attend to the ordinary in our lives.

An Invitation

Make a poem from a common action, or object, in your life, and follow the wonders it generates for you. Take a few minutes to locate an object near you—the hairbrush on your dresser, a needle and thread left near that torn scarf, the fly buzzing on the windowsill, or, look, there, on the kitchen counter and gaze at the ripening peach. Or, look closely at a photograph that is important to you, one that just happens to be near you, or one that haunts your memories. All these are objects up close and personal and readily available for exploration. You might choose instead a more expansive view—the photograph of the beach, a city-scape of rooftops, a gathering of runners preparing for a marathon. Or, a photo that turns the lens outward, toward the sky—a night photo of Orion, a bird flying, or a sunset captured in cumulo.

Take some time to jot words or phrases that come to mind as you look closely, look again, ask questions, make statements of "what if" questions with your gaze centered on the object or photo. We invite you to look back at the words, phrases, and statements and to write a few lines of a poem, capturing your experiences with this close observation.

For me, the moment in 1972 when I first saw the photograph taken from outer space, looking from a distance at our Earth-home, has never quite left my mind's eye. I have a copy of the photo on a wall near my desk, and it always reminds me of how perspectives change. As I gaze, I am reminded of Stevens's stanza and my wonderings about the relationship between what is visible and what is imagined, so I travel with these thoughts into the following exploration of the visible and invisible:

Nothing Is Hidden Except the Visible

Full Disk Earth, Apollo 17, 1972

That photograph of Earth—placid, no beating heart of
yearning, nothing moving on a rubble of continents conquered
and named by those who never had this god's-eye view. No
signs of borders on the land; the axis of a spinning globe cycling
day into night. Indigo waters roil as islands bob and glaciers melt.
An almost invisible ship struggles through wisps of clouds turned
perfect storm. Its mast splinters as the camera shutters its release.

Forgive me for searching shades of umbre, indigo, the glaucous
mists floating in shadows as if sunken Atlantis might suddenly
appear with its own Crusoe planting foot on stone, as if a pirate
in repose found buried bounty in the hidden made visible, as if
a convergence of obsidian and ice could murmur in the dark, as if
a kingfisher found its way to dip and rise in oceans of sky to cradle
earth against a sudden fall or falter.

Full Disk Earth—a reminder of how we miss the curves to focus
on the flatness, not listening to the polar silences, not hearing
whispers of gravity's edge as we hold tight, astonished by a spinning
vertigo as aperture gives way to bursts of light and momentary blindness
shanks the earth akilter to become a marble hidden in a ball of dust,
encased in fur tangles. Dusted off and gleaming, it hangs suspended
between the thumb and index finger of some imagined god.

Once your eyes adjust and clouds of understanding gather, you see
the pretense everywhere. Look closely—a fisherman leans against
his starboard bow, not seeing the cracks-in-wood where water might
seep through. Imagine my two dogs lying, perfectly still looking up at me.
Suddenly, there are three. The absent one from long ago returns for only
a moment. In the silence—a strange humming. How the heart swells
as the secret reveals itself: nothing is hidden except the visible.

Our ways of seeing take on the experiential and imaginative aspects of our lives differently. By encouraging us to wonder at the relational aspects of real and imagined and the visible and invisible, poetry becomes a mode of invention, experimentation, and play as well as a place to examine our experiences and those beyond us. As we have conceived poems of the everyday (as with noticing the blackbird at our feet), we find ordinary actions, objects, and words a powerful reminder of the wonderment in the ordinary that seems so much a part of the working of poems.

Wonderment: The Ordinary and Extraordinary as One

As Adrienne Rich (1995) points out, the tools for making poetry are ordinary too:

Take that old, material utensil, language, found all about you, blank with familiarity, smeared with daily use, and make it into something that means more than it says. What poetry is made of is so old, so familiar, that it's easy to forget that it's not just the words, but polyrhythmic sounds, speech in its first endeavors (every poem breaks a silence that had to be overcome), prismatic meanings lit by each others' light, stained by each others' shadows. (p. 84)

Language—this ordinary, intimate, and multidimensional material—offers itself to poetry. Are blackbirds subject enough for a poem? Maybe they are the ordinary used to make the extraordinary. How might what Rich suggests about the ordinariness of language and its nuances—how language shifts in relation to the speaker and the writer; how it resonates with and/or against a reader; how it carries histories; how it breaks silences that need breaking—provoke and challenge us to rethink our own reading or writing of poetry?

Wonderment, then, might be the outcome of explorations of "what if" speculations and questioning. The poet Diane Ackerman (2011) writes: "Wonder is the heaviest element on the periodic table. Even a tiny fleck of it stops time" (p. 27). Going back to where we began, we bring experience and learned interpretive practices to the reading or writing of a poem. How have our schooled interpretive practices had a tendency to make golden birds out of poetry? Or maybe they just reproduce poetry as golden birds: accessible to few, precious, esoteric, decorative. In classrooms, do we cling to a "golden bird sense" of poetry—useless, frivolous, and desired—relegating the presence of those birds to a special unit in a curriculum or a relegation to "Poetry Month" (read: a time for taking pleasure in imagining something disconnected from your everyday life and from the seriousness of writing)? We have found many teachers indicate they focus study of poetry first on literary devices and figurative language as a way of explicating and discussing a poet's purposes and meaning. Poetic devices are not explored as down-to-earth workings of language, useful to us as readers and writers in the acts of composing the ordinary through the extraordinary or the extraordinary through the ordinary. Furthermore, the teaching of literary devices often gets linked to definition and identification. That is, we learn to define what a metaphor is and then prove we understand it by exemplifying a metaphor in writing or finding it in a poem. Meanwhile, the blackbirds roam, asking to be noticed in ways that might provoke metaphor and wonderment.

We invite you to orient your approach to poetry as acknowledgment, recognition, and a record of the dialogic of the ordinary and extraordinary. Think about how this orientation might help us to recognize in our students the poetries that we and they have not yet noticed, especially those poetries they may be making that have not been named as "poetry."

I return to Stevens's stanza and try to imagine and reimagine this thin man of Haddam whom the speaker acknowledges and tries to offer a wisdom connected to both the acknowledgment of the ordinary and extraordinary. Does the thin man need the speaker's reminder to find hope and possibility in what has become a withering or destitute life? He is one man after all—not addressed in the company of others—but living among the women and the blackbirds he may no longer be able to see. Is he thin from hunger, and, if so, are these physical and/or spiritual sources of hunger? Or is he thin with a sense of narrowness or greed? Perhaps, I say with a smile: Maybe he studied poetry in school and that took his wonderment away—the ordinary and extraordinary locked into separate realms. I cannot know this man, but I can begin—through Stevens's words—to see him and to try to understand something about the human condition through this man and what he imagines, and what this man (the speaker tells us) appears to see and not to see. I wonder at the images and the reckoning of golden birds and blackbirds brought together in the same space and in the questions asked in the stanza. From all this comes a moment of wonderment that settles in and brings pause as well as illumination: I can't quite know how things of this world and of my imaginings blur, intersect, grow together or apart, but this little stanza, in this poem, keeps my mind in motion, in wonderment as the ordinary and extraordinary fuse together and not.

Recognition of One within the Other

In his haunting ethnography *Vita: Life in a Zone of Social Abandonment* (2013), anthropologist João Biehl's traces the life of a woman he meets who lives at Vita, an institution in Brazil where the homeless, the mentally ill, the sick, and the abandoned are left to die. Like most of Vita's residents, Catarina was discarded by society and cast away by her family—an "ex-human" overly and incorrectly medicated, never properly diagnosed (until at the end of her life) with a neurological disorder, emotionally abused, abandoned by her family, and eventually left to disintegrate in Vita. As a way of staying alive, Catarina kept what she called a "dictionary"—a poetic record of the ordinary objects that form her daily, unbearable existence of 221 notebooks. It became for her a manifestation of possibility in a dead-end place. Biehl calls her writing *poetry*, and he writes that her words "are disjointed objects. What ties them together is the constant effort to address the unspeakable of the ordinary" (p. 318). Catarina's writing is an unbearable record of her ordinary: medications, desires for affection, isolation, names of diseases, names of family members she has not seen in years, her own name rewritten.

The poetic imagination and the poetry of a discarded "ex-human" like Catarina would probably never have been recognized as poetry without Biehl's ability to see her. Catarina's dictionary is indeed poetry—"I was already the powder of flower / All ate me as bread" (p. 335)—without Catarina seeing it or intending it as poetry, but Biehl and her readers know and feel it as poetry. He writes, "We might face Catarina's writing in the same way we face poetry. She introduces us to a world that is other than our own, yet close to home; and with it, we have the chance to read social life and the human condition, both hers and ours, differently" (p. 318). Catarina's story and words suggest poetry as a vital force that needs to be recognized by teachers and shaped by students. We may (un)know or have a felt-sense when something is poetic, when it is poetry, and a student may be writing something that we see is poetry even if we don't know what makes it poetry. As Biehl writes of Catarina, "In her writing, she makes us see things otherwise" (p. 190), suggesting a fundamental relationship between wonder and poetry. These words invite an ethics of recognition of one within the other.

Poems nurture veins of the illusory and potentially the non-conforming. They ask questions. They are invitations to engage with the unknown, the wondrous, and the potential pleasure of the elusiveness. Emily Dickinson (1876) identifies these qualities and resonances through an explanation we find helpful. For Dickinson (1876), "Nature is a Haunted House—but Art—a House that tries to be haunted" (p. 225). What is left behind after the poem is read as a haunting, a resonance of what lingers but what we cannot quite put into words. Hauntings, we suggest, are a way of discussing a poem or a stanza. Hauntings might be an interpretive practice associated with wonderment—all those bumps in the night and whispers that come back into our thoughts and dreams when the poem is (re)membered in whisps and fragments again. This is what we hope for our students—a poem stays with them to be revisited in moments of reading other poems, in actions they or others take in the world, or when they gaze on a blackbird or someone states a preference for golden birds.

We hope to reorient interpretive practices for our students, for you, and for us in ways that give poems staying power, hauntings, that will inform our lives long after the reading or writing of them. We can only imagine how Stevens's "Thirteen Ways of Looking at a Blackbird" will live in our or your consciousness and inform our perception of "looking" long after the close encounters with his poem in this book. Or, at some moment when you see a fisherman readying his boat to leave the dock, you might cast your eye on the starboard bow and be haunted by "cracks-in-wood" if I created enough of a haunting in my poem for it to linger with you. It is appropriate for Stevens to get the last word on this topic. He writes: "The poem must resist the intelligence/Almost successfully" (p. 350). Yes, Wallace Stevens, but the resistance created by the rational and the irrational keeps the mind haunting its own thoughts and that is a reorientation from the typical idea that we explicate poems and hunt down their meanings. It is the lingering hauntings that inform our perceptions and invade our experiences.

Exploring a Site of Wonderment

In thinking about how to reorient interpretive practices to include wonderment as a desired outcome of reading and writing poems, we experiment with ways to make visible for ourselves and with our students both the subjects and language of the ordinary and extraordinary. Not unlike the earlier Invitation in this chapter to examine an object or photo, we have found it helpful to work with odes as a poetic form that helps us examine how the ordinary and extraordinary fuse and how we or other poets might use the resources of language that Rich describes to create the conditions for wonderment.

Pablo Neruda wrote 225 odes. In "Odes to Things," he begins, "I have a crazy, /crazy love of things" (1994, p. 11). His odes celebrate the ordinary—a bed, train station, village theater, chair, onion, dictionary, artichoke salt, and a lover's hands.

An Invitation

Take a moment to determine the focus-subject of an ode of your own. Write a description. List several of the qualities, attributes, associations with the word, and, finally, what it evokes for you in speculation, insight, or metaphor. Take your preliminary writing, title your poem "Ode to . . ." (Salt, Restlessness) and use your jottings to create at least a few lines.

I chose onion. Jotted descriptions, associations, words. Then, I began my draft:

Ode to the Onion

Onions are strong willed, their roots
resist the tug and tightening of hand
by fist pulling at roots. They cling to earth—
umbilical cords by the dozens curl back
into a loamy womb until exposed

yellow, white, purple—each bulb plump
and glistening, a luminous sheen from skin
and tissue sets aglow the air around them.

Cell by cellwork they taste the air, no
cries, no gasping for breath but the first
scent of them, pungent, slowly rises. I can
almost see the air move. In my grandmother's
garden row after row piled high and roots
entwined, I wonder what sounds, what
language of the earth I cannot hear, cannot
know but take this poignant moment as
reminder of the offering we've made
of them.

We are suggesting that through our writing, we learn something about constructing wonderment. If you feel as I do right now, I don't think my ode is necessarily successful in creating wonder around the ordinary act of harvesting onions. Through the mindwork of composing this ode, however, I start to take in the magnitude of the long evolution of the onion that now sits in a basket of root vegetables on my kitchen counter. In creating this start of a poem, I attempted to capture the onion at the moment of its harvest, and while doing so, I was caught in the web of its histories. How did human beings ever recognize the value of the onion, learn to cultivate and harvest it, find ways to make it a part of the cuisines of our cultures? Magnificent are all the stories and the powers of imagination and invention. Wonderment is what I feel at this moment. I hope students find wonder as they read poems, write odes, and learn from poets ways expressing amazement with the most common of objects of experiences.

To pay attention to the ordinary and extraordinary, question, and find wonder and wonderment in poems we share Naomi Shibab Nye's (1995) beautiful poem "The Traveling Onion" as a reminder of just how simple and poignant are the commonplace things of this world:

The Traveling Onion

"It is believed that the onion originally came from India. In Egypt it was an object of worship—why I haven't been able to find out. From Egypt the onion entered Greece and on to Italy, thence into all of Europe."—Better Living Cookbook

When I think how far the onion has traveled
just to enter my stew today, I could kneel and praise
all small forgotten miracles,
crackly paper peeling on the drainboard,
pearly layers in smooth agreement,
the way the knife enters onion

and onion falls apart on the chopping block
a history revealed.
And I would never scold the onion
for causing tears.
It is right that tears fall
for something small and forgotten.
How at meal, we sit to eat,
commenting on texture of meat or herbal aroma
but never on the translucence of onion,
now limp, now divided,
or its traditionally honorable career:
For the sake of others,
disappear.

Odes facilitate those moments of pause, drawing on the daily materials of our lives, on the dialogic between visible and invisible to create those hauntings to which we referred earlier. The hidden furrows of gardens, the tangled sheets on a bed, a spoon. Sharon Olds's (2016) book *Odes* is a wonderful teaching resource that includes some very funny and poignant odes. What a multitude of wonderment around us, like roots, waiting for the tug and pull of imagination to bring vision and life to others.

And to bring joy. Enjoy this ode by Rachel M. Simon (2021):

In Praise of Queer Coaches

for Coach Young, Plano, TX

We forgive your perceived preference
for fourth grade boys, understanding avoidance
of low threshold impropriety.

We needed you, the youth
of the Bible belt, decoding
a stance from locker room benches.

We acknowledge the personal peril
of pregame speeches
spectator to offensive parenting.

We know you saw the bulge of backpack
Bibles felt the ever smoothing
texture of aging basketballs.

Thank you for the gift of scrutinizing
you, your red 300ZX, the person
in the passenger seat, haircut and hands.

You could've made your reputation in a division
welcoming to women in ill-fitting track suits,
placed shot puts, pony tails optional.

Thank you for asking us high school housesitters
we watered your plants and counted
two alarm clocks by the bed.

Bewilderment Is Not Confusion

Perhaps it seems a paradox to move our focus from wonderment to bewilderment. Reading a poem that leaves you in a state of confusion, unmoored, or in the realm of the illusory may work against what our learned interpretive practices have taught us is the outcome of reading poems. Recently, I offered my students two of my poems, ones, as best I could speculate, were grounded in a combination of identifiable signifiers to signifiers of the illusory. I was thinking that the slippage of signifiers and wondering just what or how a poem might bewilder the reader. I asked students to read the poems once, not look back, and jot down a few phrases that come to mind about the points of their focus and attention after their first reading, and to describe as best they could the emotional or imaginative experience that lingers on after the reading. I ask you to do the same.

The Thought of Wolves

Lift me, great Wind, past trees firing
red. Lay me down into the clearing where
I found them, three years ago, wolf pups
curled there blossoming alive
like blood plums, small mouths turned
toward the blue of sky. A rush of promise,
of hidden pleasure in a grove now filled only
with the thought of wolves.

Maybe we are meant to trudge among thoughts
of wolves where no wolves are. Breathe deep
that forest grove where we might run or stand or
hear birds sing—not in the shadow of madrone;
not where we might build needle beds for rest
but where we spin plums that linger on branches,
looking like the late years of splendid women
before their exquisite designs begin to fall.

Close to the earth, there is never enough time
for words. Not on the forest floor, not

in the clearing, not where we hear the work
of worms so close to Earth. Only, at the
edge of held breath do words fail. Only
then, are we caught in wonder, Only
then, can we feel the silk fur of imagined
wolves, the precision of their ripe scent upon
the heart.

Take a few minutes to think through or write down your points of focus and attention
and try to describe the experience that lingers after each reading.

Jezebel

I've always loved the name Jezebel
gently flicking off the tongue—Jezebel
smooth like the oboe's reed vibrating
B flat against the lower lip. Jezebel rides
where air creaks. A tremolo. Nothing
so beautiful as Jezebel.

Jezebel wears linen gloves. Her arms
are cedar limbs where blackbirds wait
not yet aware her hands sprout vines
to grow round hearts—prisoners to
Jezebel. No man buries his beak in her
moonlight.

Jezebel. Every woman dreams, half-afraid,
to follow her, to conjure doubling rhythms,
like a trick in scansion, weave siren songs
through branches. Gentle are the harmonies
and yet lightning and thunder roil behind.
Jezebel. Say it before the sound sours.

For the most part, students felt grounded to the narrative in "The Thought of Wolves"
and one student expressed that "the thought of wolves described how memory and
imagination work together in experience." Another student shared that he was "caught"
by the lines, "Only, at the/edge of held breath do words fail. Only/then, are we caught
in wonder, Only/then, can we feel the silk fur of imagined/wolves." He said these lines

unsteadied me from thinking that we need to find words to express meaning
or wonder, and now I am left with much to think about. I am caught in a space
between the real and the imagined wolves, and I have the feeling that is where
wonder can be experienced, spaces of the between as we have talked about in class.

"Jezebel" led to other wonderings and responses. Several students indicated they didn't know the reference to Jezebel. Two or three searched for a reference after reading and making notes. Most did not feel the need, and, as one stated: "I felt like I didn't want to locate it in another moment. I did question whether the speaker was a female or male or if it mattered, but I think it is female. It is the power of the name and the associated attributes." Another student followed with this comment: "The qualities of Jezebel were revealed through a series of metaphors of imagining, and a sense of awe that we are in the presence of something we don't fully understand. That is the purpose of poetry, I think."

And with that comment, we segue past wonderment to awe. In awe, all the questions, wonderings, resonances, and hauntings come together. To be "in awe" means what? Several of these students echoed the idea that they were left without words but with feelings, as one student suggested, "just let the feeling linger." To be "in awe" might be a gradient level above wonderment, but these states vary for each reader or writer. The common element seems to reside somewhere in the idea that we are left with what we have at the end of the poem—an *effect* and *affect,* that is, both a moment captured in thought and a feeling—a sadness, a joy, or some other feeling that lingers and cannot quite be named.

Most students did not have preferences, although the narrative line of the first poem kept them "more grounded" as one student suggested. Another enjoyed "the bird's-eye view of feminist histories" in Jezebel. And what for you? Where were you located? And, if thoughts or feelings stay after each of the poems, what are those? Any resonances, questions, wonderings? And, if you are satisfied with non-conclusive endings, what is left with you from each poem?

All this may lead us to one of the outcomes of poetry—bewilderment. Fanny Howe's (1998) lecture "Bewilderment" helps us in thinking through the dimensions and practices of bewilderment. She states: "Bewilderment is an enchantment that follows a complete collapse of reference and reconcilability. It breaks open the lock of dualism (it's this or that) and peers out into space (not this, not that)" (p. 15). Howe goes on to insist that "No monolithic answers that are not soon disproved are allowed into a bewildered poetry or life" (p. 20). By encouraging us to ask questions and question answers, poems become a mode of invention, imagination, and experimentation. From wondering to wonderment, from the extraordinary in the ordinary, to experiencing awe and bewilderment are practices of living, of being in the everyday. What does this all mean for an understanding of the poetics and practices of poetry? How do we come to value the ineffable and unanswerable? We hope to introduce interpretive practices that support you as they have encouraged your students to recognize the values of being left in a state of bewilderment and to understand the distinctions in bewilderment and confusion.

Practicing Bewilderment

We turn to the poet CAConrad for guidance on the creation of and use of som(atic) rituals to imagine differently. In the "Introduction" to their book *ECODEVIANCE:*

(Soma)tic for the Future Wilderness (2014), they came to recognize, when visiting family for a reunion, that the family's factory life and monotonous jobs had separated them from their essential selves. On a train ride home from the reunion, they reflect:

> I had an epiphany that I had been treating my poetry like a factory, an assembly line, and doing so in many different ways, from how I constructed the poems, to my tabbed and sequenced folders for submissions to magazines, . . . The more I thought about this the more I realized this was what the factory robbed my family of the most, and the thing that frightened me the most, this not being aware of place in the present. That morning I started what I now call (Soma)tics, ritualized structures where being anything but present was next to impossible. These rituals create what I refer to as an "extreme present" where the many facets of what is around me wherever I am can come together through a sharper lens. (page xi)

CAConrad's call to acute mindfulness is a way to confront the unexpected, wonder and wonderment, and traffic in the extreme present in which we might experience awe and bewilderment. (Soma)tic rituals, inviting bewildering prompts to provoke fully present experiences with the material of everyday life, shake at the ground of familiarity and move us to the unfamiliar. Simultaneously they are grounded in an almost visceral reality. Conrad's blog "(Soma)tic Poetry Rituals" provides examples, as does the recent book *JUPITER ALIGNMENT: (Soma)tic Poetry Rituals* (Ignota Books, 2020).

An Invitation

You might be inspired with guidance from CAConrad to visit (literally or figuratively) the home of a deceased or living poet and imagine what you might take away and what you might do as ritual with what you have taken or borrowed. Then, as CAConrad suggests, decide what your poet teaches you about how to look at the world around you. Don't censor or edit yourself as you write. How about adapting a ritual for your commute? Write down three phrases you overhear and use each as dialogue for conversation in a poem? We encourage students to write these, too, as a way of freeing them to crack open their cautions and learned habits of logic.

What are some objects in your life you might form rituals around? For CAConrad, crystals, chocolate, a bucket of water, pennies, a red magic marker, among countless other things, become tools for wild rituals.

Write your own ritual, utilizing at least one tangible object in your life and use your practice of that ritual to create a poem. The dictionary definition of bewilder is "to cause to lose one's sense of where one is." Maybe bewilderment isn't being lost in the woods, but, as with the dictionary definition, it may center on the "sense" of lostness, of not quite knowing where we are—unsteady. Fannie Howe describes bewilderment as an altered state where "an explosion of parts, the quotidian smeared" (para. 43).

What if we asked ourselves or students a question that tries to get to the heart of the smear, the explosion: What does this poem blossom in your mind? Try to answer this question after reading the following poem by CAConrad (2015), who has taken residence as a vital part of this exploration of bewilderment:

Slaves of Hope Live Only for Tomorrow

photo of United States from
outer space in trash
green fire held to
everything as
everyone
whirls into abs-
tr-
action
a moment with the
crystal and the weight of the house is released
we hold fast
we hold one another
we hold to the vigor of the street
pain of picked flower our frame
reckless but never monochrome
everything the speed and
tension of eloping
saunter past
barricades
waking not
sleeping to
dream

What does this poem blossom in your mind? As a reminder, the dictionary definition of bewilder is "to cause to lose one's sense of where one is." The blossoming of the loss of "one's senses of where one is" might be a way to think through and talk about how this poem releases one detail only to open others in an intensification of losing the center of the blossom (Howe's altered state of explosions and smeared quotidian). Only then, after these considerations might we take up the question: How does the constructing use of language, rhythm, sound, image produce the blossoming that has vibrations into the philosophical, aesthetic, and political discourses?

Both CAConrad and Howe see bewilderment as a practice for living and seem to argue that an approach to living cannot be separated from one's poetics, at least for the poet. Howe describes bewilderment as both a poetics and an ethics. Howe's lecture is worth reading in its entirety. The lecture itself is bewildering, filled with unanticipated meditations and connections, forming a pastiche of thoughts about bewilderment. And, in the end, Howe's statement about bewilderment as an ethics is ultimately bewildering and worthy of exploration.

The blossoming of bewilderment may be accompanied by a heightened awareness that complacency is not possible, that resistance is necessary, that absence and excess and abuse are experiences of the everyday, and that to hold to these, to gaze intently on each, is a state of bewilderment. In the end, the emotional effect may be tied to hope, to an ethics of caring for the planet and all it holds to its center. And, potentially, in the end, we might take up Yeats's (1920) poem as an ending and beginning of our attention to wondering, wonder, and bewilderment. "Second Coming" blossoms bewilderment through a complete collapse of reference and reconcilability where "the centre cannot hold" in broad circulation of the "widening gyre" that bewilders Yeats, his speaker, and us through numerous circuits and flows of experience and imagination. Let's let Yeats have the last say in this chapter.

The Second Coming

Turning and turning in the widening gyre
The falcon cannot hear the falconer;
Things fall apart; the centre cannot hold;
Mere anarchy is loosed upon the world,
The blood-dimmed tide is loosed, and everywhere
The ceremony of innocence is drowned;
The best lack all conviction, while the worst
Are full of passionate intensity.

Surely some revelation is at hand;
Surely the Second Coming is at hand.
The Second Coming! Hardly are those words out
When a vast image out of Spiritus Mundi
Troubles my sight: somewhere in sands of the desert
A shape with lion body and the head of a man,
A gaze blank and pitiless as the sun,
Is moving its slow thighs, while all about it
Reel shadows of the indignant desert birds.
The darkness drops again; but now I know
That twenty centuries of stony sleep
Were vexed to nightmare by a rocking cradle,
And what rough beast, its hour come round at last,
Slouches towards Bethlehem to be born?

CHAPTER 8
CARE FOR THE MORE-THAN-HUMAN

VIII
I know noble accents
And lucid, inescapable rhythms;
But I know, too,
That the blackbird is involved
In what I know.

How is the blackbird involved in "what I know"? Another way of asking this question may be, "How is my knowing entangled with the blackbird?" Extending from there we might ask, "How is my knowing entangled with the blackbird, the branch it perches on, the soil nourishing the tree's roots, and the wind that makes both branch and blackbird sway?" Perhaps each of us *knows* that we are interconnected and interdependent creatures comprising, affecting, and affected by more-than-human elements. But how/ do our literacy practices reflect this knowing? How can a poetry practice contribute to this understand and to the ways we enact a kind of literacy unbound by human-dominant directives and norms?

We invite you to reflect on the materials that play a part in your everyday acts of reading and writing. Take a moment to list them. Consider all the elements that tend to constitute your literacy experiences. Your inventory might include tools, space, atmosphere, visible and invisible elements—all those things, often taken for granted, that go into the "literacy situation," as Nathan Snaza calls it in his vibrant book *Animate Literacies* (2019). Snaza defines the "literacy situation" as "how a whole host of actants and agents animate literacy in scenes of pre- or aconscious collision and affective contact" (p. 4). With that sense of literacy in mind—a situation, or event, animated by a diverse ecosystem of congealing elements—list those elements, actants, agents, that create your literacy situations and practices. What more-than-human elements and materials have you come to know as a reader and writer?

I pause for a moment to try out this invitational prompt myself. When I think of those actants/agents/elements that manifest my own acts of literacy, I arrive at the following: pencil, lead, eraser, the pencil's waxy polish, paper, computer, electrical cord, the computer's keyboard with a broken "e" that needs a forceful pressing to work, my external keyboard for when that effort becomes frustrating, a desk, a glass of water, air, a chair, my Muji pen, its ink, plastic, my child's interruption, the sudden feel of her arm's eczema against mine.

As I write the word "paper," I pause to consider the Buddhist monk Thích Nhất Hạnh's wise words, reminding me of what goes into a piece of paper—all those actants that I frequently failed to notice or care for when I sit down to write:

> If you are a poet, you will see clearly that there is a cloud floating in this sheet of paper. Without a cloud, there will be no rain; without rain, the trees cannot grow: and without trees, we cannot make paper. The cloud is essential for the paper to exist. If the cloud is not here, the sheet of paper cannot be here either. So we can say that the cloud and the paper inter-are. (para. 1)

It is interesting that Thích Nhất Hạnh specifies that it is a poet who sees these things clearly. We also feel there is something in the act of poetry—becoming a "poet" in the sense of continual practice and desire—that enables us to see the things that make a thing, to better sense where something comes from and via what processes it emerges, including sociopolitical systems and inequities, and to note the more-than-human elements that comprise our being, our societies, and our literacies. By "poet" we do not mean, and we imagine Thích Nhất Hạnh does not mean, a "professional" author who has published books of poems. We—and we think he, too—are talking about a way of being in the world. An approach. An orientation. Something each of us is capable of, has within us, and can/does awaken to through a practice of poetry. As Maxine Park Hong writes in her book *To Be the Poet*, "I want poetry to be the way it used to come when I was a child. The Muse flew; I flew" (2002, p. 4). I think of my own six-year-old daughter's blurring of art, science, math, reading—how knowledge intra-is, fresh and unencumbered by the constructed divisions that cleave human from material, mind from body, subject from subject matter. We've all been there, flying with our Muses, in one way or another, sensing the paper's cloud.

In the opening chapter of *Animate Literacies* Snaza argues for a "freeing up of energies to begin making sense of this bizarre, extensive, and extremely fragile ecology of things, events, and actants" (p. 5). Our own experiences as teachers and teacher educators have been in classrooms where we and others tend to center the human as something separate from the nonhuman, often at the cost of diminishing, if not totally ignoring, the more-than-human elements that shape our classrooms and ourselves: the air conditioner's drone, the desk's melamine, the linoleum tiles, the sunlight heating the window, the snapped-up shades, neon Post-its, sharpened pencils, dust, bacteria, stacks of circulating books with an occasional student's name scrawled in Sharpie, the squeak of sneaker on floor. We *know* these elements are there, but rarely do we (at least we authors of this book) think to teach with-them, from-them, or toward-them.

Just as theories of education can become too strong, normalizing human-centric approaches that prevent teachers and educational researchers from experiencing or imagining a classroom as a space of more-than-human force and agency (Niccolini and Pindyck, 2015), so, too, are orientations toward literacy. Matter is vibrant (Bennett, 2010). We encounter it in assemblage with/as us, our classrooms, our broader social-historical contexts, and all that congeal to make a thing a thing, a situation a situation, a classroom a classroom, a person a person. We are inspired by Jane Bennett's book *Vibrant Matter* (2010), especially its concluding assertions: "I believe that this pluriverse is traversed by heterogeneities that are continually *doing things*. . . . I believe that encounters with lively matter can chasten my fantasies of human mastery, highlight the common materiality of all that is, expose a wider distribution of agency, and reshape the self and its interests" (p. 122). Extending from Bennett, re-encounters with matter toward the making of poetry can be an opportunity for intentional and caring engagements with all the parts that collaborate to create what we eventually name a "poem" and to inspire broader conceptualizations of what poetry can be and how and where and for whom/ for what. Our literacy practices can speak to our more-than-human entanglements and move (with) them—and a practice of reading and writing poetry can be a particularly inviting, grounding, and creative way of consciously engaging those entanglements.

A rhythm re-grounds the memory of a burst of wind tapping against an open window; a variegated accent brings a tree swallow's song to mind. The reciprocity of human and nonhuman associations contains entangling threads. Driven by a recognition that many poems shape unexpected and often tender ways of knowing the *anima* that is within and surrounds us, poetry can attune us to the more than human. Karen Barad suggests, "We are a part of that nature that we seek to understand" in reference to Niels Bohr's (1963) underlying conception of matter in quantum physics (2007, p. 67). A poem's meaning, too, lives in relation to its material qualities—whether in the quiet pages of a book, displayed on a poster in a subway car, or spoken aloud on a stage; we receive the poem, always, in its more-than-human materiality.

From this ground, we wonder about the ways poems foreground webs of relations between human and more-than-human worlds, drawing attention to affective ways of knowing rather than conceptual or symbolic ones. Let's explore the questions and beliefs sprouting in this chapter through some experimental practices.

Staying with the Poem's Trouble

Make a moment to read this poem "Anything with Eyes" by poet Ama Codjoe, author of *Blood of the Air* (Northwestern University Press, 2020), winner of the Drinking Gourd Chapbook Poetry Prize, and *Bluest Nude* (Milkweed Press, 2022).

Anything with Eyes

My mother doesn't know why, as a girl, she killed
the slugs with salt. Coming home in the dark,
after a storm, I avoid their slow, tender bodies.

This is how it is when caution outlines
the eyes with kohl. When darkness itself wears
a black eye. There was a calf I saw once

drinking from its mother. For long minutes
I watched it take and suck and swallow.
When the beast swung its tail like a tired rope

I felt compassion for anything with eyes,
anything with a mother. The cows glowed
slightly in the pasture, chewing the grass

they trampled. Soon the cattle would drift
uphill, into the forest, a fleet of ships
unanchored. The calf's many stomachs

full of its mother like a pendulous udder,
aching. Inside my chest my mother's breast
is punched by the man who told her she was

beautiful. Hurt throbs like a pulsing star.
By its fire I warm my hands. By its light
I decipher the words, one from the other:

daughter, butcher, father. I remember so little:
the color of the calf's coat, the science of salt,
who was the first to tell me, You're beautiful.

There are hours when the body spreads like
a starfish, days when I'm a damp encyclopedia
of forgetting. How careful my remembering.

How precious my forgetfulness. How precise.
Such measured steps. And the pages left
with my wet clothes on the radiator to dry.

We invite you to interpret this poem with love, tending to the questions and gaps it seeds for you. As Snaza puts it:

> Interpretation bears love and continues to nourish it. Love then emerges from questions, from a gap between what one thinks one knows and a singularity from which we cannot divert our attention. . . . I interpret literature not to understand it, or to present readings of it as if those were things that could be accomplished, but to "stay with the trouble" that is literature, to use Donna Haraway's (2016) beautiful phrase. (p. 25)

So with that orientation toward a loving interpretation and a desire to "stay with the trouble," to echo again Haraway's words, consider what questions Codjoe's poem raises for you and what gaps it animates. What do you make of the relationship between speaker and calf, between speaker and her mother, between the speaker's mother and the slugs, between the mother's breast and "the man who told her she was /beautiful"? What trouble does this poem invite for you and where does staying with the poem's trouble take you?

For me, questions flower open in the beautiful moves the poem makes from cattle to aching udder to the speaker's mother's breast punched by the man, to the speaker's own memory, her body, to "the pages left/ with my wet clothes on the radiator to dry." Human and more-than-human pain feel entirely one thing in this poem. The poem is happening, opening itself to us, and it invites us to feel all these elements at once—mother, dead slugs, salt, pulsing star, calf, udder, human body—elements that shape the poem's more-than-human wisdom. I stay with the poem's trouble longer, rereading it less for meaning and more to be with the points of contact the poem makes and transfers to its reader.

In the opening paragraph of *Staying with the Trouble*, Haraway asserts that we live in troubling, disturbing times. The task, she states, "is to make kin in lines of inventive connection as a practice of learning to live and die well with each other in a thick present" (p. 1). This claim enables us to envision the classroom as an interconnected ecosystem and the sense of community we, as teachers, aspire to create with our students through acts of literacy. Drawing a connecting line to Haraway's provocative sentence, we consider how metaphor can enable us to imagine the design of our literacy practices as a collaborative and communal *learning-with* that unsettles human-centric orientations to literacy. Metaphor can be a way in—of both imagining and actualizing alternative ways of being, reading, and writing (with others). As Katherine McKittrick (2021) reminds us in her electric book *Dear Science and Other Stories*: "Metaphors offer an entwined material and imagined future that has not yet arrived and the future we live and have already lived through" (p. 11). What metaphors for literacy bring us to new imaginings and orientations of that practice? What futures do our metaphors yield?

In "As Spiders Make Webs: Constructing Sites for Multidisciplinary Learning" (2018), Ruth offers "orb-weaving-as-metaphor" as "one demonstration of how a learner/researcher 'moves through the world' and discursive practices that shape the learning" (p. 2). She urges us to consider the ways we construct sites, or design environments, to facilitate our abilities "to read and see more and differently" (p. 1) and fleshes out the orb-weaving metaphor to ground possibilities for multi- and interdisciplinary research and learning. We need metaphors to make inventive connections and inspire new ways of living, working, reading, and writing together. As teachers, we must keep in mind the interconnected nature of the metaphorical and the material when we think about learning.

This thinking about metaphor's capacities to radically reshape classroom literacy practices as a more-than-human endeavor (and thinking about metaphor's trouble-making qualities) brings us back to context and community. How can we build/weave/invent new sites of learning by way of writing-with each other in the places we are? What metaphors move you toward a different literacy-orientation in your classroom and/or school community?

Sympoiesis

Haraway opens the third chapter of *Staying with the Trouble* with a discussion of "sympoiesis," which she introduces as a simple word that means "making-with. Nothing makes itself. Nothing is really autopoietic or self-organizing. . . . It is a word for worlding-with, in company" (p. 58). Haraway's thinking inspires an orientation toward poetry as worlding-with others, always, and intentionally via poetry practices.

An Invitation

Shift gears and material, for a moment, to world a poem other-than-usual. Step outside. Note the weather, the temperature, the atmosphere, the sounds, smells, all the elements surrounding and "intra-acting" with you ("intra-acting" is Karen Barad's term to signal the ways that we are mutually constituted and constituting in relation to other things—this is a departure from "interaction" that assumes two entities engage without fundamentally changing in the process). As you stand outside, take stock of where you are and what lives in relation to you. With what material could you write a poem and where? For what/whom? What might it mean for you to write with/from your current environment and to consider the collaborative potentials of unusual suspects/actants in the making of a poem? With what tools? On what surface? Following what rhythm, pattern, or texture? We invite you to make a poem from different materials than usual and in collaboration with this sudden community—human and/or more than human. If you don't have time to make that poem now, or even this year, or if it's too cold outside and you need to get back inside, map out where and how you'd make this imagined poem, with whom and with what and how.

Now think even bigger. Consider the interdisciplinary knowledges and collaborative possibilities that could help to bring a dream-poem into fruition. Where would you like to see poetry in the world? Who in your community is already making poetry—and what sounds, sights, smells, already "read" to you like poetry? How might you draw that "poetry" to the surface of its environment so that others might better see and appreciate it? Where have you noticed unexpected interfacings of material, place, and written word?

We encourage you to explore interdisciplinary artist Jen Bervin's (2016) silk poems, documented and described on her website. As Bervin explains, she collaborated with scientists, extending from their research on the uses of liquefied silk and the development of a silk biosensor. Bervin wrote a poem made of strands "modeled on silk at the DNA level—the six-character repeat in the silk genome is the basis for the poem's six-letter line." Bervin describes the poem's action as "a kind of talisman, written from the perspective of the silkworm, addressed to the person with the silk biosensor implanted in their body." Moving from/with Bervin's interdisciplinary experiments, how do you imagine poetry's work interfacing with other histories, contexts, disciplines, tools, and machines, and other more-than-human conspirators? What wild possibilities spring to your mind? What work do you want poetry to do? What work is it doing—or might it need to do—in your community?

In 2014, I attended a presentation by Marcus Young at the Open Engagement Conference at the Queens Museum in New York, where he shared his Sidewalk Poetry project (2008) as part of Public Art Saint Paul. The project's website describes Sidewalk Poetry as follows:

Sidewalk Poetry is a systems-based work that allows city residents to claim the sidewalks as their book pages. This project re-imagines Saint Paul's annual sidewalk maintenance program with Public Works, as the department repairs 10 miles of sidewalk each year. We have stamped more than 1,000 poems from a collection that now includes 54 individual pieces all written by Saint Paul residents. Today, everyone in Saint Paul now lives within a 10-minute walk of a Sidewalk Poem.

How incredible! Imagine the breadth of this sympoiesis—the collaboration of elements and systems that went into this project: the sidewalk's concrete, the poems written by residents, the tools for stamping the text into wet asphalt, the sun that dried the asphalt, the maintenance workers, all the sneakered feet pausing on their walk to read a poem on the sidewalk's open page. Young's place-based project prompts us to consider how place and history intersect with the "more-than-human-materiality" of the present moment. Through his work, we wonder about the unspoken and unwritten histories of Saint Paul. Something about imprinting publicly and legibly the words of its current residents sparks in us a curiosity about the city's past people and environment. A focus on the "more-than-human" in literacy practices is also a focus on the place (in its various past, present, and future iterations) in which, through which, with which one reads and writes.

Inspired in part by Young's work, I collaborated with the artist Jessica Houston on *Light on Sound* (2015) for and at the Lewis H. Latimer House Museum in Flushing, Queens (New York). The collaboration involved the NYC Department of Transportation, residents of Flushing, and two translators (who translated poems into Mandarin Chinese), among a range of more-than-human elements: street signs, lamps, blue bulbs, sound recordings, a box hiding the equipment, speakers, and countless other actants. For this project, Jessica and I led poetry workshops in the Latimer House and collected both written poems and recordings of workshop participants reading their poems. We then installed the work, comprising various elements, both inside the Latimer House Museum and outside, throughout the neighborhood: lamps that when turned on played recordings of the spoken poems; Department of Transportation street signs with poems written on them in English, Spanish, and Mandarin, the most common languages spoken in that neighborhood; street signs with a phone number to call to hear a poem spoken and to record your own poem. The event included a kick-off with musical performances and readings by people in the community and workshop participants. It was an ambitious project and pushed me to consider how poetry can come alive off the page and in dynamic relation to a public place.

An Invitation

How would you design a poem, or an experience with poetry, that consciously collaborates with a diverse range of partners? We invite you to map out a new design for poetry. Maybe think of a place and how poetry could interface with that place. As you do so, carry with you these words by Haraway: "I care about art-design-activist practices that join diverse people and varied critters in shared, often vexed public spaces" (Haraway, 2016, p. 133). What do you care about, and how might your pedagogical design reflect this?

Your work doesn't need to be grand, complicated, or expensive. In an interview with Kirsta Tippett (2016), the poet Naomi Shihab Nye recalls suggesting to a school principal who desired more poetry in his life that he read a poem each morning on the loudspeaker. She returned to that school and learned that the suggested practice became an instilled tradition—and something the students look forward to each morning, listening for the day's poem to be read aloud. It can be as simple (and as beautiful) as that. Consider, too, the simple move of taking several lines of an existing poem that you find particularly moving and changing its scale, material, and context, as artists Mildred Beltre and Oasa DuVerney did with Lucille Clifton's "come celebrate with me/ that everyday something has/ tried to kill me and has failed" in their "Inspired By 'What Is Left,'" which was on view in Prospect Park, Brooklyn, from October 2020 to June 2021 IG: #celebratewithme.

En/Countering the Material Logics

"It's really weird that poets come out of any high school in America. Or this country. We're like oil drops floating around the water."—Marie Howe (interview with Alie Liebigott, *The Believer Magazine* [online], "Road Trip: Marie Howe," March 19, 2019)

Classroom literacy practices continually negotiate their own material logics, whether named or unnamed. By "material logics" we mean dominant and dominating uses of material toward learning or knowledge production. For example, the materials we imagine as necessary to make a poem—pencil, pen, paper, computer, desk, chair, tablet—are the ones we usually use to make a poem. We are not saying these materials need to change (there's nothing wrong with the materials, with any material to make a poem), but we want to bring forward some commonsense beliefs that quietly undergird classroom uses of materials for literacy, beliefs persisting as an assuming backdrop to most classroom literacy practices *that treat nonhuman material as separate from and not part of the human.*

Commonsense approaches to materials span both reading and writing practices. One example of commonsense use of material in a reading practice would be annotating a text for meaning. In this practice, one works over a text, usually with a pencil, pen, or highlighter, to emphasize what the reader deems important or significant in the text. Sometimes main ideas are highlighted; sometimes personal connections are underlined or written briefly in the margins. We point this out not to criticize practices of annotation—there is certainly value to marking a text in order to understand and/or connect with it—but to invite our readers to better see the commonsense logic behind a common reading practice in classrooms and to potentially disorient and reorient themselves toward creative possibilities. Sidenote: We encourage you to (re)read Billy Collins's (1996) poem "Marginalia" for a playful perspective on annotative practices!

Commonsense material logic guides writing practices, too. "The overall assumption guiding writing practices in schools could be articulated this way: You have an idea and you put that idea on the page. In other words, the page is a blank surface upon which to project your ideas and plop down words" (Pindyck, 2017, p. 59). The page gets treated as an inert, inanimate surface whose worth depends on how humans use it. It is seen as a means to an end in most classrooms rather than a collaborative actant in the "literacy situation," to bring back Snaza's term. What might a different orientation to the page as a living palimpsest of histories, processes, and texts (past-present-future) do to and for a classroom literacy practice? What ideas spring to mind when you imagine engaging the page in more dynamic, intra-active ways? What metaphors? Take note of both existing and imaginative practices that surface in your mind.

Erasure Poetry

The poet Jennie Panchy offers us this haunting erasure of a text:

Erasure

(Pages 53–5)

Clearly her first
was masterful

Ordered her four if she did not—
corn-pounding, pea-shelling

Violently, utterly clear—
finally *somewhere*

Consider how the palpable silences—the absent text, the strange and wide gaps in meaning—
work in relation to what remains here: the poem. Erasure poetry can be a way of drawing
out another possibility from an existing source, collaborating with that source, and even
reclaiming that source. Panchy leaves us with a sharp sensation through a process of erasure.
The initial source haunts the poem, whether or not we can know or name it. We suggest
also reading Tracy K. Smith's (2018) poem "Declaration" (an erasure of the Declaration of
Independence) and Nicole Sealey's "Pages 1-4, an excerpt from The Ferguson Report: An
Erasure" (2021), both available online. Sealey's title more directly points to its source—there
is no question about the initial source (*The Ferguson Report*) and which pages from it she
erased to make this poem. Note the haunting presence of the erased report: barely visible
and legible in its initial form, now, by way of the surfaced words. Erasure poems can reorient
us to consider our active relationships to texts and to what, as readers and writers, we are
capable of noticing, disrupting, and collaborating with across different times and places.

In her brilliant essay "The Race within Erasure," Robin Coste Lewis describes the
process of poetic erasure (and connects it to reading) as follows:

> As readers, it is our responsibility to pay attention to everything in a book—not
> only the way a writer wants us to read her project, but we should also attend
> scrupulously to the parts of the book to which the writer is wholly unaware.
> . . . Like a photograph, a poem or story erases what is outside of its frame—but
> here's the curious part, also like a photograph, it captures the unintended, and
> sometimes that turns out to be the most engaging part of a text: its accidents.. . .
> Erasure is a collaboration of time and intent. Erasure often erases intent. Ironically,
> sometimes by removing text from its source, erasure can even magnify the original
> writer's intent. When it is really, really, really good, erasure can reveal more about
> the projects of both writers."

Source: https://literary-arts.org/archive/robin-coste-lewis-2/

Erasure poetry, sometimes called "blackout poetry" or "found poetry," involves explicit
engagement with an already-written page. It is quite amazing to us what erasure poetry
can do. We love how Mary Ruefle describes this creative process for herself in her essay
"On Erasure": "the words rise above the page, by say an eighth of an inch, and hover there
in space, singly and unconnected, and they form a kind of field, and from this field I pick
my words as if they were flowers" (para. 21).

Reader, we invite you to create from a page and its field of possibility your own words/
flowers. Select for yourself text from a book, any book, or a newspaper or magazine or

advertisement or manual or pamphlet. The point being: any text will do, and the more random—the wider the gap (or the "dissonance," as one of my students put it) between this text and "poetry"—the better. Now pick a tool to work with. Consider the marks this tool makes. Soft pencil lines? Jagged cuts? An adhesive covering, like masking tape? A thick, black line? A pasty white streak with a toxic scent? Page by page begin erasing your text.

What is your poetry made of? How does the poetry you made interface with the initial text? Is the relationship arbitrary, purposeful, and/or surprising in any way?

Those of you who wish to incorporate visual art into your erasure may be inspired by the website of Tom Phillips's *A Humument*, an ongoing labor of love since 1966.

Reorienting toward More-Than-Human Knowledge

We conclude by beginning with this poem, "Singularity," by Marissa Davis, written in 2020:

Singularity

after Marie Howe
in the wordless beginning
iguana & myrrh
magma & reef   ghost moth
& the cordyceps tickling its nerves
& cedar & archipelago & anemone
dodo bird & cardinal waiting for its red
ocean salt & crude oil   now black
muck now most naïve fumbling plankton
every egg clutched in the copycat soft
of me unwomaned unraced
unsexed   as the ecstatic prokaryote
that would rage my uncle's blood
or the bacterium that will widow
your eldest daughter's eldest son
my uncle, her son   our mammoth sun
& her uncountable siblings   & dust mite & peat
apatosaurus & nile river
& maple green & nude & chill-blushed &
yeasty keratined bug-gutted i & you
spleen & femur seven-year refreshed
seven-year shedding & taking & being this dust
& my children & your children
& their children & the children

of the black bears & gladiolus & pink florida grapefruit
here not allied but the same   perpetual breath
held fast to each other as each other's own skin
cold-dormant & rotting & birthing & being born
in the olympus   of the smallest
possible once before once

We have emerged from our pandemic in a world where our interconnected nature has visibly surfaced in terrible, painful, and hopeful ways. People's everyday actions (building up to broader systems of care, or lack thereof) have unavoidable impacts, emphasized by the realities of the pandemic. Meanwhile, according to *The National Geographic* online, sea turtles experienced a baby boom (Scott, 2020, October 22); the pause in human activity contributed to the survival of more-than-human species, including the critically endangered. The consequences of what scientists call "the anthropause" are complex, and there are no clear answers about the positive and negative effects of the pandemic on other species (Yuhas, 2021, March 9). What has been thrown into sharp relief, however, is our intra-dependent and intra-connected nature to other humans, more-than-human friends, communities, and ecosystems. We cannot turn away. Our habitual ways of life have become upended, and we have an opportunity as teachers to respond to this reality through our literacy practices. What we notice, how we read, write, know, for who/what/why are questions we need to take up in conscious, active, metaphor-inducing, and community-oriented ways.

I remember reading, or listening to, a conversation with Marie Howe where she talks about assigning her students the exercise of researching an animal they find disgusting throughout the course of the semester. She has them find out as much as they can about this animal that repels them. At least I think that's the prompt. I have tried searching for it, and cannot find it anywhere—maybe I imagined it? I'm pretty sure it's real, but anyways—the goal is to cultivate an empathetic relationship with that animal through research and writing. To disorient one's relationship to a "disgusting" animal. When I heard this/read this/imagined this, I thought of Elizabeth Acevedo's wonderful rat ode and how it reclaims the rat's noble accents and raises up its distinct qualities:

For the Poet Who Told Me Rats Aren't Noble Enough Creatures for a Poem

Because you are not the admired nightingale.
Because you are not the noble doe.
Because you are not the blackbird,
picturesque ermine, armadillo, or bat.
They've been written, and I don't know their song
the way I know your scuttling between walls.
The scent of your collapsed corpse bloating
beneath floorboards. Your frantic squeals
as you wrestle your own fur from glue traps.

Because in July of '97, you birthed a legion
on 109th, swarmed from behind dumpsters,
made our street infamous for something
other than crack. We nicknamed you "Cat-
killer," raced with you through open hydrants,
screeched like you when Siete blasted
aluminum bat into your brethren's skull—
the sound: slapped down dominoes. You reigned
that summer, Rat; knocked down the viejo's Heinekens,
your screech erupting with the cry of *Capicu!*
And even when they sent exterminators,
set flame to garbage, half dead, and on fire, you
pushed on.
Because you may be inelegant, simple,
a mammal bottom-feeder, always fucking famished,
little ugly thing that feasts on what crumbs fall
from the corner of our mouths, but you live
uncuddled, uncoddled, can't be bought at Petco
and fed to fat snakes because you're not the maze-rat
of labs: pale, pretty-eyed, trained.
You raise yourself sharp fanged, clawed, scarred,
patched dark—because of this alone they should
love you. So, when they tell you to crawl home
take your gutter, your dirt coat, your underbelly that
scrapes against street, concrete, squeak and filth this
page, Rat.

We discussed odes in a previous chapter, and this may be a good place to revive the ode as a practice of praising our more-than-human partners-in-life—especially, maybe, the ones that terrify us, disgust us, and/or are socially deemed unworthy of praise. What is an animal that disgusts you, or that you have been taught is disgusting? What ode do you dare write to shift a commonsense orientation to a more-than-human creature? Writing my own ode to the cockroach helped me sense it a little differently and come a little closer to that creature, one that has terrified me all my life. My fear is not as intense as it used to be, but I still have work to do. I still jump (and sometimes scream) when I see them. I should probably write a second ode to the cockroach and see how/if it changes our relationship.

As I write these words, I kid you not, I see a black bird perched in the branches of the tree outside my window (!), as if calling me back. The bird stays for a few seconds, swaying on the branch, then flies away. Was it a crow? A blackbird? I can feel my wonder—and my writing, as I place that sight here, on this page—creeping into what I know and what I desire to know in more expansive, connecting ways. I fly back and toward another "Singularity," Marie Howe's:

Singularity

> (*after Stephen Hawking*)

Do you sometimes want to wake up to the singularity
we once were?

so compact nobody
needed a bed, or food or money—

nobody hiding in the school bathroom
or home alone

pulling open the drawer
where the pills are kept.

For every atom belonging to me as good
Belongs to you. Remember?
There was no *Nature.* No
them. No tests
to determine if the elephant
grieves her calf or if

the coral reef feels pain. Trashed
oceans don't speak English or Farsi or French;

would that we could wake up to what we were
—when we were ocean and before that
to when sky was earth, and animal was energy, and rock was
liquid and stars were space and space was not

at all—nothing

before we came to believe humans were so important
before this awful loneliness.

Can molecules recall it?
what once was? before anything happened?

No I, no We, no one. No was
No verb no noun
only a tiny tiny dot brimming with

is is is is is
All everything home

We began and ended this section with two poems, each building off the work of another person; Marie Howe's "Singularity" extends from the work of Stephen Hawking, and Marissa Davis's "Singularity" springs from Howe's poem. We invite you now, at the end of this chapter, to return to write your own poem "Singularity," offshooting from one, or both, of these poems, or another sense of singularity you wish to world for your reader—a future public that was, is, and will become in relation to your worldings. Your poetry has work to do. Find your pencil, paper, its cloud, the sidewalk, a blackbird, the rain, your always-lingering staphylococcus, and go forth!

CHAPTER 9
WORKING AT THE EDGES AND PERIPHERIES

IX
When the blackbird flew out of sight,
It marked the edge
Of one of many circles.

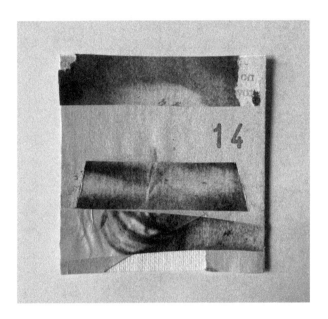

Walk into a room as the haze of sunset traps itself in the near corner. See the calico cat doze in the window nearest the fading light. Smile at the thought of her chasing a firefly, circling and whirling last night, in the dark of this same room. And, what floats just beyond the window ledge? It *is* and *is not* there. Perception is a matter of choice. Or attention. *What if* a thought becomes matter. *What if* just beyond the corner of your eye you see yourself chasing a firefly. Take a breath. The wind is blowing confetti onto the window and its markings take shape as a calico cat. No firefly in sight. Just a glint of ice on the window glass catches a last ray toward night. Engaging peripheral vision is a way of imagining and de-centering or seeing what is just out of sight or reason. Check again—just beyond where sight takes you—gaze above the cloud haze into unknown registers, or follow the trail of breadcrumbs leading, where?

When the blackbird flew out of sight,
It marked the edge
Of one of many circles.

Take a minute to let the image in this stanza enter your mind's eye. What do you see in the spaces of the blackbird's absence? At the edge and beyond? In the one of many circles?

The Responsive Eye

Sense the *presence of the blackbird without the blackbird present.* Peripheries—the just beyond the see-able, say-able, know-able. In geometry, the outside boundary of a closed figure, the circumference of a circle, is labeled the periphery or perimeter. What can we perceive just beyond the edge? And now I cannot help but ask: what does the blackbird see just beyond my seeing? Are there circles from the bird's-eye view that are beyond my sight? And this limitlessness of infinite perspectives carries me back to the periphery, of what I almost see out of the corner of my eye in the just-beyond-view. I am reminded of the spatial limits of my seeing and my knowing, but this is also a reminder of the capacity to imagine. Is this not one of the purposes of poetry—to provoke, reorient perspective, move attention from one circle to another just out of sight? All and more are the subjects of poetry's peripheries.

A poem is *poiesis*, that is, *the activity of bringing something into existence that did not exist before.* Take a moment to think about that as a way of coming to poetry: "This poem I am about to read did not exist before the activity of reading it." For the reader of a poem, we are standing on the edge of the poem's creation. What lurks in the moment before our reading, on the periphery of our vision or imaginings? How will the poem that is soon-to-be read reconfigure and reorient our attention? Take these questions to your reading of this little fragment composed at some point around 600 BC on the Island of Lesbos. Having survived through whatever machinations in time and space, multiple ways of sharing with generation upon generation of readers and listeners, it arrives in this moment on this page where you now hesitate on the edge of Sappho's poem and "You" are called to attend:

Fragment 105(a)

You: an Achilles' apple
Blushing sweet on a high branch
At the tip of the tallest tree.
You escaped those who would pluck your fruit.
Not that they didn't try. No,
They could not forget you
Poised beyond their reach.

What comes into view? What questions linger on the periphery? Is it that desire is sweeter when not attained? The unachievable? The ever-elusive? And, to the sweet apples that in many cultures are more than apples and become fruits of desire. I cannot look at an apple without seeing its histories. Out of the corner of my eye I wonder what led Sappho to this imagining? Perhaps, Sappho's apple is not really an apple—the specificity might be a vague signifier of any fruit in translation. And, Achilles's apple? Just what is on the edge of my imaginings—the weak point, the Achilles's heel?

A poem should elude our grasp for certainty. If we think of a poem not as object to be deciphered but more akin to the butterfly effect of chaos theory, the poem sets into motion multiple and indeterminate vectors that create ripples and motion, offering up an unruliness that competes with a center of fixed meaning or experience. The irony is that the more we may long for a center, away from the peripheries of uncertainty, the more the poem demands us to the edge or ledge of the known. This seductive instability continuously reorients our attention and experience with the poem. For poet and critic Joan Retallack (2004) this would mean reading a poem on the edge (or ledges she will say) of meaning: "Every philosophy, every narrative, every poem, every piece of visual art or music organizes our noticing according to its implicit and enacted geometries of attention" (p. 175). *In praxis*, that is, *the processes of production in the reading or writing of poems*, an aesthetic focused on peripheries will challenge our trusted habits of perception and attention that too often serve as near blinders to what we cannot see, feel, hear, or imagine. Just over the edge, in the spaces beyond the ledge, the poem tempts the reader beyond fixed meaning, holding firm against certainty in the just beyond of "one of many circles." What might all of this mean to us as readers, writers, or teachers of poetry?

Potentially in rereading a poem, the following adage has relevance: You cannot step in the same river twice, but you learn from each return. I emphasize this idea with my students as a way of thinking about what it means to experience a poem, and how the poem stays with us, how we might come back to it in the most particular and unexpected ways. Just suppose this morning the grass outside your window is bending toward the sunlight, a single ant has found her way to the honeycomb cube that sweetened your tea, or, you see crows with all black tails near the window, and you think again of Sappho's line "You, an Achilles' apple"—an idea you cannot quite reach out and touch. The poem is not the same river this morning as before, but you are learning and experiencing it with each return.

But there is more. You cannot step in the same river twice, but you learn from each return. This may also be a useful reminder for living a life with poetry in it. Poetry informs the way I look at and make sense of the world. A sense of knowing does not come all at once, but ebbs and flows with experiences and sensations. So, too, a poem. We parse and add and rethink. We orient our attentions, and, in so doing, our habits of attunement to the periphery grow with each poem, with each reading. I wonder at the simplicity of Sappho's poem. And still, I cannot reach out and touch the fullness of the idea, but I am satisfied holding on the edge or ledge of the peripheries, waiting to be taken up again when a thought or image catches me in the poem's web.

Poems insinuate. Poets nudge and nurture at the edges of sight and insight. They probe at the peripheries, finding image, language, or sound to explore the nooks and crannies of the small and personal: the sound of rain against a leaf, the last apple hanging high in a tree, the loss of a child, or the blackbird flying just beyond sight. Poets capture the ineffable and expansive, too—memories and stories, mythologies, those forgotten who live on the peripheries both human and nonhuman, terrains beyond the borders of our recognition or imaginings, and the beyond-human worlds.

Questions of Insolubility

Recognition is enriched by encounters with insolubility from poet's who practice honing their peripheral vision. Consider Shakespeare's "To be or not to be?" or Langston Hughes's "What happens to a dream deferred?" Lifelong questions without answers operate on the periphery. In a playful, yet mind-dizzying, collection, Pablo Neruda's *Book of Questions* (1974), composed of 316 unanswerable questions, moves among the poignant, surreal, haunting, and comic. Each poem has three to six questions. This manuscript, one of eight that lay on Neruda's desk after his death, contains hundreds of exhilarating nods to the intent of the Greek word *peripheria*, literally, "a carrying around, a revolving." The unanswerable questions that revolve and do not resolve are part of the continuous explorations of the periphery. Many begin with "Why." For example, Neruda questions: Why doesn't Thursday talk its way into coming after Friday? Why do trees hide the beauty of their roots?

Why indeed? Do these seem nonsensical questions to you? Is it possible that these questions set into motion other questions, other explorations that cause you to question the order of days of the week or month, or, of roots concealed?

An Invitation

Take a look at Neruda's question poems online if you like. Write a series of two-line questions following Neruda's example. This might be good practice for all of us each morning as we awaken. I introduced examples of Neruda's question poems to a group of eighth graders. Several were inspired to write their own. Neruda provided inspiration that freed students to explore beyond the commonsense or commonplace:

Here was Rosa's poem question:

Why is a wild Iris named wild
When her feet are stuck to the ground?

Max asked:

What color is a hug
After flames of angry words?

Rashida wrote four question poems. Here was her favorite:

> If war is endless in the Ghaza,
> What is life for?

There are chords of familiarity and strangeness in these question poems—sometimes off putting, funny, sad, poignant, and provocative. For these eighth graders, I found a near-electric energy in their surprise at what they created and imagined through such a simple form. Wide grins of shared delight accompanied the transgressions and provocations that came from practicing their peripheral vision. The peripheries help us explore the world just beyond our sight, the just out of reach of our imaginations and the many circles not quite visible.

Working by Distraction

Part of the allure or lore of poets is built on speculations about where they get ideas for poems. In the Greek legend, Sappho was informed by muses and given the title of Tenth Muse; Poe's work might suggest ideas come at midnight unsolicited, and in the traditions of Robert Browning we have a frenzy of fevered-dreams. Basho communed with often unnoticed aspects of nature; Edmund Spenser searched within the less than beautiful for sources of ideal beauty. Nikki Giovanni found inspiration in the glow of meaning from her mother's storytelling; Gabriela Mistral torments her own lyrical voice to envision the harshness and lack of mercy in human rights and for the disadvantaged. These very different ways of describing creative imagination or peripheral vision may arise when typical forms of attention challenge the common.

Roland Barthes (1975), the French literary critic and essayist, thinks of it in this way: "To be with the one I love and to think of something else: this is how I have my best ideas" (p. 24). Developing a practice of distraction doesn't simply mean shifting attention from one thing to another. The word itself carries negative connotations as in "that person is very distracted." Distracted from what? Do we assume all distractions take us away from some central attention on which we should be focused? If I say to you in reference to a friend, "She is a person on whom nothing is lost," what comes to mind when you hear this statement? What qualities do you attribute to a person about whom this statement refers? Or, I might say this about another friend: "She cannot seem to concentrate on anything. Her head is always in the clouds." What notion of my friend is carried through this description? For each friend, the descriptions of their capacities for engagement suggest a valuing of what is present, what is visible, often with focus on the task or subject at hand.

Noting that we are surrounded with continuous stimuli and information, it is worthy of note that we seem not to have the capacity to take everything in and make sense of it. As with the descriptions of the poets named at the beginning of this section, there are those who practice and learn ways of being distracted from the flow of information and the visible and hone their capacities to see the lesser, the unavailable, the hidden. Poets develop practices to achieve these peripheral visions and work by distraction.

Let's probe how distraction might be of interest in both the reading and writing of poetry. Information floods our senses but, as neuroscientists have determined, the brain is intimately involved in how and why attention is enhanced in some cases and not in others. How is it that you can hear one voice out of dozens in conversation even those that person is across the room? How is it that you can spot that one book you were looking for in piles of stacked books, or smell coriander through other spices flooding a multitude of smells in a spice shop?

For decades, the idea was that attention worked similarly to a spotlight, illuminating what was of interest and darkening or dulling what was surrounding the point of focus. Interestingly, as neuroscientists have pursued this idea recently, the research studies indicate it might be just the opposite. That is, the searchlight metaphor does not explain what actually happens in the brain. If the spotlight effect describes the way our brain works, then it would appear we are not open to the unexpected, and we have much evidence this isn't true. Recent work of Fiebelkorn (2018) now suggests that the brain seems to cast not a steady illumination or spotlight, but it works more like a blinking light as compensation to ward off over-focusing on a single event or stimuli in the environment. It is in these moments of the spotlight's flicker (in animals about four times per second) that Fiebelkorn suggests *peripheral stimuli* receive a boost and can distract focus. We are, then, inherently distractible if this view in neuroscience holds up to further scrutiny. What difference does the idea of distractibility make in our exploration of peripheral vision for poets and in poetry?

This recent work in neuroscience reminds me of the qualities I have admired in poets who seem to have an uncanny sense of a world just beyond my grasp. Their poems draw attention to the tension between common ways of seeing and attention shifted to a very different way of perceiving beyond the habitual. "Uncanny" is the word that comes to mind here. It is not that attention has simply shifted from one thing to another, but it is *the way* it shifts, bringing surprising connections, penetrating truths deeper than the commonsense way of seeing or interpreting stimuli or ideas. The third eye metaphor comes to mind, using the terms from neuroscience, as the receptor of peripheral stimuli. The capacity for penetrating the strange into the common seems nurtured by a certain type of distractedness when our capacity of vision outruns itself, leading me back to a better understanding of the third eye.

An Invitation

Here is an exercise I've given to both high school and graduate students. Try this out yourself and see where it takes you. Create the pauses you need and that you find productive.

(1) Take a look around the room where you are reading this book. Scan first and take time to see the room, capture the feeling of the space, consider its

significance to you, if any. Start writing about the room without editing. Capture the stream of consciousness as best you can.

(2) Stop somewhere mid-sentence. Close your two eyes and see something or someone in the room that/who isn't there, or, imagine sounds coming into the room, a voice from long ago or somewhere else that you barely recognize. Start writing and let this take you wherever it might. Again, write and don't edit. Let your third eye move your points of focus miles away from this room and back into it. Your third eye needs to work against the temporal/spatial logics.

(3) Stop mid-sentence or end of sentence and veer or swerve to describe what histories—no longer visible—inform this room? What comes to mind? Your history with this space? Those before you? Who built this place? Record whatever random thoughts on this come to mind. What histories have you sensed, heard about, or on which you speculate?

(4) Stop again. Take the last word you wrote and use it as the first word in a paragraph and just write without editing for about five minutes. Then stop, take a deep breath and start a new paragraph.

(5) Now with actual knowledge or just imagining, take up these questions. Who originally lived on this land? Are there seen and unseen presences of those first or other inhabitants in the circles of widening explorations beyond the room where you are? How would you describe how you feel about this space to someone else? How do the histories co-mingle with your thoughts? Pick up the last word you wrote again and make it the first sentence in a new paragraph as you start again.

(6) Now, move to the future. Describe this space fifty years from now. Keep exercising that third eye. Close your two eyes. Wake up in the same room and open your third eye. Let it do the looking around the room of the future.

To generate your own prompt on this, or for further inspiration, you might look at what Margaret Atwood (1983) does in *Murder in the Dark*, a wonderfully rich collection of poems, essays, thoughts, and instructions that I go back to often when I need to remind myself how to practice and trust my third eye.

Additionally, Gertrude Stein's experiments and explorations into attention and distraction come to mind. Perhaps because of her interest in studies on the operations of mind and body when attention is distracted or because she herself honed her own practices in distraction, her poems offer us a look inside a study on distraction. Her experiments evidence her desire to find the values of distraction more than its liabilities and her poetics and poems demonstrate this focus and exploration.

Stein's (2012) *Stanzas in Meditation* evidence these explorations. Check out examples on poets.org or poetryfoundation.org. There are more than 149 pages and 164 stanzas of her experimentations/meditations on the relationship between attention and distraction. In Part V, Stanza XXXVIII, she begins: "Which I wish to say is this/There is no beginning to an end/But there is a beginning and an end" (p. 215).

Where is your attention drawn? How might you describe what Stein is doing here if you and another person were talking about this beginning of this ten line stanza? I see this stanza as a stream of consciousness that starts in the middle of a thought ("Which I wish") linked to a conceptual idea ("There is no beginning to an end") moved forward by a play off the words, using words to draw attention briefly only to deflect through distraction. And, yet the unpredictability of the distraction meets a point of attention to offer a look back at the original thought as well as a moving to some other iteration of the original. The openness to allow near-random thoughts to take form temporarily seems to include—or to inspire—a sense of freedom and a sideways glance at what was not there before. In some odd turn, working by distraction emphasizes what is lacking in our focused attention rather than the more typical notion that distraction keeps us from paying attention. Through her *Meditations in Stanzas*, Stein offers guidance and permission to lose the thread of thought and attention, to see distractibility itself as a particular form of attention worthy of practice in developing peripheral vision. Stein's *Meditations* are provocations to see out of the corner of the eye, and be accomplices in trafficking with the peripheries and the invisible through the exercising of our third eye.

An Invitation

Now might be the time to create a *found poem*, a Stanza of Meditation of your own, from the writing you generated from the prompts on third eye exercising earlier in this chapter. Circle words or phrases that are of particular interest to you but do not think about a logical sequence or a temporal or spatial logic. You might randomly pull words or phrases and juxtapose lines without much thought and see what comes of it. Let ideas bounce one into another, trusting the rhyme or rhythm and not the reason. No planning for now.

Take a few minutes to experiment. You might start with Stein's "Which I wish to say is. . ." and see what poem can be found in your third eye writing. Here is my poem from my writing about a space, a small alcove room overlooking the Aegean Sea, from a visit there some two years ago now.

The roaring never stops, never the waves
the earth by language never arrives to cripple
beauty, never speaks to the olive tree by luck
to the olive tree roaring its love for the stone
fountain roaring its water back to the sea, unwinds
are winding far, they drink the sea dry, the fountain
flies, and Poseidon dreams round the break of sky,
the roaring stops, never waves again, arriving
a cripple beauty of the future and round a roaring
arrives the roaring never stops never the waves
the earth speaks olive trees in the future, they drink,

they fly by my room, my room, pie in the sky,
I remember

This little exercise demonstrates how entangled and simultaneous are the experiential, affective, sensual, and spiritual landscapes of past, present, and future. The work of poets is to draw our attention to dimensions not so easily within our grasp and to call those out and invite us into the moments. Take a look back at what you wrote and see if there are places which surprise you in the connections made. Much that happens around us never enters our conscious level but runs somewhere like an underground spring that feeds a pond. That spring may bubble to our attention when conditions are ripe.

Sometimes it seems the poem exists to remind us that the invisible is in plain sight. These missing and invisible places, these peripheries, are lessons for us—to attend, to look from the corner of our eye or with our third eye, to gaze more deeply at what has been hidden or blurred. Just maybe poems exist to remind us how to be more mindful of distraction, of the capacities of our third eye.

Poets teach us what neuroscientists articulate as well. Sensory experiences, physical movements, and consciousness are deeply and inextricably intertwined, and we are overloaded every moment with impressions and information on the sensory level. I only hear the ticking of the clock when I turn my attention to listen. The hum of the fan in my writing space is not noticeable unless I attend to it. Even the city sounds of sirens, people singing on the street, the screech of air brakes on the garbage trucks are just beyond my hearing unless I stop to listen, to find that little blink between the steady illumination of the spotlight. I had not noticed before this moment that I can feel the tag in my shirt against my neck if my attention dissolves from writing this sentence as I wait for the sensory to catch up in that little gap away from intention. Does this matter? Is it important? I suspect it depends. As we explore the peripheries, Wordsworth perhaps says something of the importance related to the burdens and purposes of nurturing our peripheral visions and working in the spaces of distraction.

The World Is Too Much with Us

The world is too much with us; late and soon,
Getting and spending, we lay waste our powers;—
Little we see in Nature that is ours;
We have given our hearts away, a sordid boon!
This Sea that bares her bosom to the moon;
The winds that will be howling at all hours,
And are up-gathered now like sleeping flowers;
For this, for everything, we are out of tune;
It moves us not. Great God! I'd rather be
A Pagan suckled in a creed outworn;

So might I, standing on this pleasant lea,
Have glimpses that would make me less forlorn;
Have sight of Proteus rising from the sea;
Or hear old Triton blow his wreathèd horn.

Glimpses of a world too common, too known. Wordsworth (1807) longs for the cracks and crevices of peripheral vision to remind us of the richness of attempts to explain the inexplicable and to see the invisible—all these are evident in the restless imaginings of poets who inspire others poets and call us to hone capacities toward the peripheral. Pay attention. Look to your left. Look skyward. Look in the blink. Into the myths we have created. Stand on the edges. And, as Wordsworth suggests, the world is richer in the glimpses of imagination and possibility and even the outworn beliefs than it is if we are not using our powers to see more than what is in front of us.

Poetic Practices on the Periphery

How does a poet render images and imaginings from the peripheries, the invisible in the visible, or non-thought inside of thought? What are the resources of language and device that support ways to help a reader experience background noise, the spaces between the blinking light, or the just over the edge and out of sight? How do imaginings that seem hard to translate into words become poems? Trust the poets. They have found their ways.

Perhaps Emily Dickinson (1896) starts us in this exploration:

I heard a Fly buzz—when I died—
The Stillness in the Room
Was like the Stillness in the Air—
Between the Heaves of Storm—

The Eyes around—had wrung them dry—
And Breaths were gathering firm
For that last Onset—when the King
Be witnessed—in the Room—

I willed my Keepsakes—Signed away
What portion of me be
Assignable—and then it was
There interposed a Fly—

With Blue—uncertain—stumbling Buzz—
Between the light—and me—
And then the Windows failed—and then
I could not see to see—

What stays with you? If you read, taught, or studied this poem before, how does the focus of this chapter on distraction and peripheries influence your attention and focus?

In the moment of dying, a fly with a "stumbling Buzz" comes between "the light—and me—. . ." It seems so simple. And, yet, in the gravity of the moment of dying, what can we make of the imposition of a fly buzzing, and not only buzzing, but with a "stumbling" buzz? It may be my mood this particular morning, but there is a hyperawareness here of what often goes unnoticed in our typical routines of life—a fly buzzing near the window or in the next room. In a moment of impending death, does it seem odd to notice the "stumbling Buzz" of a fly? In the context of the focus of this chapter on peripheries and distraction, I come to this poem differently and find it intensifies my experience with the poem. I read this poem as potentially Dickinson's own exploration of distraction, of periphery. Of course, that is my reading, at this moment.

I was taught to read this poem differently, however. The first time, Miss Jackson, ninth grade: "As you read, determine *the* theme of this poem. Dickinson imagines the transition between life and death. The first stanza sets up the impending death. The fly *is* death. How do you know this and what is the theme?" Silence. We were each left to read on our own. I vaguely remember hearing a buzzing fly and there seemed a phrase off-kilter that I couldn't understand: "the Windows failed." Is that the light disappearing with the onset of death? Is it that light cannot enter the room or leave it? I was struggling with that and wondering about all the dashes? My interests were soon distracted by Miss Jackson's voice again: "This is a poem spoken by a dead person. Please note the past tense of 'died' in the first line. The speaker is already dead and is telling us about what happened as she died." I remember that Miss Jackson continued to summarize the poem. I learned later this is called exposition. "Now," said Miss Jackson, her voice alone having framed our reading before and after reading of the poem, "take this theme on the fly as death and write a paragraph about how you can prove it is the theme. Let's take ten minutes." I was still a bit stuck on the "stumbling" and the windows but no matter. I figured a way to state how the fly was death and found phrases to suggest how that was so. I still do not believe the fly is death here, and, even more as I write this chapter, I believe the fly may be a way of reminding us of the awareness and capacity we have, even in an ultimate moment like death, of noticing what often goes unnoticed. I am still not certain about windows failing. I cannot explain why Dickinson used all the dashes, but I can name the effect for me now—a halting, stumbling, like the fly—a moment of—trying—to—catch—breath—in—the—dying. And one dash after words fail, at the very end, to hold the moment in stillness, perhaps? Even now, Dickinson leaves me with much to think about.

The Engines of Ingenuity and Invention

Poetic imagination requires more than nurturing peripheral vision. Attending to what is not present and drawing on a combination of experience and imagination requires utilizing the tools of poetic craft with ingenuity and invention to produce the unfolding of experience. If a poem is left with spaces and crevices for exploration, the richness of interpretive and experiential possibilities blossoms. How our experiences are shaped during and after the reading depends on *how* the poet brings us to attend, spurs us to think and to experience the poem *in concert with* the context of the reading and the readers' proclivities. The interplay is intricate, recursive, and iterative. Too much information or direction from the poet may not leave enough room for the reader to imagine and experience. Overuse of figurative language, abstraction, repetition, or any poetic devices may keep the reader at a distance, and, unless that is the intention, it will impede the reader's experience.

The equation I have found useful is to work *from effect and affect of the poets' craft*, that is: To what effect (for me as reader not trying to state motivations of the poet) is the use of this metaphor, this particular line or stanza break, rhythm or rhyme or any other devices identifiable? To what effect on my experience as a reader? Starting there, I begin to note particular crafting techniques and how these affect my reading and my experience with the poem. How does the craft cause me to think, digress, feel, or experience with the poem and its poet? As readers, we work in responsive relation to the poet. There are times when I hear a poet whispering between the words or lines of a poem: "Don't you see how poetry and the real world are inextricably merged in your perceptions? Did you notice how this phrase or image tugs at your shirt sleeve and deserves attention? Look to your left—right now, here in this space between words. Look skyward, right there where I have placed that lonely little cloud." The poet urges me to pay attention through the crafting, to move with the experience as I read and after.

Take a moment to consider the difference in framing our students' readings of poems as well as our own with the three questions asked in the preceding paragraph rather than Miss Jackson's "look for the theme." To what effect on my experience as a reader? How does the craft of the poem cause me to think, digress, feel, or experience with the poem and its poet? This reorients both intent and focus. Of course, these questions come after the original reorientation we have stressed in earlier chapters: experience the poem first; breathe it in; and take time to notice and become alert to the experience the poem conjures.

While each poem engages the conceptually, emotionally, or experientially with different emphases, all poems elaborate a degree of recombination of attention in direct and peripheral ways. Whether in its musicality, verisimilitude, imagism, sensorium, or whatever combinations, the poem is a point of intersection for perception and imagination, taking us back to Stevens:

When the blackbird flew out of sight,
It marked the edge
Of one of many circles.

Perception tells us the blackbird is out of sight, but imagination takes us to the edge and beyond into the "one of many circles." For Stevens (1965), "The imagination loses its vitality as it ceases to adhere to what is real. When it adheres to the unreal and intensifies what is unreal, while its first effect may be extraordinary, that effect is the maximum effect that it will ever have" (p. 6). If we follow Stevens's thinking here, perception and imagination are inseparable and craft will serve to enhance and enrich the interdependence.

Let's take a close look at this striking poem by Jennie Panchy (2021):

Spring

> I would not think to touch the sky with two arms
>
> Sappho

I want—

deer at the woods-edge,
pulse within—

not possible to become

who would know our ankles,
our restlessness

wearing a country dress

cream dipped from the pail
behind the barn

yes you know well

a farmer plants grain then cuts it down
a butcher cuts meat

As we read and reread this poem, we sense a distinct pulse that has something to do with the relationship between the down-to-earth images that ground the poem (the country dress, the cream dripped from the pail, the butcher cutting the meat) and the more airy, imaginative space that the epigraph by Sappho seems to speak to, emphasized in the poem's spaces—its sparse form and vibrant silences. The poem seems to become more grounded in earth as it goes while navigating that open, imaginative space. We see imagination and perception as inseparable in this poem. Together these offer a distinct sense of spring.

Let's come back to the questions asked earlier to reorient the ways we understand our experiences with this poem: What are the particular aspects of craft that I notice? To what effect do those identified have on my encounter and experience at the moment and after? For example, to what effect are the shapes and placement of lines in this poem, of particular lines or stanza breaks, of the juxtaposition of commonplace and the peripheral? What do I notice about how temporal and spatial shifts are crafted, and how do these shifts guide my encounter? How do particular moves of the poet cause me to think, digress, feel, or experience with the poem and its poet? Certainly, we can read the poem without this deeper examination of craft and effect/affect, but what this offers us is an opportunity to probe the *performance* of the poem. Just what does Panchy suggest about perception and imagination as these brush against each other in this particular performance? If poems are a medium for examining and exploring the world, how does her poem nurture your alertness, openness, and desire to engage in the significance of "Spring"?

Perhaps, Significance Is the Point

Here is a proposition: if we think of a poem as a performance, in the sense of a poet crafting perception and imagination to share with others, and if readers are in *concert with, are co-constructers* of the experience then, perhaps, we might imagine ourselves as readers leaving the performance. What do we take away? How do we describe what we carry away? Perhaps, *significance* is the point more than meaning. For poet, essayist, and translator Lyn Hejinian (2000), co-production is the goal:

> For a writer, it is language that carries thought, perception, and meaning. And it does so through a largely metonymic process, through the discovery and invention of associations and connections. Though it may seem merely technical, the notion of linkage—of forging connections—has in my mind, a concomitant political and social dimension. Communities of phrases spark the communities of ideas in which communities of persons live and work. (p. 166)

As you turn away from your reading of Panchy's poem, or any other poem for that matter, *what is the significance you carry with you*? Perhaps this is a question we ask of both ourselves and our students. In the context of peripheral vision, the commonsense search for theme or meaning might be replaced by the word *significance*. The dictionary definition of significance is: *the quality of being worthy of attention; importance*. Perhaps, we understand a poem has a life force of its own, but that is not simply to intellectualize the poem into theme or meaning. We understand a poem is not all about muses and inspiration. Perhaps thought, word, and feeling are inseparable as are perception and imagination. Perhaps all are firmly connected to the craft work of shaping the encounter. Into significance.

Peripheries and the Ethical Turn

> "We are responsible for boundaries; we are they."
>
> *(Haraway, p. 180)*

Haraway (1988) provides us with a stark reminder that our actions and responsibility have created the boundaries and borders that imagine, shape, and interrogate the peripheries. We created the lines between what we notice or do not notice through our habitual practices and varied cultural practices and world views. In this chapter, we have examined the productive and imaginative forces at the edge and into the peripheries, but we want to refocus our thinking now on how peripheral spaces, their mobilities and aesthetics are also taken up in poetic theory, practices, and poems in ways intended to shed light on critical understandings as well. "We are responsible for boundaries," Haraway reminds us. Border and boundaries of all types exist because of actions, long-held beliefs which shape practices and values, conquests of lands and people, hierarchies, racism, discrimination, marginalization of cultures and communities, and repressed histories— all made so by action, inaction, and the ethical stances that shaped our collective and individual histories. It is more to take in than the heart and mind can bear. Borders and boundaries exist because of various acts of colonization including of our planet's lands and resources. Both geo-cultures and eco-cultures receive attention. We are responsible. Many poets have been vocal that the peripheral of the political, economic, and cultural aspects should be made visible. These poets crack open spaces of the peripheral, creating alternative perspectives that highlight imagination, innovation, and futurity to counter the lingering normalization and colonization. Our exploration of peripheries moves now to the poet's role in highlighting the normalizing influences through their use of critique, experimental techniques and devices, and subversive practices employed to resee and reshape the horizon of peripheries and awaken possibilities of what *might be* (other)wise.

The Earth as More than a Supply Yard

The development of *ecopoetry* reflects one more push at the peripheral boundaries as it takes critical and ethical lenses toward humanity's relationship with the planet. Rather than rely upon nature writing where the poet-observer honors and praises nature, *ecopoetry* strips away the illusion of our observer status as recorders of natural occurrences and the purpose of these observations to commune with, honor or praise nature. In ecopoetics, humans *are* nature, entangled and implicated in all aspects. Jonathan Skinner's (2001) journal consolidates this focus on ecopoems. As Skinner writes in his first editorial statement: "Eco" here signals no more and no less the house we share with several million other species, our planet Earth. "Poetics" is used as poesis or making, not necessarily to emphasize the critical over the creative act (nor vice versa). Thus: ecopoetics is a house making (p. 7).

The poet Gary Snyder (2021) deserves our opening focus as his poems explore humanity's relationship to the Earth, and from the early 1960s on, he has continued to hone his own peripheral and ethical visions in his astonishing body of poems. Fitting into what has now become the ecopoetry movement, Snyder developed a new ethic and aesthetic that draws on Japanese, Chinese, Zen Buddhism, and Native American relationships with Earth to create his unique practice of ecological focus that is also intended to promote ecological consciousness.

In stark simplicity, Snyder draws us in:

A Dent in a Bucket

Hammering a dent out of a bucket
  a woodpecker
        answers from the woods

An Invitation

Take a few moments to tap into your own peripheral noticing and listening—you and the earth in communication. Notice in Snyder's poem how unexpected are moments of illumination. After recording a few notices, you might look at that blank space on your computer screen or in a little notebook and compose a few three-line poems. Simplicity may be the ethical virtue here.

Ethics of Human Action

The poet Juliana Spahr came to an interest in ecopoetics by way of Jonathan Skinner's journal and the ideas he had about ecopoetics as "house-making." For her, the poetics and poets who were working to challenge the common divisions between nature and culture informed a new direction in her thinking and in the poetry. Spahr (2011) determined a need for poets to pay attention not only to the beautiful bird but also to the bulldozer that might destroy its habitat (p. 69). Spahr's poems are inventions of peripheral imagining that focus on the outcomes of human machinery, that is, the destruction or transformation of both human and nonhuman habitats. The ethical mind of Spahr confronts how entanglements are ecological and political and underscore ecopoets' investigations into nature. Her vision of the beautiful bird and bulldozer is a powerful image of peripheral vision extending our view and the ethical implications of our ways of seeing and how we perform in the world ethically.

Interventions in "Distribution of the Sensible"

For the French philosopher Jacques Rancière, art's capacity to interrupt and reorient the established "distribution of the sensible" is certainly at work in ecopoetry as well as in and on the edge of peripheral visions. An aesthetic is constituted that, following Rancière's theorizing, creates a condition that redistributes the sensible to make new sense possible. If we think of all the ways the poets included in this chapter have challenged the visible and commonplace, we can imagine a new aesthetic that is intended to break consensus thinking, complacency, and action by working the peripheries. This is much like a form of *dissensus* that Rancière (2010) describes as the accepted "cartography of the sensible and the thinkable" that creates "a new partition of the perceptible" (p. 143 and p. 124).

The ethical imperative is to attend to the edges, traffic in peripheral visions, and keep searching in spaces between the dark and the blinking lights. These spaces are fertile ground for multiple dimensions of interpretive practices. Attention to gaps and the in-between-ness and to unexpected convergences and collisions can augment our explorations of poetry for ourselves and with our students. These become our explorations through poetry and with our students as readers and writers of poetry. Attend to what is beyond sight—ghosts, hauntings, traces left behind, what is almost in your sideways glance. Periphery of *context* not quite within sight. Periphery in *words* as a *word* is never just the word but all the histories of the word embodied or embedded within it. Periphery in *story or myth* waits, almost invisible, avoiding the reductiveness of bringing them into clear view.

Attend to peripheral vibrancies in reading and writing poems. Approach the "blank page of paper" and the words that will be placed on it as filled already with histories, materials morphing and changing (cloud, light, seed, wood), and possibilities for writing. One practice we emphasize here is how a poet is to insinuate the nooks and crannies of memory, of histories or myth, and of context in the search of the ineffable.

When the blackbird flew out of sight,
It marked the edge
Of one of many circles.

CHAPTER 10
TAPPING SENSATION'S SAP

X
At the sight of blackbirds
Flying in a green light,
Even the bawds of euphony
Would cry out sharply.

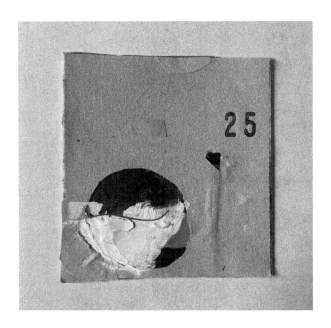

A memory pricks the conscience. Blood drums through ears. Skin prickles. The weight of fear. Sensations resist description and spare logic. Emily Dickinson (1870) wrote vividly about poetry as sensation: "If I read a book and it makes my whole body so cold no fire can warm me, I know that is poetry. If I feel physically as if the top of my head were taken off, I know that is poetry. These are the only ways I know it. Is there any other way?" (para. 50). We know exactly what she means, even though it feels impossible to explain sensation. As Dickinson suggests, there's a sensational urgency to poetry—an urgency that perhaps exceeds and evades our capacities for understanding. People talk about poetry saving their lives and turn to poems in the face of intense grief, loss, and love. People want poems read at wedding ceremonies and funerals. Bodily sensations sometimes perform what words cannot capture; therefore, we concur, poems must be more than clusters of words. It's fitting that in a letter Wallace Stevens (1928) said of *Thirteen Ways of Looking at a Blackbird*, "This group of poems is not meant to be a collection of epigrams or of ideas, but of sensations" (p. 251).

Sensation and Craft

Extending from a long tradition of poets writing about poetry, we believe what enables us to feel the sensations that Dickinson define as poetry is a fusion of what Frederico García Lorca (2007) called "duende" (what he described as "a mysterious force that everyone feels and no philosopher has explained") and the poem's structure, or craft—how the poem is assembled, including where the line breaks, the poem's underlying rhythm, or a sudden shift in point of view (para. 7). By way of these choices, we receive and feel a poem. Mary Oliver, in *A Poetry Handbook* (1994), writes, "Everyone knows that poets are born and not made in school" (p. 1). She argues that poetry possesses a mysterious quality that can't be dissected and reproduced. She notes that a poem is both a mystical and a written document, and there is much that can—and must—be learned about a poem's craft. Her book is dedicated to craft: the part of poetry that can be learned and practiced. In this chapter, we argue for the importance of studying and practicing craft, and we explore the relationship between a study of craft and sensation, including those where "Even the bawds of euphony would cry out sharply."

Before we dive further into this chapter, we pause to acknowledge and address our skeptical readers who may already be shaking their heads at our claims, perhaps having never felt much of anything when reading poetry. To the high school English teacher who once said to us, "Poetry's not my thing," we hear you. When we talk about sensation, we are not talking about cause and effect (e.g., "Read this poem and you will feel X"), nor are we saying that everyone experiences sensations in the same poems. That would be an absurd claim. If we see poetry as "the poem-as-evoked" (p. 128)—the "event," which is the transactional experience between reader, poem, and text, to draw from Louise Rosenblatt's (1964) theorizing—then our ability to feel a poem depends on whether we show up for this event as distinct readers with varying experiences and histories. Hopefully, we can agree that the more we read and write, the more attuned we become to the workings of language and, perhaps, the more curious we become about language's capacities. So, what if poetry isn't about the reader's identity or preference or style ("my thing"), or a genre that a person does or doesn't connect to? What if we think of poetry as a carefully crafted body encountering a human body, crafted by particular value systems and practices? What if poetry is a body carefully made (holding, of course, beautiful accidents and unintentional readings) for reception? How might you participate in the event that is poetry—that uncanny happening between you and the poem? You need to be open to receive it, and it seems the poem that you receive must be made with care for you to care for it.

If we begin from an understanding of a poem as a distinct, irreproducible event that occurs, as Rosenblatt suggests, between you, reader, and poem, we might consider how learning elements of craft enable us to participate in sense-provoking, sense-inducing, and sense-making capacities of poetry. That feeling of sensation that we recognize but struggle to articulate cannot be separated from a poem's structure—the principles of craft that give the poem its physical presence. We receive the poem as we do a piece of music, a painting, a carefully chiseled sculpture. When we read a poem, we are not reading a cloud of fog (though perhaps a poem invokes that feeling); we are reading an assemblage that someone crafted out of words, lines, spaces, silences, or stanzas. There is no poem "itself"—the poem "is," always, in an act of reception, interfacing with the feelings, mind(s), and experiences of the reader/listener—or Massumi's (2002) "thinking-feeling" (p. 145) of its reader/listener.

An Invitation

We invite you to return to a favorite poem of yours. Think of a poem you love for whatever reason. Reread it. As you read it, track your bodily experiences. Where do you pause to catch your breath? What prompts a sensation of goose bumps? What line or phrase or moment in the poem hits you most forcefully? Where do you pause and reread? Make a "body map" of your experience, making visual, sonic, and/or written notation of what you feel and where.

Now study that poem more closely. What about the poem's craft might be prompting these sensations for you? Try to locate without separating multiple possibilities. Consider how the poet made the poem—that line, rhythm, rhyme, space, break as your focus— and note what about its craft you're now sensing. Is it the sudden enjambment between two lines? Is it a simple comma, directing the line's meaning? Is it the poem's "alchemy of language," to use author Jason Reynolds's description (in *On Being* podcast interview with Krista Tippett from 2020)—what words make when placed together? (My six-year-old's language-play from yesterday springs to mind as I write this: "solar system sandwich! Moon maze melon!") Or, is a sudden shift in point of view burning you?

Once you've noted what moves you in your selected poem, use the material of craft that is singing to you (enjambment, the two words you love the sound of together, the single couplet in the poem, that sudden dash) as you write your own poem. See what happens when you move with the elements of craft whose power you have come to sense.

Making Sense

I remember first reading Rilke's (1995) "The Archaic Torso of Apollo" and needing to catch my breath when I arrived at that surprising last line: "You must change your life" (p. 67). If someone just said that to me, that line alone, I would say, "OK, that's a cliché" and probably be unmoved by the statement. But the placement of that line at the end of Rilke's poem makes a powerful, heart-hitting action. I feel the directive with an urgency made possible by the particular assemblage of what he says and how he says it: his poem: the lines, how he orders them, where he breaks them, their length, the poem's lyric moments, its language, its size and shape, what precedes the last line, and so on. A poem is an assemblage as much as it is an event. Fine-tuning our abilities to sense and receive these elements of craft affects how we participate in the sensorium opened by poetry.

One of my earliest experiences of falling in love with a poem was in high school when reading (and memorizing) Emily Dickinson's (1862) "Much Madness Is Divinest Sense." The subject matter spoke to me. I was obsessed with the question of madness and the tensions between society and the artist who chooses not to conform. My favorite book at the time was Sylvia Plath's *The Bell Jar* (1963), and I remember the sharp feeling of wanting to assert my identities in relation to social and cultural norms that felt to me stale and/or problematic. Dickinson's poem blew me away. She was saying what I wanted to say in such a way that I wanted to shout her words from a rooftop. I had found a poetry-sister! It felt like she was speaking directly to me.

Much Madness Is divinest Sense—(620)

Much Madness is divinest Sense—
To a discerning Eye—
Much Sense—the starkest Madness—
'Tis the Majority
In this, as all, prevail—
Assent—and you are sane—
Demur—you're straightway dangerous—
And handled with a Chain—

Never mind that I didn't understand what "discerning" "assent" or "demur" meant and only kinda understood what "prevail" meant when I first read this poem. Eventually I looked those words up, but the poem had an impact on me before I could understand what all the words meant. I could feel its impact and message without complete knowledge of the poem's vocabulary. As a crafted assemblage, the poem speaks on multiple, lateral levels, which include its lyricism or sonic force, message, diction, tone, cadence, its gem-like shape, and those dashes—we can sense a poem sharply (and softly) on any of these levels. Memorizing this poem enabled me to carry it in my body, to feel its breath and movement, differently than I had when I first encountered it.

Years later, I practiced what I loved so much about Dickinson's poetry—specifically its brevity, lyricism, and what the dashes do to each line's movement—and subconsciously borrowed those elements in my own poems. I wasn't reading much of her work at the time, but I could recognize her influence on me from the love affair I had with her poetry in high school. I returned to her work and felt the love affair revive anew, especially encountering her *Envelope Poems* (2016), seeing how she wrote so many of them on envelopes scraps. I was struck by the stunning visual presence of her writing on those small scraps and wondered about how the process and material affected how Dickinson composed her poetry. And how have acts of translating them to the space of an 8.5/11 page shaped how they dominantly get read today?

Our claims should not be confused with Formalism. Unlike Formalist claims that form structures meaning and that this meaning is universal, bearing a "correct" interpretation, we are arguing that a poem's form guides sensation—and those feelings of sensation are both shared (overlapping) and distinct as the personal "event" that creates the poem. In her book *The Forms of the Affects*, Eugenie Brinkema (2014) argues that a study of form opens up a study of sensation and for "a new approach to affectivity that regards its exteriority in textual form as something that commands a reading" (p. 4). Brinkema even says that "the more rigorously structured the text, the more affective it is" (p. 178). In other words, a poem's carefully crafted structure has a capacity that evades our systems of measurement. Spinning off from Spinoza's truth paraphrased by Deleuze (1998)—"No one knows what a body can do" (p. 17), Brinkema concludes her book with, "We do not yet know all it is that form can do" (p. 261). Form then is not something that can be dissected and rationally grasped. It *does* something that affects us—shapes us, even—and a study of craft can intensify sensory experiences with poetry, for both readers and writers.

We advocate for a study of craft rooted in the question of affective capacity as writers and affective response as readers. As Felicia Rose Chavez (2021) reflects in her brilliant book *The Anti-Racist Writing Workshop*,

> I encourage my workshop participants to *feel* their way through a text. When they hit upon an embodied response—a bark of a laugh, a sigh, a wandering mind—it's up to them to interrogate why. What was it, exactly, that evoked the response? I want them to put the text up on blocks, so to speak, and deconstruct its insides: How does this thing function as a work of art? We read for craft. (p. 119)

These orientations challenge a widespread sentiment in schools that what makes a poem moving is simply its authenticity for the student; that the poem speaks to the student's raw experience, oftentimes, seems to be enough, reproducing a sense of poetry as a formless, cathartic release where anything goes or should be embraced.

We have no intention of suffocating the experience of poetry into a definition of poetry. At the same time, we believe it is necessary to reorient attention to form from a route to accessing a shared meaning, the Formalist claim for shared meaning, to understanding form as a tool for prompting distinct, bodily sensations (sometimes—eerily oftentimes—shared), as Chavez suggests. This approach to form honors our powers as writers to create sensations through the ways we go about making a poem and, as readers, to attune ourselves to a poem's existing architecture—what that architecture *does*. From this orientation, the alchemic process of the "event" of a poem is entangled with the question of how we come to feel (and grow to more finely feel) a poem's working. Therefore, we argue that classroom approaches to poetry as unstructured, emotional catharsis may be important for the writing process, but they cannot end there if the writer wants their poem to communicate to a broader audience. Poets are unlikely to provoke sensation in/ with their reader without any care or attention to a poem's structure—the *how* through which the poem becomes received.

What a Body Can Do

What body is reading this book? What is the body you read doing? What body might you make?

An Invitation

Turn to a piece of your writing. It need not be poetry—any writing will do: personal essay, academic article, graduation speech, a letter to a friend or colleague, an unfinished Op/Ed you eventually submit to a newspaper. Consider the form. Who was your imagined audience? How did you navigate the language, the spacing, the tone to communicate as effectively as possible (consciously or not)? On a separate sheet, map what you notice about the moves you make in this piece of writing. What elements of craft do you locate and how might you articulate them? You can use existing vocabulary or make up your own. Following Chavez's (2021) guidance, approach craft as an "assembled living archive" (p. 120) of tools that we collect as readers and writers and that continues to grow. Elements of craft are not predefined, static identifiers; we come to define and refine them in relation to the works we encounter and the sensations these surface. Write down where you feel "voice" in your writing, without worrying about whether your sense of "voice" corresponds to an existing definition of "voice." Maybe you feel something in your writing that you call "Flying in a green light," like those blackbirds, based on what you notice in your writing, assemble your ever-expanding craft toolkit.

We invite you now to put aside that text and your notes on craft and go to your refrigerator or to the fruit bowl sitting on your counter. Select a piece of fruit. Perhaps a berry, a peach, an apple, part of a peeled banana. If you're allergic to fruits, pick a bite-sized vegetable or part of a vegetable. You get the point. Now follow this simple, sensory exercise, first introduced to me in 2007 by educator and scholar Alyssa Niccolini:

(1) Look at the strawberry [or insert here your fruit of choice]. Notice its details. Write down everything you see. Note the color, any specks, misshapen parts, or leaves. Describe what you see in as much detail as possible. Embrace similes and metaphors.

(2) Now smell the strawberry. What does it smell like? What memories, places, things does that smell evoke for you? Write everything that comes to mind.

(3) Now touch the strawberry. What does it feel like? How would you describe its texture? Again, take detailed notes and don't hold back on any associations.

(4) Finally—taste the strawberry! What does it taste like? What images, memories, things spring to mind as you savor it? You might also jot down the sounds of eating the strawberry.

(5) Compile your notes and make them into a poem.

In the past few years I've been bringing in blackberries or blueberries to class. Recently, I took notes on my experiences eating a blackberry while doing this exercise with my students, and when I came home, I shaped my notes into this poem:

blackberry

meadow night's
guts

smash of river
engorged

Voldemort's good heart
(if he only knew!)

my true Jew
black with life

pimple-bushed
lucky pluck

you who sees
through all your eyes

after you turn
to tooth-caught
grain

do you still have
your dream in you?

As I reread this poem, I consider how the exercise invites us to follow the intelligence of sensation. That intelligence is one of intuition, of feeling around in the dark and trusting the images and words that come to you. There's a familiar alchemic process happening, too. One's experience of seeing, smelling, touching a strawberry transforms into something else: a poem.

Working Intensities

We write poems and turn to written poems in times of intense sensation. Anger. Grief. Joy. Suffering. Renewal. We hear poems recited at weddings and funerals. We seek poems in times of need, in times of great affective intensity. We write them furiously in response to difficult experiences. We hold on to them to stay sane. We read them to make sense of a crazy world. It's like a call and response. It's as if poems know we need them—like they've been written for us across time and space, jolting our current moment.

We offer you two very different poems to read about a father-son relationship. Pause for a moment to sit with this first poem "The Lost Son" by poet and editor Geoff Babbitt, author of *Appendices Pulled from a Study on Light* (Spuyten Duyvil, 2018).

The Lost Son

My father and I have had a longstanding disagreement
about Colin Kaepernick, whom I love,
and the day before Thanksgiving, a few years back,
that disagreement came to a boil. Now,
I should tell you that this
was before the diagnosis;
we knew he's inattentive and
hard of hearing, and those two facts
prevented serious concern. So here
we are, arguing away on a level playing field,
I think, when the whole thing
spins out of control—I'm spewing
statistics about police violence, he's challenging
the sources, the bottom
is falling out. What happens next
I can't reconstruct—hindsight
isn't twenty-twenty. He brings up
army glory days that never happened
and things that actually happened
when he was a U of Chicago law student
living in the South Side in the 70s—I'm still ineffectively
rattling off stats, from my phone by now—when he says,
"you should have seen how they live," a statement
that raises a thousand barbed objections,
and I have a fraction of a second to decide whether or not
to let the switch inside me flip, so I think
about white privilege and confronting racism
even in the case of a hopeless septuagenarian—
changing his mind doesn't matter, I have to, I tell myself—and I tear into him
for the racist he is and has always been.
I reduce him.
I feel a flash of pride
for holding his feet to the fire,
for not making an exception for my dad,
when I see him look at me

like a lost child, as if I'm an abusive parent
who's going to hit him—
because I am going to hit him,
I think, and I almost do, but instead,
I poke his sternum with my pointer finger,
punctuating each word, and he
shrinks in fear, wondering how
he got here, how things
got to be this way. So helpless. A few months later,
he'd be diagnosed with Alzheimer's,
Stage 4. Already.
When I look back, I know
that the cause was right, but I
feel so small.
I'm so glad I didn't
abuse a sick elderly man,
even if he might have deserved it.

Where does this poem hold you? How does it map onto your body? Where do you feel it most intensely—which lines? What feelings rise in you?

For me, Babbitt's "The Lost Son" conveys an unsettling moment between father and son. I feel like I'm witnessing a shameful experience, and it's hard to look away. I feel uncomfortable, especially in my stomach, but I also feel a sense of relief that this reality—one that is widely shared (lots of people have family members with racist beliefs)—is talked about and actively wrestled with. The poem carries a refreshing honesty that can't be separated from its emotional charge. I imagine this was both a difficult poem to write and one that needed to be written. Even though the speaker seems to have come to a sort of resolution at the end of the poem, the poem's emotional quality feels unresolved, like it's squirming in its skin, still saddened and boiling in the aftermath of this exchange.

Now turn to the poem "Homecoming" by poet and translator Kaveh Bassiri, author of the chapbook *99 Names of Exile*. "Homecoming" was first published in *Shenandoah* and later in *Best New Poets* 2020.

Homecoming

When everyone as gone, while the clouds still
argue loud with the stars, I sit near him,
wipe his shoulders, dip my hand in the small
of his back, unbutton the pump, the drainage.
I unwrap the blue robe, like candy. Scent
of moldered covers pours on the floor, I
rise over my father, lunate, plant bulbs
In his eye sockets, winnow heart from lungs.

I groom him for shahrazad, who's waiting.
Irises, tulips are sprouting. Patiently
holding to his spine, I shake the branches,
pluck arms, legs, the tongue, his penis. I lift
his chest; the latches fall as I open
the shutters. Splayed, his pelvis fills with leaves.

Reading and rereading this poem, I keep coming to the question: Is the father alive? Is he dying? Real or imagined? Is the speaker caring for his father in life, in a dream? The answers to these questions do not matter to me. In fact, not knowing, the ambiguity haunting the precise images, is part of what moves this poem for/in me. I read an act of tenderness—sense of longing and labor and love. The heartbreak intensifies as this is the kind of care that many of us (will) experience. This poem pulls at my heart and throat. Rather than convey a story, as Babbitt does, Bassiri conveys this sensation through images. Both poems illuminate and create sensations that travel into my body in feeling their sadnesses.

An Invitation

Consider a sensation that lingers for you when you recall an argument, a moment of sadness, a terrible loss, an intense joy, or even a simple act of kindness that swells your heart. How might you convey that sensation in a poem? Try. Perhaps you tell the story in a straightforward way as Babbit does, or maybe you focus more on images and metaphors that evoke the sensation. Maybe you try both ways.

I am reminded of Rachel Eliza Griffiths's poem "Elegy, Surrounded by Seven Trees" (2019), which we encourage you to find online and/or read in her hybrid collection of poems and photographs, *Seeing the Body* (2020). Though I have not experienced the loss of a mother, as Griffiths describes in her poem, I can feel something of that loss in how the poem is crafted. The truth of loss expressed in this poem haunts me, sits in both my heart and my gut. And the feeling of holding absence—I know it in my body and can feel my understanding of loss, of absence, of my relationship to my own mother changing in the presence of the poem's language. How to convey the wild terror of facing death and the expansiveness of this moment—mother and universe, one thing—birth and death, touching? How would you convey such a moment, based on your experiences?

I return to Stevens.

Even the bawds of euphony
would cry out sharply.

CHAPTER 11
WRESTLING WITH THE MIND'S *MAYBE*

XI

He rode over Connecticut
In a glass coach.
Once, a fear pierced him,
In that he mistook
The shadow of his equipage
For blackbirds.

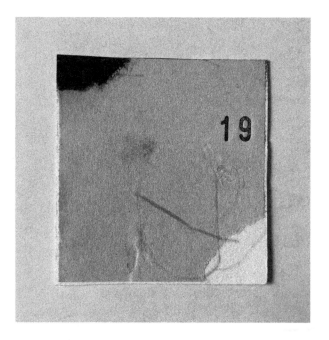

Have you ever mistaken the sound of footsteps behind you in the forest and turned around to see a tree quivering? Has thirst led you to mistake a shadow just beyond the grove of trees for a pond? How can a blue light emanate sadness? Just what is Rimbaud's "mercury mouth"? This chapter investigates how poems offer us fresh ways of attending to the world as these fallibilities and mistakes are crafted into poems. Double-takes (seeing "figures" of one thing *as* or *in* another), illusion (a "deception" of the senses), and bricolage (the dissimilar intermingle, collide, juxtapose, or create disjunctions) are ways to express and explore the spontaneous combustion of imagination that occurs in the *mind's maybe*. This *is* the stuff of poetry. Poems both shape and reflect these mental processes into reconfigurations of the impossible strangeness of living and feeling in the world. There is something satisfying and mysterious about seeing a shadow as blackbirds, but this stanza invites confusion—a glass coach, a piercing fear—and leads to a sense of the ineffable in wrestling ideas into words.

One night a cloud shrouding the Big Dipper dissipated to reveal what seemed like millions of stars spilling into the night sky. I realized my mind was playing some beautiful trickery:

> Tonight, the Big Dipper spills
> her stars into the dark ocean of sky.

Among the millions, suspended apart from the others, a brief flash, and as suddenly as I had seen stars spill from the Big Dipper, I saw fireflies appear through the glow of darkness:

> Tonight, the Big Dipper spills
> fireflies into the dark ocean of sky.

My double-take, seeing "figures" of one thing *as* or *in* another, was triggering my imaginings. First, a grouping of stars forms into a figure of a Big Dipper (a ladle, scooping up stars from the sky). Now the dipper spills its contents of stars, and these morph into fireflies. Stars are now *figured* as fireflies through my double-take, and the night sky has become an ocean. All this through comparisons that animate one figure as another.

With a sudden gust of wind and spatters of raindrops on my face, Venus comes into view. I feel the breeze on my skin which turns into Venus's breath, her unique mix of gases and droplets of sulfuric and acidic crystals, blowing me and the Big Dipper and the fireflies end over end, and sky over stars over end and into fireflies until we all tumble and bump into Cassiopeia. I write this sensory deception:

> Just now a chilly gaze from Venus pierces the Big
> Dipper, sends it tumbling, fireflies and all, and knocks into
> Cassiopeia, sending her on her rump before the whole sky
> falters and quakes.

How is it that Venus can have a chilly gaze? How can this gaze pierce the Big Dipper? This intermingling of modalities creates an intermingling of the senses as a way of playing out the *illusion* of Venus blowing gases into the night sky, creating chaos in what was otherwise an orderly and quiet night. And, this trafficking in my *mind's maybe* could be viewed as a failed attempt. I learned something about the resources of language available to me as I tried to language the comparisons and sensations traveling through my mind. My attention to double-takes, illusions, and a little lean into bricolage makes me more attentive to how I come to read others' poems and the resources available to me to craft my own.

As a teacher and student of poetry, I want to experiment and encourage my students to do the same for their own satisfaction and enjoyment but also to help them experiment with the resources of language that give us access to and help us as readers. Poetry invites us *to attend* to language, compressed expression, and the specialized features of poetry. It does more, too. Poems challenge us to experience the more halting and disruptive features of living—wicked wit, biting candor, or relevance to public action and political attention—all to emphasize the fallibility of language, perspective, and the impossibility of a poem to leave more than a residue.

Embracing Fallibilities

Without mistakes, failures, or evidence of fallibility, a work of art or poetry can be too sure of itself, too confident, or too pedantic. It loses its poetry. In the context of visual art, a computer-generated graphic mark does not give way to stain, bleed, or accident and leaves instead a flawless mark. Something of the hand has been lost. The difference between a graphic line and poetry, we argue, is a matter of connection: hand, eye, and other sensorium. Through experimentation we don't always make the mark. It's what distinguishes us (currently, at least, though this seems to be rapidly changing) from machines. We need the glitch, the stutter, the eraser's trace, and the stain, to feel a work's humanity. Possibly there is something about the human spirit wrestling ideas and imagination into language that needs to be demonstrated in its own search for expression.

Trusting the Less Good Idea

Artist William Kentridge founded the Centre for the Less Good Idea in Maboneng, Johannesburg (South Africa) to create a space for collaborative and experimental artworks across disciplines. The point of the Centre is described on its website (which you can find at lessgoodidea/com/about):

> Often you start with a good idea. It might seem crystal clear at first, but when you take it off the proverbial drawing board, cracks and fissures emerge in its surface, and they cannot be ignored. It is in following the secondary ideas, those less good ideas coined to address the first idea's cracks, that the Centre nurtures, arguing that in the act of playing with an idea, you can recognise those things you didn't know in advance but knew somewhere inside of you.

Consider how antithetical the spirit of this Centre is to the aim of a perfect, glossy reading or writing of a work. Poetry—the written art that is the focus of this book—comes out of a process of human connection *to* something uneasy, unpolished, and still open, something beyond the "I" who writes. Imagine what our classroom might look like if we encourage students to follow their "less good ideas." What would this mean to us? To them? What if revision were thought of as radically generating something out of one idea's mistakes, fissures, failures and of tapping into an understanding that poets may not be able to fully grasp but wish *to make something of* their attempts to articulate imaginings?

We see these fallibilities as generative, as necessary ingredients for a poem to move, for its questions to stay open, for its lines to stir or jolt its reader or surprise its writer. The same fallibilities are part of readers' and writers' repertoire as they produce and interpret the *mind's maybe*, utter sounds from sights and sensations from cracks and fissures, or a mystery at the feet of an accepted idea. One of our functions as teachers, and clearly a pedagogical challenge, is to open students to multiple possibilities, especially those students who have been overtrained in interpreting poetry. They often find poetry obtuse and are afraid of giving the wrong response. We work in various ways to ease their hesitations, and we demonstrate that poets continuously challenge rules or "right" ways through experimentation that oftentimes leads to the less good idea but that brings pleasure and knowledge through experimentation.

Wordplay

It is challenging to build confidence in fallibility and trust the stutters, stops, and even failures. As you have experienced throughout this book, we work inductively through Invitations to experiments with ideas and language—letting language loose and loosening ourselves up to play with language. We exercise ourselves and invite our students to do the same in attempts to follow the *mind's maybes* and not let our *mind's censor* work against the freedom of exploration.

An Invitation

In *Poetics of Space*, Gaston Bachelard (1994) writes:

> Words are little houses, each with its cellar and garret. Common-sense lives on the ground floor, always ready to engage in "foreign commerce" on the same level as the others, as the passers-by, who are never dreamers. To go upstairs in the word house is to withdraw step by step; while to go down to the cellar is to dream, it is losing oneself in the distant corridors of an obscure etymology, looking for treasures that cannot be found in words. To mount and descend in the words themselves—this is potentially an important trigger for writing. To mount too high or descend too low is allowed and potentially brings earth and sky together. (p. 147)

Choose a word (or let one find you) that offers room to play from ground floor to attic to basement and back again. Maybe it is the sounds, the feelings that vibrate off the tongue, a sentiment it carries, an image, a sound, a memory, or, a word of witnessing. A word—

write it on a piece of paper or on a blank screen and play out its "little houses," find its hidden treasures, its links to other words. Let the censor go quiet and enjoy the random free play, mistakes, illusions, or collisions.

(Re)Inventing a "Make It New" Mindset

Once we are willing to take risks, there are particular resources available that help us present our fallibilities and all the other unfinished and fragmentary ways of being in and composing our experiences, imaginings, and visions. The *mind's maybe* has some connection to that often-quoted statement attributed to the poet Ezra Pound, "Make it new." Of course, as with so much of what we know about wrestling with ideas, Pound found the phrase in two key Chinese texts. In both Confucian moral philosophy, the *Da Xue*, and in an older classic Chinese history, *T'ung-Chien Kang-Mu*, the imperative exists. And, if we think of wrestling ideas into language, it is interesting to note that the translator of both texts was Zhu Xi, a neo-Confucian scholar, from about 1130 to 1200 CE, who may have articulated the idea differently than in either of the preceding texts. I often relate this history to student writers of poetry, reminding them and me, of the entanglements and complexities of any ideas and to give them confidence to play and experiment, recognizing that we value invention and fresh takes on seemingly old ideas. Even in this small recounting we are not finished with the inventions around "Make it new." The source of this understanding apparently came from nature and the explanation in the *Da Xue* offered a double-take on "Make it new" with a comparison to renewal evidenced "like a tree shoot," reminding us that nature teaches and demonstrates the principle of make it new. This idea also appears in the Roman poet Ovid's narrative poem *Metamorphoses*, written in approximately 8 CE. Ovid emphasized nothing perishes but is adapted, reshaped, recirculated into new forms. Ovid's idea is that nature is inventive, continuously producing one shape from another and is a vital teacher of invention and change. Our imaginings work on us, potentially boosted by our own perception of the natural world's renewals and mutations, to find ways to express anew and to craft our *mind's maybes*.

Double-Takes

Double-takes, those surprising and oftentimes spontaneous comparisons that come to mind, are sometimes transformed into figurative language including simile, metaphor, allegory, or symbol. These comparisons nudge and nurture both poets and their readers to see the shimmering and shifting of any one thing by all the strange and wonderful ways it exists not only as itself but also in other things. Poems serve *as thresholds* to step into experience with fresh expressiveness and perception. As writers of poetry, how might we use all these versions of double-takes to create unexpected images—blackbirds for example—or dissolving presences of privileged connections? Even though we frequently use this language (capturing voice, catching an image), we recognize the necessary gap between what inspires a poem—our "triggering subjects" to return to Richard Hugo's (1979) phrase—and the slant kind of seeing that can bring that subject to mysterious life.

When we hold a word or idea to its accepted meaning, it might not be very interesting. So, too, with an event, object, or emotion. Poets wrestle with how to see fresh and new and yet work in relation to the world in which they find themselves. Sometimes the poem's power is in its recursive struggle to say what needs to be said—to communicate something that remains wrapped in questions, and to embrace the "failure" of smooth and rational language.

Read Rebecca Keith's poem "Voyager 2":

Voyager 2

When you were twenty-six another poet
published a poem about the gold record
sent into space. And then another. Before you—
how do you say *too late* in moonspeak?
You could translate bitter into a hundred tongues,
paralyzed into one. When did you become
someone who hides in the second person?
A meta-failure. Can't even admit I
drink too much watch too much TV
spent all my energy plumping my ovaries
and getting another degree instead of
soldiering on with the work I said was mine.
Okay, I remember, when I crossed the border
into late thirties, shifted laser focus
to my geriatric uterus. That's what they do
to us. So many keep their art intact
but I don't know. The part they cut out
for endometriosis. Maybe that tissue housed
every last image I had left. Maybe the overgrowth
was my process, the manic tendencies I tempered
with medication for the brain migrated
to my core. My legacy removed to make room
for a more tangible one of downy hair and gap-toothed smile
a dozen sounds that mean hello. Is she the record
and I the voyager that brought her to this planet?
Each trill and gurgle a different animal inside her—
all the people she could be.

The poem offers evidence of a mind in motion and creates a temporal and spatial blend of feeling and events. What is the effect for you? What if you try to articulate *in simile* what experience or feeling this poem evokes in you? Where does your *mind's maybe* take you with this comparison?

Keith notes that though this poem is spoken to her daughter, the "you" is the writer in the beginning of the poem. Consider what this shift in address does for you, as a reader. What do you make of this double "you" carried by the poem, its blending of "yous," the movement of a "you" that turns from mother to daughter? What imaginings does this spark?

An Invitation

Take a phrase that you hear often and blast and ballast it with wonder as you let comparisons go wild. Let go. The censor in you has hidden behind the pleasure of wrestling the idea in your mind. Just keep drawing comparisons to the original words or new ones that come up as you continue to write.

Here are several Invitations we offer our students. Each is intended to work against the censor and toward fresh takes on seeing one thing in another. Take any one of the following invitations into your own writing and exercise or offer these to your students:

(1) Take an existing poem of your own or one you've read, shuffle its lines, and write from that discombobulated state, drawing as wild comparisons as your mind will allow. There is no such thing as a mistake unless that mistake is caution. Think of simile as a way of exploring double-takes on likenesses, on resemblances—one image, object, feeling caught in a surprising moment, a discovery of sorts where *some thing* becomes likened to *some thing* else (a simile).

(2) Search through either your journal writing or recent draft of a poem and find similes already present in your thinking; that is, find likenesses and resemblances already there. If you find none, can you circle and identify places where a simile might help draw an apt comparison or likeness. Such a search may be futile. We could say that IF you don't recognize the resemblance in the first place, it rings hollow to add it. Only you will know. Does what you have tried add to the effect you hope to achieve? Crafting double-takes often demonstrates our ongoing attempts to articulate what seems nearly impossible to put into words.

(3) Take the word *Hope*. Place the word on paper or your computer screen. Make a list of all the possible similes that come to mind. Set a goal of at least three comparisons (in the form of simile) that are double-takes on the word Hope.

Hope is like_____. Hope is like_____. Hope is like_____.

Choose your favorite simile and make it the first line of a poem. Write two or three of lines as you work out where this comparison might take you. Then, take away the "like," the simile, and this simple change transforms the simile into a metaphor.

Hope is_____. Does this small change make it necessary or lead you to change the other line or two you have written? If so, why? How does such a seemingly simple change such as omitting "like" change the nature of the comparison you have drawn?

Here is an example from Jamie, an eleventh-grade student:

Hope is like a click of the heels, like a light piercing fog.

Hope is a click of the heels, a light piercing fog.

Once you write the two versions, examine the differences in effect. Jamie wrote her thoughts about the distinctions:

I was thinking how suddenly hope comes over me. It's like a surprise that cascades over my body, so I thought of how the click of heels is sudden. When I read my simile, the use of "like" is a reminder that this is a comparison. When "like" is omitted, the comparison collapses and hope becomes the click and the pierce.

Here is Emily Dickinson's (1891) poem "Hope Is the Thing with Feathers":

Hope Is the Thing with Feathers

"Hope" is the thing with feathers—
That perches in the soul—
And sings the tune without the words—
And never stops—at all—

And sweetest—in the Gale—is heard—
And sore must be the storm—
That could abash the little Bird
That kept so many warm—

I've heard it in the chillest land—
And on the strangest Sea—
Yet—never—in Extremity,
It asked a crumb—of me.

Anything that strikes you as a fresh way to conceive of hope in the comparisons made in Dickinson's poem? Take a moment to remind yourself that her poem, like any of ours, is an attempt to wrestle the mind's wonderings into words. The success is perhaps best determined by how for herself and her reader an abstract concept—hope—is illuminated.

Illusion's Deceptions

Fleeting and momentary discovery is unstable and shifting. The unseen makes an appearance. Logic dissolves. Sensory responses take over. How might a poet express such ever-moving, changing, and shifting perception in a poem that is intended to resist closure? By paying attention to slippages that yield momentary grounding, a discovery holds for a moment only to shimmer away to reveal yet another surprising connection or disjuncture that overcomes complacency in the reader's attention. *It's bitter cold*. How can it be bitter cold? Bitterness is a taste and cold is a tactile sensation. Or, *I smell trouble*. How can that be? *Actions speak louder than words. Loud colors. Dark sounds*. On full display in these often-used examples are imaginings and inner workings of the mind. The sweetness of understanding comes from temporary illusions that rely on a deception of the senses to feel uncertainty of vividness in what we are sensing.

Illusions stretch and exaggerate the senses through synesthesia and other sense-defying means. Consider poems that work against a taxidermy of the senses. The aural, emotional, and visual float without clear signifiers when illusion blossoms to the foreground. Such poems feel like a sleight of hand as one sense overlaps or takes the place of another to challenge our sense-making. When teaching, we emphasize that working with illusions, and particularly synesthesia, requires the censor in us to take a back seat to the *mind's maybe*. Yes, many attempts fail to capture the essence or have the effect we hoped. But, the satisfaction is in trying. Follow Frost's (1939) dictum, "no surprise for the writer, no surprise for the reader" (pp. 394–5), and we circle back to the importance of experimentation, willingness to show the mind's wrestling with ideas, and how playfulness might lead to interesting surprises.

I owe Irene, an eleventh grader in one of my classes from years ago, gratitude for her playfulness in wrestling with synesthesia. Over a three-day period, I asked students to bring in one sticky note per day for three days on which they had written a one phrase or sentence example of synesthesia. Those were all posted on one classroom wall. With 3 classes participating, approximately 270 examples, a range from the mundane to the exhilarating, dressed the otherwise drab wall. This warm-up to the mind's wrestling with synesthesia led to an invitation to students on the fourth day to create *an occasion* at the beginning of a poem in which they would offer a series of examples of synesthesia. From a letter to a friend, a conversation with a dead poet, a used car advertisement, students offered surprisingly clever and generative reasons to use or extend their three-day play with synesthesia or "borrow" any from the gallery of examples. At this moment, I feel compelled to share Irene's opening lines. Surprising, risky, and oh, so satisfying:

Doctor Liberty, please offer a remedy. I am afflicted
with a case of synesthesia.

And in this moment of writing this section on synesthesia, I borrow her lines and continue with my own mind's wrestling with synesthesia:

> *Doctor Liberty, please offer a remedy. I am afflicted*
> *with a case of synesthesia.* How do I know? Your voice
> is burnt orange. My loud tongue laughs when I'm accused
> of wearing my heart on my sleeve although my chest seems
> unable to awaken any taste for desire. I am suffering from
> humdrum sentiments and I too often listen to the sunset
> lurch toward sleep. I confess. I smell of damaged goods.
> I have synesthesia but I am trying to keep my fear quiet.

Thank you, Irene, for freeing my censor to play with synesthesia. I offer Irene's lines, in gratitude to her for the ways in which this context challenges the censor.

An Invitation

Take a moment and (1) try Irene's invitation to experiment with synesthesia and shed your censor as best you can. Other versions of this Invitation are (2) to create a poem based on an illusion of fierce movement in the midst of quiet to defy the senses. Or, (3) upend an existing poem of your own or one you've read, shuffle its lines, and write from that discombobulated state. There is no such thing as a mistake unless that mistake is caution or a too-thought-through push to say something unusual.

It's interesting to take a look at the poetry of Jean Toomer and his experiments with synesthesia. As a person of European and African American descent, living from 1894 to 1967, he explored racial fluidity in ways that challenge us to see differently. In his novel *Cane* and through his poetry, he depicts consciousness ever-in-motion. Monotony for him, the lack of fluidity through certainty, signaled a death of the intellect. Consider how he challenges fixed conceptions through this poem written in 1923.

Storm Ending

Thunder blossoms gorgeously above our heads,
Great, hollow, bell-like flowers,
Rumbling in the wind,
Stretching clappers to strike our ears . . .
Full-lipped flowers
Bitten by the sun
Bleeding rain
Dripping rain like golden honey—
And the sweet earth flying from the thunder.

What image lingers for you? What sounds? What is the effect of the *ing*? The "ing" is a grammatical synesthesia, making verb forms out of nouns and adjectives and vice versa.

In creating this link of gerunds and participles, I am reminded of Toomer's constant attention to fluidity, his continuous search to wrestle into words the fallibility of trying to find the words. We hope this invitation to think with synesthesia offers you the opportunity to wrestle your commitments and imaginings into language.

Bricolage Is Tinkering

What image comes to mind with the word *bricolage*? If you were asked to make a bricolage to represent your reading and experience with two poems that puzzle you or strike you as strange or ambiguous, what poems might you choose? How might you represent, through bricolage, your experiences and feelings about the poems, what you don't quite understand, or how these poems speak to you?

Bricolage in common usage is the concept of making one thing by recombining other things into some *thing* new. Bricolage comes from the French word for tinkering. If we think of bricolage in innovation, it is the act of taking underutilized resources and recombining them into a productive resource. In poetry, it might be combining poems into one—a patch up! The idea here is taking preexisting things and putting them together in new ways. Or, combining lines from the poem with lines of your own. Do other possibilities come to mind?

In keeping with our focus in this chapter, bricolage demonstrates provisional and shifting meanings. The bricoleur does not search out or find ways to present a stable meaning or a fixed truth or value but uses *what is* to challenge and create new ways to think what *might be*. Emphasis falls on play, fluidity, and indeterminacy rather than the stability and determinacy often valued in Western culture. Bricolage is one way of uncovering the world, the mind, a poem, or even a single word by emphasizing the provisional, the fallible, the wrestling with yet another resource for "making it new."

As we move into reading and writing bricolage in poetry and this idea of stitching or melding together, I am reminded of Stephen Reusser, a twelfth-grade student, who presented himself as an interpretation of Stevens's "Thirteen Ways of Looking at a Blackbird." Yes, the poem serves as dialogic bricolage, in conversation with, nurturing, and often provoking our pedagogical expedition in writing this book. I asked students to create a bricolage that combined, in whatever ways, a reading of a poem or combination of poems they were puzzled by, loved, or stayed with them. How might they make "material" a bricolage of their experiences with poetry through stitching together poems of their choice? Stephen walked through the door of the classroom, a rustle of multi-sized sheets of paper, ribbons on which words and phrases were attached. Pinned to his shirt, pants, tie, belt, socks, and a black skull cap (intended to be a blackbird's head) were words from Stevens's poem, and, we would come to learn, Stephen's thirteen-stanza poem on John Lennon. He stitched his own stanzas as interplays over Stevens's stanzas, sketched images from both his and Stevens's poem, again as overlay or underlay to written lines and stanzas. Intricate, though temporary, tattoos of images and words covered the skin on his cheeks, forehead, and hands. His makeshift pair of glasses "filmed" his view with the right eye: 13 Ways. And the left: Of Seeing. Yes, earrings, too, and three rings on fingers, each with images taken from both poems mixed together. When he walked into the room, I was reminded of Bradbury's story *Illustrated Man*. What a remarkable class session! He was one of thirty students, each with their own bricolage to express the provisional and playful understanding of their experiences with poetry.

An Invitation

Now, it is your turn. Let's go back to the original questions in this section: If you were asked to make a bricolage to represent your reading and experience with two poems that puzzle you or strike you as strange or ambiguous, what poems might you choose? How might you represent, through bricolage, your experiences and feelings about the poems, what you do not quite understand, or how these poems speak to you?

Take a deep breath and send your censor to run errands for a couple of hours. Pick at least two poems that puzzle or interest you for particular reasons and print out a copy of each on separate pieces of paper. Don't overthink this. A little impulsiveness is a good thing. Read through each poem on the printed copies and highlight or circle anything that interests you—words, phrases, a particular quirk in formatting. Right now, mark anything of interest. I have sometimes circled or highlighted as many as twenty to thirty words or phrases in a less-than-page-long poem.

Now, in whatever random order, make a new list of all the words and phrases you marked from both poems into one document (use a font of at least fourteen points and a different font type for each poem) or write each word or phrase on a blank piece of paper (to show distinctions of one poem from the other you might use cursive for one and print the other). Distinguish for now to see the balance from each poem might be of interest to you later.

Scissors come next. Cut out each word or phrase so that you have a little stack of words and phrases. This might look something like the magnetic poetry after cutting. You may decide to cut some phrases down into smaller parts.

I used cork boards and pins to play with bricolage in my classes. It is not so easy to find these any longer, but it was more trapping than necessity to emphasize that the words and phrases were fluid, in motion, and moveable on impulse. To avoid the censor, I have sometimes recommended a simple lift and scatter first. Sometimes words are upside down or one far apart from the others. All offer the imagination possibilities for the *mind's maybes*. Then, come some exploration and play. Move pieces around. Join random words. Notice how your two different poems (fonts and handwriting) mingle and merge. Resist overthinking. You might even close your eyes and feel the movement of paper. Open and see the new combinations. Once you are ready, you might begin to bring pieces together. You do not need to use every word or phrase from your first list. Eliminate into a separate stack as you go.

After some initial moving around and reorganizing, you might set some creative constraints for yourself. Again, the little pieces of paper are fluid, in motion. Whatever you try can be undone and redone. What if you work with all nouns? All adjectives? All verbs? Or, you might group words by a mood created. Where is the energy? A strange and new image being created as you move the pieces around? Read aloud. Rearrange. Read again. Take a look at balance in the two texts. Take a risk and take out two or three words or phrases you love best and, at random, replace them with two others in your pile. Now what? Yes, you can go back to the original if the urge to do so is overpowering.

Take a break. Leave the pieces there. How I wish a small wind would blow over them just now and rearrange while you are not looking. Just then, you might see other possibilities if you are locking into one version too quickly. When you come back to see what you have, you might add, eliminate, move pieces around. Then, write out or type a version. Title your poem. Take a moment to read again and experience what you created as a bricolage, the "Make it new," of two other poems.

A Fallibility Workshop: (Re)Orienting Revision

As teachers, we have long struggled with making revision meaningful to our students. We find many students resist revising their work and/or conflate revision with editing. We believe there is something about how revision gets taught in schools that may have lost the sense of *re-vision*, to see again, to play with possibilities, to imagine differently. What if we think of (re)vision as multiple takes—a version of mistakes? One of the ways we challenge this belief about revision is to study revisions that poets share in both drafts of poems and commentary. We offer here a gift from poet Dan Chu, both his final, published poem and his commentary on revision. His poem "Cemetery Picnic" (2021) was published in *Bennington Review*:

Cemetery Picnic

In Ghent, gloved hands coat gold onto a strand
of bacterial DNA and shoot it into a corn cell.
It's readily accepted by the nucleus—
c'mon it's glittered with gold—and the whole family
changes forever, transgenic, toxic to worms.
Division's stimulated, the mass hardens
into turquoise seeds, wingtipped neon green.
Now stalks in an Iowa field, they are eaten
by the combine, kernels gushing like golden water
into the truck. At the country elevator, a man in a harness
opens the roof of a hopper car and the grain chutes
from silo to rail, rides past glancing towns,
and arrives at a mill outside Dallas to be ground.
The refugees dump the feed for the caged chickens
to feast—they're going out gluttonous—the protein of the corn

builds the muscles of the chickens, upside down
they go into darkness, a plastic pad rubs their breasts
to calm them right before the saw whizzes,
and the parts are packaged, and shipped frozen
to Justin, who is stoned, in Brooklyn. He drenches
the pieces in the desert of flour, herbs, and spices.
I buy a thirty-piece box, steady its warmth in my lap
as my dad drives us to the cemetery. Upon your grave,
I offer it to you, Grandma. You said they wouldn't have
Popeyes where you'll be—I pray the chicken there
would be free range, organic, and fair trade.
But there's something about big and juicy pieces
of fried chicken, like the ones you brought
when we came with you here to visit your own mother.
We still share this meal together.
Do you remember how crunchy this is, Grandma?
The uncles, aunts, and cousins eagerly come
for a piece—it's been a year since we've all seen
each other—divorce, that family moved to Jersey,
or we're all our own people, but none of this matters
as we catch up, blast your favorite opera, and eat Popeyes
with the hoods of our car trunks as tables.
Grandma, I'm not religious like you,
but I know what matters can't be created
or destroyed—it just changes form
at this picnic in the cemetery.

Commentary from Dan

Like the corn cell in its first line, "Cemetery Picnic" undergoes a transformation as it progresses. The first two-thirds of the poem detail the creation, growth, and change of a cell of corn as it travels through its industrial journey. The last third of the poem shifts to a personal scene where the speaker visits his grandmother's grave at a cemetery. The ending provides an opportunity to play off the two different strands of the poem—the corn's journey and the speaker's cemetery visit. In the first draft, the poem ended with:

I'm not religious
like you are, but I know that matter
can't be created or destroyed—it just changes form
like you did at this picnic in the cemetery,
back to the basic unit of life.

There is a tendency, especially in early drafts, to summarize the poem in its last few lines. This can create a flat ending since you end up taking the readers out of the poem by telling them exactly what to think. You worry that poem you just wrote might be misunderstood so you try to connect the dots for the reader. If that's the case, it's better to look at the beginning of the poem to see that the dots are connecting in the first place. If that's working, the solution might be directly up: many times, an opening for the ending can be found a few lines above from where an initial draft ends.

A starting point for a revision of a flat ending can then be really simple: cut out the last one to two lines of the poem, especially if it begins to lapse toward summary. The "basic unit of life" was a summary of what "matter" is, a definition that does not need to be reiterated. I wanted to reconnect the corn strand of the poem into the ending, but ended up stating the obvious. It took me until the final draft to move away from "matter" as a noun—I realized that the word itself was tonally too scientific and clinical for an ending that should be centered on the speaker's personal relationship with his grandmother. Again, I was being too heavy-handed in forcing the connection between the corn and the cemetery strands in the poem. Rather than ending on a science lesson, the change from "that matter" to "what matters" keeps the moment between the speaker and his grandmother in focus. Of course, the idea of matter changing form is still evoked, now a bit more indirectly, which is enough for the reader to make the connection back to the first two-thirds of the poem. There is surprise in seeing how the impersonal and predictable journey of industrialized corn can lead to a moment of personal remembrance and celebration of those who have left us.

Failure. Fallibility. Double-take. Illusion. Glitch. Stutter. Stammer. Smudge. Rethink. Revise. Trip-Up. Human connection. Without these things we have dogmatism, certainty, hard-headedness, final answers, outlines, borders, divisions, gloss, advertisements—a polish refusing the reality that it will someday crack. All are part of revision!

William Stafford (1962, p. 344) ends a poem titled "Vocation" (he is speaking of the poet's vocation) with the line: "Your job is *to find what the world is trying to be*." And though it may be presumptuous, this may finally be what trying to articulate the fallibilities and mistakes is all about.

CHAPTER 12
SPECULATIVE POSSIBILITIES

XII
The river is moving.
The blackbird must be flying.

As an aphorism, "The river is moving . . . the blackbird must be flying" sounds a tone of certainty. But the self-assurance could easily have a question mark at the end. Does the flow of the river inherently cause the flight of the blackbird? Is the blackbird flying so the river must be moving too? Is it a simple depiction of the coming of spring? With these questions, the ground beneath our feet shifts. The mirrored two lines try to muscle a truth, but it is a cover-up for uncertainty. You can't get to the bottom of this speculation; it stands as a complexity, and no easy aphorism provides assurance. Speculative possibilities pull, like gravity, to a different kind of openness where breadcrumbs of description, event, action, emotion, or causality present themselves in life and in poems.

Intersecting Landscapes

This chapter extends our understanding of poems as historical and cultural landscapes intersecting with our experiences, our entanglements of what we think are truths and speculative possibilities as we encounter them in the present moment. We turn our attention to the shifting ground beneath us—to the landscapes and histories embedded in our bodies and in our reading and writing of each poem. Rather than treat context as information for a better understanding of the poem, we invite you to work context as a way to be alert to the situated and speculative possibilities in our readings as times and places intersect.

The river is moving. I think back to my most recent memory of swimming in a river. I must have been a child. The last time I walked by a river was more recent—and from that memory I can recall its soft currents, ripples, deep green and browns. The flow of water, moving, always moving. Natalie Diaz's book *Postcolonial Love Poem* bubbles to mind; the river threads throughout it, entangled with love, landscape, and desire. I think of her poem "From the Desire Field"—how she describes her desire for her lover. These lines, especially:

I am struck in the witched hours of want—

I want her green life. Her inside me
in a green hour I can't stop.
      Green vein in her throat green wing in my mouth

green thorn in my eye. I want her like a river goes, bending.
Green moving green, moving.

In these lines and throughout this book by Diaz, I can feel the river inside me, gesturing at a way of seeing and wanting. "Like a river goes, bending."

An Invitation

Where are you in relation to the river? When you think of, remember, or imagine a river, what words come to mind? Make a moment to jot down memories, associations, even sights, smells, sounds, especially if you have a river near you—actual and/or metaphoric.

Now look around you. What objects, sights, smells, sounds surround you in this moment? List those on the same page as your river thoughts. See how you might bring those two places together: the ongoing river you've known in your past and that lives, now, in your present consciousness and those things you've come to notice that tangibly form your present moment. What might you make with these materials? Perhaps you are reading this in your classroom, or from your home, or at a local coffee shop. Take note of the sensations and materials constituting your current place. Track its currents.

Another way of phrasing this invitation is: *What happens when the river's current meets your current context? Make a poem from this intersecting moment of river and context.* (We are, of course, brought back to Suzanne Gardinier's striking poem "Some Manhattan Rivers.")

Meeting Points of Place and Time

It seems worth mentioning that Stevens's stanza just led me to that invitation. I've never tried it out before, and I came up with it as an experiment in bridging something that exists across time and space—a river—that can reference a shared feeling like desire and the particularities of our present moments within our local contexts. I pause to see where the makeshift exercise takes me, attempting to reorient my treatment of context as an educator, which has mostly been as a way to situate a text *within* a sociohistorical context. From that position, I stand outside a text, seeing how the social and cultural norms of the past manifest in the text and deepen my understanding of it. This is important work, for sure, but we see poetry inviting another orientation: to stand with(in) the text and feel times and places (contexts) collapse at their meeting points. This collapse foregrounds both historical patterns and the feelings that cut across times and spaces, leading us to a sense of connection. It is from this place of connection that we may be able to sense our futures more keenly and tend to the work that needs to be done today in our interconnected world/ local communities. With that in mind, I return to the river as languaged by Stevens and by Diaz—a river which need not be as far away as I first imagined. Perhaps it's our imagining that affects how close or far we are from this source of life.

When I think of rivers I have known, these words well up: deep brown, green, twig, flow, ripple, current, going and going, a leaf floating, carrying, not holding anything, shadow of trees, shadows of leaning humans tossing stones, river bank, family, river bed, pebbles, and so on. I like the internal rhyme that bounces between *river bed and pebbles* when they are near each other, so I linger there for a moment before turning to my current context.

Current context: kitchen—round wooden table, green plastic cup, tie-dyed bathing suit drying, six chairs—one almost broken, the sound of the kitchen timer, the smell of roasted broccoli, smell of sweet woods (the broccoli), the refrigerator's hum, and so on.

The river is moving. I bring this statement to my current environment, as I sit at my kitchen table: my partner's childhood kitchen table, with its cracked grooves, dry paths once flowing with conversation, or deadened by heavy silences. Where am I as I write, now, of rivers? Sudden landscapes emerge from the table, and I track the dried-up rivulets with my fingers.

I begin the bones of a potential poem:

If the river holds nothing, carries only
its body, deep & shallow, wanting & going
nowhere with a fallen leaf, how long

will the cup's curved handles
casting a shadow on my kitchen table
last? How long will its water?
The table's wood, parched, cracks deeper,
broken by its memories of a family
blind to the river bed and pebbles
tossed by an empty hand. Still
I hear the kitchen timer singing.
It must be singing.

I try listening again to the flying blackbird. To the moving river. I look for a relationship between the two. I fold in something sensed in Diaz's lines. Invent a possibility.

We invite you to consider other ways of reorienting your present moment to explore another dimension of time and space. Maybe you begin with the river. Maybe with the blackbird. Maybe with the blackboard streaked with clouds—the one you've been meaning to wash.

Endangered Blackbirds: Encountering Our Present Tense

A sudden swerve away from the beauty and flow of the river to address our harsh ecological reality that entangles with the river's survival. A reality embodied by ongoing wildfires, floods, and droughts across the planet, diminishing ecosystems, and the disappearance of species. According to the website *Our World in Data*, within the last 5 centuries alone more than 900 species have gone extinct. We are waist deep—no, full body deep—in an ecological crisis, and it appears very likely our own species will become extinct, perhaps sooner than we imagine. The blackbird must be flying. It also must by dying.

Part of what has contributed to this devastating reality is the separations we humans have created and reproduced between ourselves and nature, treating the natural world not as an essential part of who we are as humans but as something to be used, commodified, and profited from. Each of us has a responsibility to the future. As poets and educators, ours may be a matter of what we make, how we teach, and what we do with our knowledge, resources, and contexts. Response-ability: an ability to respond, something each of us has. What you say and how—and how you read and listen to what others are saying— is, in some sense, everything. There can be no right action without responsiveness and no responsiveness without listening. When we listen to our environmental crisis, perhaps through the words and actions of the Extinction Rebellion movement, or of young activists Greta Thunberg, Autumn Peltier, and Zeena Abdulkarim, we cannot not respond. We may respond through our own form of "ecopoetry," loosely defined as poetry with an ecological message and based on a belief in connections between the writing of poetry and the environments we create, and/or we may respond through other forms of activism that may or may not be rooted in our literacy practices. Either way, we invite you to reorient your literacy practices toward a listening-with-others to our planet and the role of our species. Where might that listening carry you?

Experience this poem by writer and editor Hila Ratzabi, author of the chapbook *The Apparatus of Visible Things* (2009). The poem was first published in *About Place*:

Of the Veritable Ocean

I trace the jagged residue

        with my feet

    The sand

presses grains to skin

    and I press back so the sand

        feels wanted

Waves fall

    like the word *what*--

    What what

        is happening

to me?

    And *how*

how how will all

    my creatures go?

Who by oil, who

    by bomb

Who by storm

    Who by dry land by famine

Who by *what*

    what water

I feel the people

    wade and wallow

into my open throat

I cough a question

    and swallow it back

Which one of you

    can hear me?

Water pools around my feet

    singing *you you*--

        but *who*?

As Ratzabi notes in a reflection about the poem, which she created for the Avodah Institute for Social Change, "I remember the sensation that inspired the poem . . . I was standing at the shore and looking at the jagged line in the sand left by a receding wave, tracing it with my toes. This physical act became an invitation to contemplate my relationship to the earth at that moment" (H. Ratzabi, personal communication). She offers a related writing exercise titled "Listening to the Earth's Call" rooted in ecopoetry's invitation to see the human as part of the natural world and to ask,

> Who am "I" as speaker in relation to the voices that arise from the natural world? *Exercise:* Go to a natural area alone, whether a beach, forest, lake, mountain, or other location. Explore the surroundings mindfully with all your senses, looking, listening, touching, until something feels like it is calling to you. It might be the texture of tree bark, the sound of waves, the movement of an insect, the play of light among leaves. Stay with this object/experience/sensation until a sound, image, or word arrives to you. Follow its lead. What is the earth trying to say to you and through you? Try to remove your "self" as speaker and make space to allow the object or sensation to speak.

Where have you located a truth about your species and your relationship to the natural world? In what common pleasure, curiosity, or experience?

From my kitchen in Philadelphia, I listen again to the flying blackbird and its relationship to the moving river. I want to study something close to me, find a pattern, make of it a future thought form. This table, maybe.

Imagining Utopias

We begin this section with Jean Valentine's (2007) short poem "Mare and Newborn Foal" from her collection *Door in the Mountain: New & Collected Poems* (p. 250). Make a moment to read it and, as it probably goes without saying at this point in the book, to read it again.

Mare and Newborn Foal

When you die
there are bales of hay
heaped high in space
mean while
with my tongue
I draw the black straw
out of you
mean while
with your tongue
you draw the black straw out of me.

What do you make of the "black straw" in the poem's action, at the moment of death? Does this poem carry for you any tenderness, any hope, something else?

Something about this poem speaks to me of human connection and care, even though, as the title suggests, it is about a mare and newborn foal and, as the first line suggests, it is speaking about what happens when we/you die. I recognize in this poem a tenderness that I have both known and yearn for in my life—the "you" feels spoken to me, any reader who picks up and reads the poem, at this moment, and also to a reader who may know something of death, who perhaps carries a deeper insight into this experience. It reads to me as such a beautifully odd and quiet poem, as many of Jean's poems do. The fact of our mortality and the possibility of death involving "bales of hay/ heaped high in space" strike me as a reminder that our life, too, is what we make of and imagine it to be. What does it/could it mean to teach and write from this pared down place of tender exchange? Is the poem a strange, unsettling utopia we've entered?

The word "utopia" comes from the Greek "ou-topos," meaning "nowhere" or "no place"—echoing the Greek word "eu-topos," or "a good place." We need to imagine utopias, not as striving for perfection, but from an understanding that our acts of imagining have power to materialize worlds. History shows us the truth of this: Imagining a hierarchy of humans created the horrific realities of slavery and genocide. Imagining humans as higher than and separate from nature created environmental atrocities. Imagining religion created continued wars and divisions within our species. We need not look far to find history's ongoing demonstration of human imaginations creating brutal systems, unlivable environments, ongoing violence, and deeply unequal social structures. At the same time, art/literature continues to show us the capacities of human imagination to resist those structures and create new ones—worlds whose beauty depends on an acceptance of human flaw/accident/error, as the Japanese wisdom of wabi-sabi teaches us, and whose sense of beauty cannot be separated from a sense of justice (Elaine Scarry, 2000, *On Beauty and Being Just*). As Scarry argues, beauty and justice have an interconnected relationship; beauty moves us to recognize an "esthetic of fairness" that is also an "ethical fairness" (p. 109) and decenters us through a process of absorption. Perhaps it is in such moments of absorption encouraged by art/literature that we can more keenly sense the imbalances in our world and imagine alternatives.

Speculative poetry is a genre in itself, and one that overlaps with science-fiction, mythology, and various forms of fantasy writing. It can provide students a way to wildly imagine alternative worlds, realities, and dimensions in their writing. Though we do not focus on speculative poetry as a genre in this chapter, we want to emphasize how the power of imagination central to speculative poetry extends to everyday poetry writing practices, reminding us of the life-affirming work of the imagination. Jason Reynolds, in the interview with Krista Tippett of the podcast *On Being*, from 2020 referenced earlier, discusses the relationship between imagination and fortitude, arguing for the collective necessity of young people being able to activate their imaginations:

if, by the time you're out of high school, your imagination is shot, we're in trouble, bigtime. . . . But how does one keep an imagination fresh in a world that works double-time to suck it away? How does one keep an imagination firing off when we live in a nation that is constantly vacuuming it from them? And I think the answer is, one must live a curious life.

Reynolds connects this sense of living a curious life to poetry and what he calls "the alchemy of language" (how one word near another word makes someone feel), and to drawing from the resources of our lives: books read, conversations with friends, things noticed on a walk down a different route than usual, and so on. He suggests this sense of curiosity is crucial to our ability to recognize each other's humanity and create a just world: "What if you were to try to walk into a situation, free of preconceived notion, just once? Once a day, just walk in and say, 'I don't know what's going to happen, and let's see. Let me give this person the benefit of the doubt—to be a human.'" It seems to us an intuitive truth that a literacy practice invested in imagination contributes to a common good.

An Invitation

We invite you to watch Tim Morton's recent lecture on YouTube, from November 2020 during Covid, "Lockdown Is Reopening, Reopening Is Lockdown." Then, as an exercise, mobilize the same refrain ("Imagine. . .") and see where it takes you. Imagine a future you hope for. A future you can envision. A future that could repair our present. A future undoing the brutal realities we've created. Imagine that future. Imagine something that need not feel far away. Write a poem/litany that begins with "Imagine," working the power of repetition and its meditative qualities.

I try this exercise out myself:

Imagine no war.
Imagine enough food and flowers for everyone.
Imagine no nation. No tribe.
Imagine no "us" to preserve from the hatred of others.
Imagine a country made of static and wind.
Imagine the girl still alive, flicking her sharp wrists.
Imagine no piles of bodies and braids.
Imagine no trauma carried by offspring.
Imagine no notion of perfection.
Imagine the sheep taking over the empty streets
Imagine thousands of cicadas emerging from the ground.
Imagine a girl wanting to look like herself and not like the doll inside the box.
Imagine clear skies.

Once you've written your own list, pick one that feels particularly close to home and urgent. Maybe choose an "imagine" that is down to earth and tangible. Maybe it's an image that shouldn't need imagining. What poem might you make from it? Begin writing.

Put your poem aside for a moment, and turn to this poem "Imagine" by the incredible Kamilah Aisha Moon whose books *Starshine & Clay* and *She Has a Name* we urge you to read.

Imagine

after the news of the dead
whether or not we knew them we are saying thank you
       —W. S. Merwin

A blanket of fresh snow
makes any neighborhood idyllic.
Dearborn Heights indistinguishable from Baldwin Hills,
South Central even—
until a thawing happens and residents emerge
into the light. But it almost never snows in L.A.,
and snows often in this part of Michigan—
a declining wonderland, a place not to stand out
or be stranded like Renisha was.
Imagine a blonde daughter with a busted car
in a suburb where a brown homeowner
(not taking any chances)
blasts through a locked door first,
checks things out after—
around the clock coverage and the country beside itself
instead of the way it is now,
so quiet like a snowy night
and only the grief of a brown family (again)
around the Christmas tree, recalling
memories of Renisha playing
on the front porch, or catching flakes
as they fall and disappear
on her tongue.
They are left to imagine
what her life might have been.
We are left to imagine the day
it won't require imagination
to care about all of the others.

What have we become that we need to imagine this? Moon's poem leaves us with the devastating reality of racist seeing, born from a nation's imagination. Her poem "Imagine" is rooted in our present day. We (you, reader and I) need to "imagine the day it won't require imagination to care about all of the others." Return to your poem. Locate where it lives in relation to your everyday life and community.

An Invitation

Circle back to Stevens's poem. List thirteen ways of looking at the future, rooted in the poem you just wrote. Try bringing in your version of blackbirds and rivers, using them as symbols to animate your own imagining. Consider the role of hope and affirmation in your list. If you narrow your list to a short poem—a prayer of sorts—what is important to say? Danez Smith's poem provides a poignant example:

little prayer

let ruin end here
let him find honey
where there was once a slaughter
let him enter the lion's cage
& find a field of lilacs
let this be the healing
& if not   let it be

Note the simple pleasures in Smith's poem. Honey. A field of lilacs. How it speaks to finding beauty in the aftermath of violence or imminent danger through hope and healing.

The utopic impulse of our imaginations and what we allow ourselves to notice *do* important work even if they don't "fix" our world—and perhaps we need to release ourselves from the grandiose idea that art/poetry needs to be a solution to our problems. In a recent interview with the *Poetry Society of America* (2021), poet Maggie Smith speaks to the simple, earth-bound work of poetry: "Any world worth living in and fighting for is a world full of art. So we do our work, whatever it looks or sounds like, without expecting it to heal someone. We just do our work, and perhaps it will mean something to someone else, the way we find art that means something to us." The paradox may be the intensity of an impact free from *knowing* the effect of one's work—and in this way poetry's work seems to share a kinship with the butterfly effect. Who knows what ripples the flapping of wings—or the joining of two unlike things to make a metaphor—might do. A futures-oriented literacy practice, then, may be less about preparing our students for a future we claim to know than about giving them the tools and invitational prompts to do the necessary work of imaginative shaping.

Dear Future

In 2018, artist Jessica Houston invited me to contribute to her project "Letters to the Future" (2019). She describes the project as follows on her website:

Letters to the Future is a photograph, video and sound installation based on an actual time capsule buried in an Antarctic glacier in 2019, containing letters written to the future. No one from the present has seen the letters, except the authors themselves. . . . Letters to the Future uses images, sounds, ice and text—the words in the ice, and those spoken by the contributors—as materials. This affirmative, collective gesture provokes consideration of our present and the possibilities for our future.

I remember sitting at my desk, gazing out the window at the synagogue across the street, as I wrote my letter to the future—a letter that only I, at least in my lifetime, would ever read. The exercise prompted pedagogical questions for me that I had not considered. *What does it mean to write something to be read far into the future, even if that writing may never be read, or read in a way that I cannot even recognize? What is my relationship to the future—1,000 years or longer past my lifetime—as a writer and reader of poetry? As a teacher? And what might the meeting of words and glacier do to the words, to the glacier?* I am brought back to some of the ideas and questions raised in our chapter on more-than-human materialities, thinking again about the form of the classroom, its existing material nature and the future forms it might take on, depending, maybe, on how we teach, read, and write.

An Invitation

Consider for a moment your own letter to a future you won't be alive to experience. What would you write and how? Try this exercise with your students and collectively bury or sink your letters for a future unearthing. When I was a high school student, we wrote letters to our future selves—a kind of prediction of who we will become as "adults"—and buried them in a time capsule. Houston's prompt, on the other hand, invites us to write to and for a future far beyond our lifetime, and in this sense, we leave ourselves behind to reach an imagined reader in a world we will never know. Something about writing to the future 1,000 years from now feels different from writing to an older version of myself (the person I desire myself to become), even though the exercises share a kinship in their orientation. Writing my "letter to the future" provoked me to consider what message I wanted to carry and leave in a world, even though I will personally never experience that future.

Wording as Worlding

If you were to express the words "I love you" to someone, but had to use an image to substitute it for those words, what would you say? A clichéd image might be a dozen roses and a Valentine's Day heart. Let's break away from cliché and come up with our own wild alternatives. When you think of "love" what specific memory or association comes to mind?

I love you = mint leaves boiling into tea

I love you = a plate of dates and cashews set out at exactly 3:00 each afternoon

I love you = a swarm of red ants sharing the last crumb

I love you = one hand giving another hand a soft tickle on the walk to school

As processes of reading and writing teach us, there is no *what* we say that lives apart from *how* we say it. The *how* shapes the *what*. "I love you" may seem like an innocuously good thing to say to someone, but it can become a meaningless phrase depending on how it is said and the relationship behind the saying. It can become an empty cliché, a saying of something that means nothing without the action, tone, and demonstration of love behind the words.

I remember one of my most inspiring teachers in graduate school, the poet Suzanne Gardinier, offering us "the orchard" as an alternative to "I love you," prompting us to come up with our own languaging of this feeling beyond cliché. She provoked us to find and articulate our own "how" to express love. That expression comes to life when rooted in our everyday world.

Turn for a moment to the opening lines of Aracelis Girmay's poem "You Are Who I Love" and seek out her amazing books: *Teeth*; *Kingdom Animalia*; and *the black maria*.

You Are Who I Love

You, selling roses out of a silver grocery cart

You, in the park, feeding the pigeons
You cheering for the bees

You with cats in your voice in the morning, feeding cats

You protecting the river You are who I love
delivering babies, nursing the sick

You with henna on your feet and a gold star in your nose

You taking your medicine, reading the magazines.

You looking into the faces of young people as they pass, smiling and
saying, *Alright!* which, they know it, means *I see you, Family. I love you.
Keep on.*

You dancing in the kitchen, on the sidewalk, in the subway waiting for the
train because Stevie Wonder, Héctor Lavoe, La Lupe

You stirring the pot of beans, you, washing your father's feet

How would you continue this poem? Who is the "you" you love—for what actions, what noticed vibrancy? Reading Girmay's poem, I am in those scenes, seeing those spotlighted "yous" and recognizing something of the people I know in them. Images, experiences, and associations spring to mind. Reading her poem, I feel inspired to continue the list, to keep the declaration of love for "You" going. Maybe this way: *You walking into the classroom, seeing your students for whom they are and what they love. You reading and writing a poem.*

An Invitation

Images can invite alternative possibilities for wording what we love about the world. We invite you to return to Stevens's poem—all its stanzas—and create a tarot card deck for the images in that poem. For example: blackbird, tree, river, thin man, golden bird. Use each image/card to inspire a poem that tells the future. In other words, let the deck you made from those images be a springboard for future readings. It might be joyful to create this deck collectively with your students, each person contributing one card/image, and then distributing the cards at random to each contributor to inspire a poem.

Wording as worlding. We loop back to our opening statements in this book: How we assemble our words on the page, the tone that assemblage invokes, is an act of worlding. *Assemblage as thought, form as future* becomes a way for us to reorient our literacy practices toward speculation, hope, and affirmation—toward a future we may feel in our present moment, perhaps when we are most present. There are no ladders arriving to this future, no reading levels determining achievement. Instead a recursive, speculative, and imaginative shaping that becomes the poem arriving at the page and the thoughts, feelings, images form in the reader's mind-heart.

We leave you with "Toward Midnight" by poet Jean Hartig (author the chapbook *Ave, Materia* 2008), which evokes a sense of love that we cannot put into words:

Toward Midnight

The hour we've left each other
you and I held within this sliver
of dark earth. Net of concern fractures
among the low roofs, far towers cradling
cells of light. Pure interiority.

Will dos, I love yous, anxious tasks
in the absence of light to draw them, those
articulated sorrows collapse.

Protection here, where all across
the faded land, sea of surfaces
our costumes more familiar, post capital
post performance. Swerving dreams
of children and animals.

Fold of their quilt
comfort of their star.

I have chosen to be alone.
This hour I lie between
the mirror of my choices
and the window that reports:
   You are standing in a field, you are a fog
    among the others.

I tell myself:
  Listen. Your listening will wind you
   into the earth.
Your listening will gather you above it
will collect in you states even lighter
than this, cool sheet designed to hold you.
Collected lightness, pale pink.

Children with their paths unordered
wild provinces shifting, their spinning maps.
How fragile, I can't help but think
one star mirroring another
hour over hour to this.

Where boundaries of my station in the world collapse
human again, small, pulsing and sufficient.

Poem as Gratitude and Gift Giving

During my first semester as a doctoral student at Teachers College, I took Ruth's doctoral seminar, which ended with an act of gift giving. Each member of the class (including Ruth, the teacher) arrived on our last day with a gift for each person. The gifts were small and, for the most part, did not cost much, if anything. A note on a piece of paper. A piece of fabric. Chocolate. A pencil case with pencils. A stone. A bookmark. Neon Post-it notes. We left class that day with abundance—gifts from all, tiny tokens, treasured thoughts, a piece of each person in the class. As I remember this moment, I wonder about the relationship to gift giving as an expression of gratitude and poetry.

Around seven years later I taught "Studies in Poetry" for the first time at Moore College of Art & Design. I decided to write my final comments on student work as haiku and to present the haiku as gifts, selecting the special paper on which to paste each typed poem. As I wrote each haiku, I thought about each student's writing that semester—the images and moments that stuck out to me. The form required me to keep it brief, and I stayed true to the three-line and 5/7/5 syllable count formal convention of the haiku. I tried to distill what I needed to say as precisely as possible—such a change from my habit of writing long-winded comments to my students! I worried about how my students would receive the haiku. *Am I saying enough about their work? Do they expect me to say more?* They expressed joy and surprise at their "final comments"/haiku, and received it as a gift, commenting on how meaningful it was for them. I realized that up until that point, I had never thought to communicate with my students through poetry. Why can't poetry also be a method for feedback or critique? Why not embody a practice of poetry in more dimensions of our literacy exchanges as teachers and students?

Poetry can also take on the form of an expression of gratitude to students. Victoria Restler, interdisciplinary artist and Assistant Professor of Educational Studies at Rhode Island College, wrote this poem for her students at the end of the semester during the pandemic in fall 2020.

Poem for Seventeen Humans and the Space We Built Together during a Time We Never Could Have Imagined

Thursday a few minutes before six
Like a gravitational pull
To a place that's not a place

Watching names and then faces appear,
Reshuffling squares
Boxes get smaller until we're all here-
complete.
Each of us meant to be, each of us holding up the walls of our space that's more
  like a feeling.

We move into the rhythms that are ours,
Undulating from big groups to small to big
Talking and wondering, cursing, cracking up
Riding the bicycle of this still new *we* that we have made and keep making
like a huge collective fingerprint.

Some of us have never seen others of us below the shoulders
And sometimes in the sky climb of belly laughter there is also a piercing loss
For the world, yes,
But also for the absence of knowing each other in the thickness of three
  dimensions-
The missing snack table we might crowd around gingerly pouring chips into a
  paper cup;
The air we don't share and the way it might change when we pushed all the chairs
  to the edge of the room to stand in a circle
Or when someone opened their heart.

And then here we are again.

Pulled back as the clock nears six.

Wondering in the intervening days if this space I can't see is real, really
    happened?

I arrive again tentative,

Popcorn bursts of black rectangles opening onto faces and homes.

And . . . yup, there it is.

Plain as day shifting ever earlier into night,

This unseeable space that we make and keep making

With our smiles and eyes and thoughts and hearts.

We must admit to ourselves truly that building an invisible home together is
    quite a feat.

We have done/ are doing this unlikely astonishing thing and we are astonishing.

And this wonder that is our unseeable home,

that is us,

Somehow pries open new space for the possibilities of other unlikely dreams and
    invisible towers.

What a way of synthesizing shared experience from a semester in a poem for the seventeen humans and space built together! This poem provokes a reorientation of poetry as an act of gift giving for and toward a future education. A making of a future space. A making inextricably linked to a tenderness expressed to our students, facilitated and beckoned by poetry.

We invite you to use poetry as a move to counter the logic of teaching as a direct act rather than as an act of communication with students. Think about it. When does poetry ever serve as the teacher in the room? This question echoes the book's first chapter, and we want to bring it here again, to emphasize our capacities as educators to "redistribute the sensible" of schooling practices. Consider all the possible purposes of poetry. When do we, as teachers, use our own poetry as gifts to students? When do we communicate to our students through poetry, speaking to issues that come up in class that we may never take up directly?

We end this section with an example of a poem to graduate students who were also teachers that Ruth wrote as a gift at the end of their semester together—a poem that we feel aptly closes a chapter on shaping and imagining different futures.

Enough Said

I have evidence that enough never seems enough
in teaching—Never enough—the room pregnant
with novels, with white boards, with questions and hands,

gasps of overfilled ideas overflowing. And you, dear ones,
do not have to stand on your heads, do not need bucketsful

of metaphors or beautiful fossils of syntax to perch on every
shoulder or thump against the heart. You have only to let
yourself imagine yourself like this poem, making yourself
anew as you go with them, these children, these futures, these
treasures. Paragraphs outlive their usefulness, but words spoken

moisten to maze the heart. Meanwhile opening upon themselves
without us, finally believing they illustrate themselves you can
believe in them, in you. Can you see through the dazzle? Can you
ferret the shapes from the shining? Can you swim through the shadow
map of illusion? Upstream the river? Forget what you failed to see
and stand in the winds of the tender world, standing on tiptoe for just
this moment in history to right and write the next sentences, the new
syntax for a world in need.

CHAPTER 13
REORIENTING PRACTICES

XIII
It was evening all afternoon.
It was snowing
And it was going to snow.
The blackbird sat
In the cedar-limbs.

---

[1]We leave you with this stanza, image, and the poem on the following page to create this Chapter 13 for yourself. See what you make of these three elements. Where does this particular assemblage orient you as a writer, reader, and teacher?.

Kindness

—Naomi Shihab-Nye

Before you know what kindness really is
you must lose things,
feel the future dissolve in a moment
like salt in a weakened broth.
What you held in your hand,
what you counted and carefully saved,
all this must go so you know
how desolate the landscape can be
between the regions of kindness.
How you ride and ride
thinking the bus will never stop,
the passengers eating maize and chicken
will stare out the window forever.
Before you learn the tender gravity of kindness
you must travel where the Indian in a white poncho
lies dead by the side of the road.
You must see how this could be you,
how he too was someone
who journeyed through the night with plans
and the simple breath that kept him alive.
Before you know kindness as the deepest thing inside,
you must know sorrow as the other deepest thing.
You must wake up with sorrow.
You must speak to it till your voice
catches the thread of all sorrows
and you see the size of the cloth.
Then it is only kindness that makes sense anymore,
only kindness that ties your shoes
and sends you out into the day to gaze at bread,
only kindness that raises its head
from the crowd of the world to say
It is I you have been looking for,
and then goes with you everywhere
like a shadow or a friend.

PART II
INVITATIONS

We offer a series of Invitations for your daily practice of writing. Curated here are examples that range from Invitations gifted to secondary and graduate students as well as teachers in professional development workshops. Often Ruth sends out these Invitations in the early morning to encourage a daily practice of noticing, attuning, and jotting—living a life with poetry in it! When circumstances make it possible, these Invitations are sent out for about two weeks before a class or workshop begins. The intention is to establish a daily practice and also to create a wellspring of daily writing that becomes the material to work with and from when the class or workshop begins. What we have learned is that the more we engage in these practices ourselves, the more agile and helpful we are to students. So, you might use these Invitations to develop a daily practice for yourself. In the spirit of this, we offer thirty Invitations that draw on various ways of attending and reorienting. Many are remixed versions of invitations offered in the preceding chapters, providing different points of access to the (re)orienting principles discussed. Often the material for these Invitations comes out of everyday experiences and the desire to attune to the world, notice more carefully, honor moments, large and small, as a way of paying attention: reflecting on books or events, moments of bewilderment, and pedagogical imaginings. We did not order these into categories deliberately. We invite you to write to these for the next thirty days, and then, you will have your own ways of thinking about how Invitations might be helpful to you—creating them for yourself and your students, and, more importantly, we encourage students to begin writing Invitation for each other once they have experience with the practice. These Invitations are not intended as "How To" examples but as ideas for expanding ways to encourage ourselves and our students to attune and attend to the world through poetry and writing.

•

Listen to the world around today—the rumble of wheels on the subway track, sounds in the hallway, a cell phone's ping nearby, or listen for new sounds that you may just not have noticed before. Tune your ear to sounds—a dog's bark outside your window, the sounds of keystrokes alive with possibility. Listen. What music do you hear? Listen again. The cries of injustices? A plea for help? The hum of something not quite nameable? Perhaps it's the rhythm of the words, cadences, or sounds that cause you to pay attention.

Gather the best of what you hear today, literal and figurative, in the pages of your notebook. Write from this Invitation or in any direction your mind or pen takes you. Attune to the world of sound for today. Listen. Hear.

•

The Rock Dove, also known as the common pigeon, has surface feathers of an almost cerulean shade of gray. It is a rat with wings, a garbage eater, a germ conveyor, an annoyance. But in those rare moments when we see it fresh, make the familiar strange, we might know it as an extraordinarily beautiful bird. Iridescence decorates its neck like a shining, ancient patina, a shard of stained glass, glowing rainbow green, spectral violets and shimmering yellow. And its mating courtship, a dance at once elegant and clown-like. Its call, a soft "who?" asks us to stop, pause, and wonder.

What exists in your daily routine that you walk past, forgetting to see the possibility within? Write, doodle, draw, capture lines, images, of questions in your new notebook in whatever way this Invitation or your day may take you.

•

As I write this Invitation, we still find ourselves in the grip of Covid even with edges of optimism for the days ahead. Other news brings grief and sadness as well as acts of strength and heroism. Behind it all are more visible understandings of injustices that are in tension with kindness and giving. This may leave us without ways to articulate our understandings, ways forward, or generative ways to take meaningful action. Ursula Le Guin (2001) writes: "One of the functions of art is to give people the words to know their own experience. There are always areas of vast silence in any culture, and part of an artist's job is to go into those areas and come back from the silence with something to say" (p. 101). It's one reason why we read poetry, because poets can give us the words we need. When we read good poetry, we might say, "yes, that's it," or "I had never thought of that before." Either way, we are provoked to think again.

Go into one of those areas of silence, a place difficult to put into words. Put your mind toward experiences, events, systemic injustices, a cultural phenomenon—moments that are hard to locate in words. Try! See where this takes you today.

•

Pablo Neruda wrote odes in everyday language about everyday things and people. By writing odes to the ordinary, he sought dignity for the commonplace. Perhaps we can use more dignity for all the commonplace now. Neruda's odes honor a wide array of objects, ideas, or people that/who we take for granted: socks, salt, the atom, a fall that resulted in an ode to his cranium; a friend, child, the woman who sits on a bench alone. There are also sardonic odes—for example, to literary criticism (we could ALL write that one!). If you read Spanish, find some original examples.

Look around you. Find one common, ordinary, and forgotten object and write an ode to it. Show your appreciation.

•

Take a moment to think about some-one, some-object, some-moment, some-current situation that you have not had enough time or have been unable to find the words to express what you are seeing, thinking, feeling, hearing, understanding (wherever the emphasis of that inability to express might reside). Rest a moment. Let that feeling, the person, the event, the object *live* in your mind/body for a few moments before you move to put this into words.

Then, start to write. Stutter. Hesitate. Mutter. Murmur. Create the web of generative understanding. Tell only part and resist telling too much.

•

Write a few lines of a poem in which you literally build and/or take apart something for your reader. Focus your attention on constructing or deconstructing your object, taking into account technical terms, instructions, perhaps even the source of your materials. The object you build or take apart may be small, like a computer mouse or nesting dolls, or it may be larger, like a house or a concept such as social justice. You may treat this very literally as Elizabeth Bishop does in her poem, "The Monument," or figuratively, as Carlos Drummond de Andrade does in his poem, "The Elephant," a work that creates an other-worldly animal from scraps and garbage. Both poems you can find readily online.

You may want to write some of the directions out first and then go back and compress to make it look like a poem or start with an intention of drafting a poem from the start.

•

Phosphorescence. Now there's a word that vibrates the tongue. Phosphorescence is a light within. Say the word over and over again. Phosphorescence. Phosphorescence. Feel in your mouth; let it tickle your tongue. Does it carry light? Sound? An experience—maybe you have happened upon phosphorescence in a cave, in a dark grove of trees? Now, write the word phosphorescence three times on a new page in your notebook. Allow the word to lead you to other words—a list of words that are triggered by phosphorescence? Words. Words. List words for at least five minutes. Don't censor. One word leads to another and maybe back to one you have listed before. Write it down a second time. A third. And on the list goes. Five minutes! That should generate a PILE of words!

Once you've exhausted yourself with words, take a look back and read the list aloud. Choose one. It is the first line of what will come next. And, then just keep writing either using the words on your list or let your first word, your first line, move forward into new words and thoughts.

•

Write a short poem in question-and-answer format. Ask a question in stanza one, and then answer it in the next stanza, or some variation? Continue the question-and-answer format throughout the poem. What if you go back after you have a draft and pay particular attention to the length of each stanza? To what effect might be consistency in number of lines of both questions and answers throughout the poem? To what effect might these stanzas vary in length?

Try a couple of different options. Or, collaborate with a partner and one of you will start with the question stanza and the other person write the answer stanza

●

Write about an idea, person, or situation that you think is misunderstood by many people. Then, take a few minutes to turn that writing into a first draft of a poem dedicated to that invisible audience whose assumptions you are arguing against, but with whom you want to create a "bridge of understanding."

Who are "they," what might you want to help them understand about your perspective through your writing, what might they say back to you, and how might you talk back to their viewpoints in ways that may not lead to agreement but lead to opening a dialogue for further conversation and perspective sharing?

●

The stars: chunks of ice reflecting the sun; lights afloat on the waters beyond the transparent dome; nails nailed to the sky; holes in the great curtain between us and the sea of light; holes in the hard shell that protects us from the inferno beyond; daughters of the sun; messengers of the gods; shaped like wheels; condensation of air with flames roaring through the spaces between the spokes. They sit in little chairs; are strewn across the sky; run errands for lovers; composed of atoms that fall through the void and entangle with one another

They are and they are . . . Keep writing about stars. . .

●

A group of larks is called an exaltation, while cheetahs cluster in a coalition. Crows in plural are known as a murder, and eagles come together as a convocation. Two or more ferrets make a fesynes. Put foxes side by side and you have a skulk. Humans form a clan (though more commonly known as family). Why are geese on the ground called a gaggle but in the air a sledge? What have I missed? The list goes on and on, from aerie to cast, badelynge to bloat. So what can you do with a fascinating menagerie? PLAY. A poem about "a pride"? A dialogue between "sedge" and "siege"?

Swarm or flock to this prompt if you are so inclined or prowl in any direction your mind and pen or keyboard or doodles take you.

●

Take time to capture a current moment in your *history* through as *detailed description* as you can muster. Is there a picture in your mind or a photograph that "holds" this moment for you or that speaks to you and provides a perspective on this moment? Is there something that has been said or repeated that stays with you? An image? Take time to write toward this moment through as much detail as you can, start in prose if helpful.

Now comes the challenge beyond capturing this moment in as much detail as you can. The *description* does the work of teaching the *History Lesson*. Make sense? Show don't tell. If it helps, the poem "History Lesson," by Natasha Trethewey, offers a provocative and powerful example of how to craft a history lesson as a poem.

•

Olivia Laing, in her 42-mile existential expedition recorded in *To The River: A Journey Beneath the Surface*, writes:

> There are sights too beautiful to swallow. They stay on the rim of the eye; it cannot contain them. . . . We talk of drinking in a sight, but what of the excess that cannot be caught? So much goes by unseen. . . . No matter how long I stayed outdoors, there was a world that would remain invisible to me, just at the cusp of perception, glimpsable only in fragments, as when the delphinium at dusk breathes back its unearthly, ultraviolet blue. (p. 30)

Try to capture what is too beautiful to swallow, what is almost there on the rim of the eye, the invisible, the cusps . . . maybe just listing a few phrases of such description or detail . . . the nearly ungrasp-able or unglimpse-able.

•

Draft a poem of nine lines that addresses itself to a relevant obsession of yours. Have at least three words, phrases, or lines that repeat at least four times throughout the poem.
Or
Draft a love poem that uses no words of endearment or adoration. Have fun. Enjoy a few laughs, a couple of frustrating moments, and some joy in what is revealed.

•

Rita Dove, in the Behn and Twitchell book of writing prompts we mentioned earlier, shares a little exercise that sounds simple. Write a poem about your mother's, relative's, friend's, or your kitchen. It helps if you actually draw the kitchen first, sketch it out.

Now to drafting the poem. Include an oven and something green and something dead in your poem. YOU are not in this poem, but someone—aunt, sister, close friend, stranger—must walk into the kitchen during the course of the poem.

•

Decide on a story that you feel the need to tell. Whether you start by narrating the story either verbally to someone else (or record on your phone) or simply write the first part of the story in prose, just get some of the images, details, feeling of the story in mind. If it is helpful, give it that "Once Upon a Time" start so you feel captured into the narrative moments of the story.

Then, take the story and try it in the form of a narrative poem—a poem that tells a story. Let's place some *creative constraints* on the poem:

(1) Pick a story you feel *the need* to tell.

(2) Make it clear in the poem that **you are telling the story to someone else or have that person the persona/narrator retelling your story**—somehow in reading your poem we know someone else is present or is retelling your story.

(3) Skip the build-up. That is, start in the MIDDLE OF THE STORY.

(4) Sweat the small stuff. Details, images, sounds—the story is alive and in the moment.

(5) No moral at the end.

•

Make a flat assertion. There are fairly easy to make: "I like yogurt. Today is Monday. I love you. I see a horse." What if you keep the tone of the matter-of-fact but add a twist? Write about the FANTASTIC (assertion of something definitely fantastical) in a matter-of-fact way, using flat assertion and perfectly plain description. Recreate a slow-paced, highly detailed, matter-of-fact relating of a fantastic event—say, the horse that is in our list of assertions above is suddenly galloping through a museum filled with . . . well, you get the idea. Humor, elements of the fantastic, abrupt juxtapositions, surprise—all the tools used in magical realism. The matter-of-factness is potentially what makes the fantastic unsettling.

You get the idea. Let your imagination run you headlong into this moment of writing.

•

I was thinking this morning about the meaning of the word *ancestor*. What comes to mind for you? Who is the first person, collective or what is the saying, ritual, myth, or object that you conjure with the word "ancestor"? So many ways to bring to life *ancestor*. Write whatever comes to mind for a few minutes.

Stop, write a first line for a poem, and keep bringing to life *ancestor*. When you are curious or need a mentor whispering in your ear, check out Jimmy Santiago Baca's "Ancestor" online.

•

A simple box. A little dreaming of what makes you who you are. I was reminded in reading Kimiko Hahn's "The Dream of a Lacquer Box" this morning of how the material informs her ways of expressing her identities, desires, histories. For now: a simple box. A little of you dreaming. Just what from your life, your culture, your family history. your identities *might* you place in this box to pass on to someone else.

Yes, you might work by setting a creative restraint on the SIZE of the box, its location, to whom it is offered, or use it as a holding place, a metaphor, for the parts of you to pass on. Hahn's poem is available online if you are curious to see her dreaming although I'd suggest working on your own poem first.

•

Dwell for a little time on a painting, a photograph, a sketch, a tapestry, a dreamcatcher—some image that draws you back to it often in your mind's eye as memory. Take time to capture the memories of this if you do not have physical access to it. Either way, find a focal point. Stay with it.

Now, create a poem that recreates this object through textures, shapes, colors. One more thing to complicate this. *What IF* the speaker in the poem (the persona) is the thing itself?

•

Imagine poetry in numbers. What's a number that everyone should know—personal, historical, philosophical—allow for no limits in where you locate your numbers. Check out Lucy Ives's "Early Poem" as she may challenge your way of thinking about numbers.

Now, communicate the story of this number or numbers in a poem.

•

Take time to think about the resources of language, spacing, punctuation, lineation, stanza breaks, and other ways in which we can create *silences* in a poem. This Invitation is intended to attune you to the resources of silence available as we craft silences. Spend a few minutes grazing a few of the poems you have written and see where you are nudged into quiet, silence, a moment to pause. Make a list, if helpful, of potential spaces where you might want to create more reverberation, echo, silences.

Then, choose one poem you have been working on and *double* the effects of silences, pauses, and quiet spaces already in the poem. Compare the EFFECT of the use of silence in your two draft poems.

•

Evidently F. Scott Fitzgerald came to believe that poetry no longer sells, but he believed in the power of poetry and indicated that his aim was to make *The Great Gatsby* a kind of prose poem. Let's dismiss the old binary. Maybe, we could learn to see how poetry is in prose and prose in poetry—only as and if we can learn to see, listen, and create one in the other.

Take a piece of prose that you have found exceptionally beautiful, memorable, poetic. No creative constraints—just *prose it* into poetry. Or, take a piece of your own prose writing and find the poem in it!

•

Forms provide us with ways to understand the resources of language and structure, so it might be interesting for you to take a poem that you have in-progress or a prose piece will work as well. The idea here is to see how it changes in emphasis and meaning if SHAPED into a particular form. Many poets indicate that they learn craft, resources of language, and structures by working with forms. So, here, you are invited to try a PANTOUM. You have probably read several poems that are Pantoums but may not recognize it by name as much as by its form. Find examples of Pantoums online and spend a few minutes examining how form (don't look at a definition of form but read several poems to speculate for yourself) influences the effect. Here are examples of Pantoums that are online: "Fortune's Pantoum" by Jane Shore, "Pantoum" by Joyce Carol Oates, "Pantoum" by John Ashbery, "Market Day" by Marilyn Hacker, and "Amnesia" by David Lehman. A Pantoum uses a **four-line stanza** in which **lines 2 and 4** are carried over, whole, to the next stanza where they become **lines 1 and 3**. You write new **lines 2 and 4** that both fit into the stanza and will be carried over into the next stanza. **The poem can be of any length and the final lines 2 and 4 are in fact lines 3 and 1 of the very first stanza.** This creates a tidy closing of the circle. Whew! Complicated, right?

Take a minute to write the line scheme on a piece of paper, so that you see what type of effect a Pantoum has by its formal use of repetition—not sounds, individual words, images, but in FULL lines. Just think for a moment what the effect of this might yield. The design:

Line 1

Line 2

Line 3

Line 4

Line 5 (repeat of line 2)

Line 6

Line 7 (repeat of line 4)

Line 8

Last stanza:

Line 2 of previous stanza

Line 3 of first stanza

Line 4 of previous stanza

Line 1 of first stanza

Now take one of your drafts of a poem and see what or if you can work it as a Pantoum. No matter how you solve the technical problems of carrying over whole lines, you resort to some form of word play—subtle and not so subtle transformations of your lines. Here are some of the possibilities: as you repeat the line you change nothing, or you change nothing but the punctuation, or you change the tense of a verb, or a noun goes from plural to singular, or you substitute words, or you use homonyms . . . or, or, or. Enjoy a day of repetition!

•

Inventory-ing: Take a few minutes and just read through some of your starts of poems. Read (aloud if you can) and let your own language seep back through you. I assume these are not finished pieces, but fragments—jottings or beginning drafts of a poem. If you have had time to do some form of daily writing, you have a substantial "body" of starts or middlings or maybe a finished draft or two for now. Just read through.

Go back and SCAN what you have written until your eyes settle on a phrase, a line, a stanza that makes you pause, causes you to smile, or be satisfied. Stop there. Take a deep breath. Pull out a line or two as the start of a new burst of writing and just write for ten minutes and see where that takes you. One version of this might be to write for ten minutes, reading it again, taking a line or phrase from it and writing out of that for another ten minutes, and repeat.

•

Take stock of your poems-in-progress or think of a particular event, mood, or experience that you would like to capture as poem. If you are working from a poem-in-progress, start at the end and make your way in reverse (really seeing and feeling the moving back over and over finding those little details not needed in moving forward). The tiniest of details may be what captures or surprises the meaning of *de lo reverso*. If you work from a completely new idea for this poem, you might find it helpful to stop and list, draw, or doodle the backwardness as a way of capturing pacing, imaging the reverse feeling of all that makes the poem. If helpful, take a look online at the wonderful poem by Victor Cruz "El Poema de lo Reversa."

•

How might you get nearer to something, to someone, to some feeling or emotion through language, image, figures? Experiment with creating nearness by taking a poem you are working on and collapsing the distance between speaker and subject, in viewpoint, or change the speaker to be in the middle of the description, images, or subject of the poem.

•

Take a few minutes to dive in, fiddle with a draft of a poem you are working on, not in to finishing, but into more drafting. It's an impulse. It just must be done with the spirit of play and not censorship. Let what-if possibilities and the *mind's maybe* reverberate in your wonderful and overfilled brain cavity all day.

●

This morning take a few minutes to play that movie in your head of some conversation, activity, exchange with family, a friend, an exchange with your pet, or the site of a deer in the yard—something yesterday that spoke to you, that causes you to (re)member this now, again this morning. Take a minute. Run the movies of yesterday in your mind. Forward. Reverso. Find in all this a space for gratitude. Then, write a *Letter as Poem* to that person, animal, hummingbird, sunset. In this classical movie version the letter is sent but never actually received. Title your poem "Letter to_____," Unsent and date it.

●

Finale. Endings are sometimes beginnings, so you are the author of these Invitations from now on. My morning practice of composing them, arising to look ahead at the day, steaming cup of coffee next to me, staring out the window contemplating this daily practice of inviting you—to what? This becomes a daily practice for me as it does for you. How do Invitations gather, orient, and shape attention? I hope these Invitations have or will at some point be helpful reminders to you about a life with poetry in it. Taking a moment to see, listen, hear, find the beginning of a day, a moment, an event, an emotion.

So, on this final, ending of Invitations from us, we invite you to begin by writing your own Invitations.

PART III
RESOURCES FOR TEACHERS
Diana Liu and Ashlynn Wittchow

Diana Liu and Ashlynn Wittchow curated this dynamic collection of resources that have supported them as they guide their students through meaningful poetry experiences. Diana is currently a 9–12 English teacher in a New York City public school, serves as a mentor to pre-service teachers, a private educational consultant, and an ELA curriculum developer within the Department of Education. Ashlynn serves as a professional development coach at the Center for Professional Education of Teachers. Prior to joining the Teachers College community, Ashlynn taught middle and high school English in South Carolina. As English teachers, Ashlynn and Diana enjoy weaving poetry across their curriculum. Both are pursuing their PhD in English Education at Teachers College, Columbia University.

They write:

This carefully curated collection is intended to assist teachers with the resources they need to plan as they invite students into poetry experiences. Covering a range of potential pedagogical needs, these resources are organized into a number of categories, including our narrative reflections as educators, sample student writing, websites, social networks, publication resources, and other collaboratives for further exploration. We offer this assemblage of resources in the hope that it will help teachers cultivate their identities as creative writers and create dialogic spaces of poetry transaction and transformation for their students.

Teacher Resources

Teacher as Reader

In this section, teachers can find resources designed to expand their library of poetry. Ranging from specialized archives to massive poetic databases, these resources were selected with the teacher as reader in mind.

Materials for Teachers from the Academy of American Poets—https://poets. org/materials-teachers

The Academy of American Poets offers resources for teachers through their *Teach This Poem* initiative, including poetry, primary sources, and a set of classroom activities. Furthermore, the *Resources for Teachers* tab hosts a comprehensive poetry glossary, select reading guides, discussion questions, essays, and anthologies.

Presidential Inaugural Poetry from the Catbird Seat Blog—https://blogs.loc.gov/catbird/2017/01/poetry-and-the-presidential-inauguration/

Presidential Inaugural Poetry explores the history of poetry and the presidential inauguration, including links to poems and archival video from each of these high-profile poetry readings.

Poetry Resources from Google Arts and Culture—https://artsandculture.google.com/

Google Arts and Culture connects the public with cultural artifacts from museums and cultural organizations around the world. Through these partner institutions, teachers can use Google Arts and Culture to access interactive virtual exhibits that merge art, poetry, and history.

***MAPS: Modern American poetry site*—https://www.modernamericanpoetry.org/dashboard**

Curated by the Department of English at University of Illinois and the Department of English at Framingham State University, the MAPS archive connects poetry with criticism and media.

The *Learn* Tab from Poetry Foundation—https://www.poetryfoundation.org/learn

The Poetry Foundation's *Learn* tab offers Poem Guides, which provide helpful historical, biographical, and structural commentary. The tab also offers resources for teens, including podcast episodes, video resources, and poem samplers.

***Poetry in Motion* by the Poetry Society of America—https://poetrysociety.org/poetry-in-motion**

Founded in 1992, Poetry in Motion © is a public arts program that places poetry in transit systems, inviting educators to consider how they could implement similar projects in motion within their own spaces.

***Resources for Educators* from The Favorite Poem Project—http://www.favoritepoem.org/**

The Favorite Poem Project was founded by Robert Pinsky, the 39th Poet Laureate of the United States. Pinsky offers guidance for teachers who wish to host their own school-wide poetry events, including the *Resources for Educators* tab, which hosts lesson plans for teachers.

The American Verse Project by the University of Michigan Humanities Text Initiative—https://quod.lib.umich.edu/a/amverse/

Born from a collaboration between the University of Michigan Humanities Text Initiative and the University of Michigan Press, the American Verse Project hosts an "electronic archive of volumes of American poetry prior to 1920." The archive includes a diverse range of poets, including works authored by African American and women poets.

"Poetry 180" and "From the Catbird Seat: Poetry & Literature" by the Library of Congress—https://blogs.loc.gov/catbird/

This blog shares poetry and literature resources alike, drawing from the extensive resources of the Library of Congress. Categories include information on the Poets Laureate program, as well as a Teacher's Corner, where educators can find suggested resources and activities from the Library of Congress.

The Scottish Poetry Library—https://www.scottishpoetrylibrary.org.uk/learning/

The Scottish Poetry Library is a "national resource and advocate for the art of poetry, and Scottish poetry in particular." The Education tab of the Scottish Poetry Library includes Learning Resources, Advice for Poets and National Poetry Day information.

Poets' Corner—https://www.theotherpages.org/poems/

Since its creation in 1994, Poets' Corner has hosted over 7,300 works by 800 poets. In addition to Author indexes, the Poets' Corner also includes additional materials like essays centered on National Poetry Month.

Australian Poetry Library—https://www.poetrylibrary.edu.au/home

A joint initiative of the University of Sydney and the Copyright Agency Limited, the Australian Poetry library hosts over 42,000 Australian poems.

Teacher as Writer

In this section, teachers will find resources that focus on the teacher as a poet. Including writing workshops and literary festivals, this section covers regional and national poetry workshops.

North America

Kundiman—http://www.kundiman.org/

Dedicated to "nurturing generations of writers and readers of Asian American literature," Kundiman offers online classes, regional writing groups, retreats, and mentorship opportunities for emerging writers of poetry.

Bard Institute for Writing and Thinking—http://writingandthinking.org/

The Bard Institute for Writing and Thinking offers a variety of programs devoted to helping teachers "develop writing practices that enliven classroom learning through writing."

Dodge Poetry Festival—https://www.dodgepoetry.org/

A four-day celebration of poetry, the Dodge Poetry Festival has been widely acknowledged as the largest poetry event in North America. Teachers and students have access to free programming via the Education Pass program, which gives full access to all festival livestreams and videos from the event.

Cave Canem: A Home for Black Poetry—https://cavecanempoets.org/

Cave Canem was founded in 1996 to "remedy the under-representation and isolation of African American poets in the literary landscape." In addition to lecture and master class series, Cave Canem offers community workshops at little to no cost to emerging poets.

Poetry in America Courses—https://www.poetryinamerica.org/about-us/

Created by Harvard professor Elisa New, Poetry in America offers online courses for undergraduates, graduate students, high school students, and educational practitioners.

The National Writing Project—https://www.nwp.org/

The National Writing Project is made up of "a network of teachers, university faculty, researchers, writers, and community educators who work to advance writing and the teaching of writing."

Mass Poetry: https://masspoetry.org/professionaldevelopment

Geared toward high school teachers, Mass Poetry offers summer professional development opportunities for teachers interested in the "the teaching of poetic craft and technique." The program offers professional development credits, which can be used toward recertification.

The Community-Word Project—http://communitywordproject.org/what-we-do/

The Community-Word Project offers professional development sessions tailored to the needs of each group, "with a particular focus on innovative ways to strengthen collaborative, creative expression and literacy skills."

The Tanka Society of America—http://www.tankasocietyofamerica.org/home

The Tanka Society of America was founded in 2000 to share the history and form of *tanka* poetry. They offer a Tanka Teachers Guide, which contains further resources about tanka poetry.

United Kingdom

The Ledbury Poetry Festival—https://www.poetry-festival.co.uk/about-the-festival/about-ledbury/

The Ledbury Poetry Festival takes place annually each summer in Ledbury, England. In 2021, the Ledbury Poetry Festival celebrated its twenty-fifth year with its first hybrid poetry festival, offering events both livestreamed online and in-person.

StAnza, Scotland's International Poetry Festival—https://stanzapoetry.org/

StAnza hosts its annual poetry festival each spring in St. Andrews, Scotland. In 2021, StAnza hosted a hybrid festival, and many of the "online talks, exhibitions, installations, and films and more" are still available online in StAnza's online Events Archive.

Lyra: Bristol Poetry Festival—https://www.lyrafest.com/

The annual Bristol Poetry Festival hosts local, national, and international poets each year in Bristol, England, and includes "poetry readings, slam competitions, poetry film screenings, poetic walking tours, digital media, discussion panels, open mics, lectures and more."

Australia

Perth Poetry Festival—https://wapoets.com/perth-poetry-festival/

Taking place in September each year, Perth Poetry Festival supports professional development through "workshops, seminars, panels and networking opportunities."

Japan

The Asian Conference of Arts & Humanities—https://acah.iafor.org/dvteam/haiku-workshop/ / https://acah.iafor.org/ (main website)

The Asian Conference on Arts & Humanities is organized by The International Academic Forum and brings people together from different cultural backgrounds to present on research. The conference hosts an annual workshop regarding teaching others the history of haiku and engaging people in readings as well as opportunities to create haikus under haiku scholars.

Teacher as Teacher

In this section, teachers can find resources dedicated to *teaching* poetry. Centered on poetry and pedagogy, these resources include links to professional organizations for teachers as well as curriculum tools.

Mark Nowak's Worker Writers School: Mobile Unit—https://creative-capital. org/projects/worker-writers-school-mobile-unit/

> The Worker Writers School offers poetry workshops directly to the working class by providing workshops near areas such as bus stops, construction sites, and other locations to provide brief poetry writing classes.

Poetry resources **from the National Council of Teachers of English—https://ncte. org/resources/poetry/**

> The National Council of Teachers of English offers Poetry Resources for teachers, including interviews with poets, poetry themed journals, poetry books, links to lesson plans from ReadWriteThink, and blogs written by NCTE members and staff.

Split This Rock (Poetry for Activism)—https://www.splitthisrock.org/

> Split This Rock advocates how poetry can be used as an agent of change. This organization offers poetry workshops, readings, festivals, community collaborations, and opportunities for publication.

The National Association for the Teaching of English Poetry Portal— https://www.nate.org.uk/poetry/

> Hosted by the UK-based National Association for the Teaching of English (NATE), the poetry portal includes a wealth of resources and opportunities for the English teaching community, including news, opportunities, poetry publications, and other resources for educators.

Literature and Language by *TEDEd*—https://ed.ted.com/search?qs=poem

> TEDEd includes numerous videos on literary topics, including recorded slam poetry, author biographies, poetry explications, mini-lectures about poetic forms, and traditional TED Talks.

The Poetry Society Education Resources—https://poetrysociety.org.uk/education/

> The Poetry Society's *Education* tab includes numerous resources of interest to teachers worldwide, including poetry lesson plans from PoetryClass as well as resources for young poets through the Young Poets Network and the Foyle Young Poets of the Year Award.

Student Resources

Student as Reader

Designed with the adolescent reader of poetry in mind, this section focuses specifically on poetry anthologies and collections for young poets.

Poetry for Teens—https://poets.org/poetry-teens

The Academy of American Poets has curated an anthology of poetry specifically for adolescent readers. It includes blog posts and interviews with advice for young poets in addition to other recommended reading, anthologies, and essays.

Young People's Poet Laureate—https://www.poetryfoundation.org/learn/young -peoples-poet-laureate

The Poetry Foundation hosts the Young People's Poet Laureate. At the time of writing, Naomi Shihab Nye is the Poetry Foundation's Young People's Poet Laureate, and the site hosts poetry, readings, and monthly suggested book picks for young readers from Naomi Shihab Nye.

Kweli Journal—http://www.kwelijournal.org/kweli-teen

Kweli is an online journal that celebrates lived experiences within communities of color. They offer online poetry written by teens to be experienced and opportunities for students to serve as editors, readers, and mentors.

Student as Writer

In this section, we provide resources where students are positioned as writers of poetry. The following resources focus on opportunities for publication and writing resources for adolescent poets.

The Student Press Initiative by *The Center for Professional Education of Teachers*—https://cpet.tc.columbia.edu/student-press-initiative.html

The Student Press Initiative connects teachers with publication coaches to implement project- and inquiry-based curricula with students culminating with student publication.

TeenInk Magazine—https://www.teenink.com/

TeenInk Magazine is a website and teen magazine for student publication opportunities in creative work ranging from writing, photos, and art. *TeenInk* offers numerous publication opportunities for teens "everything from love and family to school, current events, and self-esteem."

Scholastic Arts and Writing Competition—https://www.artandwriting.org/

The Scholastic Arts and Writing Awards offer students in grades 7–12 opportunities to publish their work in twenty-eight different categories of art and writing. There are also opportunities for direct scholarship and awards for recognition at the secondary level and college.

The Adroit Journal—**https://theadroitjournal.org/about/submissions/**

> The journal hosts the Adroit Prizes for Poetry and Prose for secondary and undergraduate writers. It also hosts summer writing workshops and a mentorship program that pairs experienced writers with students grade levels 9–12 who are interested in learning more about the creative writing process.

Ember Journal—**https://emberjournal.org/**

> The journal mostly focuses on entries of poetry, short fiction, flash fiction, and creative nonfiction from writers from ages ten to eighteen. They also offer special opportunities for teachers and the entire classroom community should educators feel inspired to create an entire class submission.

The Kenyon Review—**https://kenyonreview.org/workshops/young-writers-online/**

> Kenyon Review offers the Patricia Grodd Poetry Prize for Young Writers opportunity for high school sophomores and juniors. The Kenyon Review also offers summer writing workshops for young writers (around the ages of sixteen to eighteen) who desire to develop their craft.

New York Times Writing Resources—**https://www.nytimes.com/2018/11/15/learning /out-of-the-classroom-and-into-the-world-70-plus-places-to-publish-teenage -writing-and-art.html**

> *The New York Times* published a collection of over seventy places where students can submit their writing.

Student as Teacher

This section here recognizes students' value as educators of poetry and, as a result, offers resources of spoken word and oral performance opportunities for students.

Poetry by Heart—**https://www.poetrybyheart.org.uk/**

> Based in the UK, Poetry by Heart hosts a national poetry recitation competition for UK-based students. Teachers outside of the UK can access the gallery of poems, videos of past performances, and anthologies organized by grade-level.

Poetry Out Loud—**http://poetryoutloud.org/**

> Poetry Out Loud hosts poetry recitation competitions for high school students and offers free educational materials, including sample lesson plans, videos of past performances, contests, and resources for both teachers and students.

Power Poetry—https://powerpoetry.org/

> Power Poetry offers student opportunities for SLAM poetry and advice on how to write poetry under a specific theme.

Hip-Hop Youth Conference at TC—https://laurenleighkelly.com/hip-hop-youth-con ference

> The Hip-Hop Youth Conference (HHYRA) annual conference offers students workshop activities, performances, and presentations led by high school and college students. There are also leadership opportunities for students to serve on the HHYRA Youth Leadership board.

Alt-Text as Poetry—https://alt-text-as-poetry.net/

> This is a poetry collaboration that incorporates technology and amplifies "disability media and culture." They offer workshops to schools and focus on the needs of blind and low-vision people.

Public Art Saint Paul's Sidewalk Poetry—https://publicartstpaul.org/project/poetry /#about_the_project

> Sidewalk Poetry allows residents to produce poetry on sidewalks and to feature diverse poets in their Sidewalk Poetry Competition. Though local to St. Paul, their approach may inspire similar community-based projects.

Poetry Like Bread—https://www.bowerypoetry.com/bread

> This website focuses on the ghazal poetry form during the time of the pandemic and beyond. It features a collaborative poem revolving around bread and introduces the ghazal poetry form to others.

Closing Invitation

Poetry experiences—like other encounters with art—have the power to nourish us as readers, writers, and thinkers. Commenting on poetry as art, Alexander Potebnya writes, "Poetry, as well as prose, is first and foremost a special way of thinking and knowing" (p. 83). Though this list of resources is far from comprehensive, we hope that they serve as inspiration, feeding teachers and students alike with rich, poetic experiences. Through the sharing of poetry across its multimodal possibilities, we invite others to our experiences of the world and the word. Through shared creation, we also invite our readers to expand and understand our collective experiences and the nuances within through a continual love and exploration of poetry.

REFERENCES

Acevedo, E. (2017). For the poet who told me rats aren't noble enough creatures for a poem. *Beastgirl & other origin myths*. YesYes Books.

Ackerman, D. (2011). *The rarest of the rare: Vanishing animals, timeless worlds*. Vintage.

Adichie, C. (2009, July). The danger of a single story [Video]. *TED*. https://www.ted.com/talks/chimamanda_ngozi_adichie_the_danger_of_a_single_story/transcript?language=en

Adorno, Theodor. (1983). Cultural criticism and society. In *Prisms*, Translated from German by Samuel and Shierry Weber (pp. 17–34). MIT Press.

Alexie, S. (2011, May 9). The Facebook sonnet. *The New Yorker*. https://www.newyorker.com/magazine/2011/05/16/the-facebook-sonnet

Ali, A.S. (2002). Ghazal. *Rooms are never finished*. W. W. Norton and Company Inc.

Atwood, M. (1983). *Murder in the dark: Short fiction and prose poems*. Coach House Press.

Babbitt, G. (2018). *Appendices pulled from a study on light*. Spuyten Duyvil.

Babbitt, G. (2021). *The lost son*. Unpublished manuscript.

Baca, J.S. (1990). Ancestor. *Immigrants in our own land and selected early poems*. New Directions Publishing Corporation.

Bachelard, G. (1994). *The poetics of space*. Beacon Press.

Baldwin, J. (1998). Freaks and the American ideal of manhood. In T. Morrison (Ed.), *Baldwin: Collected essays* (pp. 814–829). Library of America.

Barad, K. (2007). *Meeting the universe halfway: Quantum physics and the entanglement of matter and meaning*. Duke University Press.

Barthes, R. (1975). *The pleasure of the text* (R. Miller, Trans.). Hill and Wang.

Basho, M. (1688). *[I come weary]* (W. G. Aston, Trans.). Poets.org. https://poets.org/poem/i-come-weary

Bassiri, K. (2019). *99 names of exile*. Newfound.

Bassiri, K. (2019) Homecoming. *Shenandoah, 68*(2). Retrieved August 30, 2021, from https://shenandoahliterary.org/682/homecoming/.

Behn, R. & Twichell, C. (1992). *The practice of poetry*. William Morrow Paperbacks.

Beltre, M. & DuVerney, O. (2020–2021). *Inspired by 'what is left'* [Exhibition]. Prospect Park, New York, NY. https://www.bricartsmedia.org/art-exhibitions/inspired-what-left

Bennett, J. (2010). *Vibrant matter: A political ecology of things*. Duke University Press Books.

Bervin, J. (2016). *Silk poems*. http://www.jenbervin.com/index.php?p=projects/silk-poems

Biehl, Jaõo. (2013). *Vita: Life in a zone of social abandonment*. University of California Press.

Bishop, E. (1939). The monument. *Poems*. Farrar, Straus and Giroux.

Bohr, N.H.D. (1963). *The philosophical writings of Niels Bohr. Vol. 1. Atomic Theory and the Description of Nature*. Ox Bow Press.

Bowery, Poetry. (2020). "Poetry like bread" ghazal. *Bowery Poetry*. https://www.bowerypoetry.com/bread

Bradbury, R. (2012). *The illustrated man*. Simon & Schuster. (Original work published 1951).

Brinkema, E. (2014). *The forms of the affects*. Duke University Press Books.

CAConrad. (2014). *ECODEVIANCE: (Soma)tic for the future wilderness*. Wave Books.

CAConrad. (2015). *Slaves of hope live only for tomorrow*. Poetry Foundation. https://www.poetryfoundation.org/poems/58067/slaves-of-hope-live-only-for-tomorrow

CAConrad. (2020). *JUPITER ALIGNMENT: (Soma)tic poetry rituals*. Ignota Books.

References

CAConrad. (2021). *(Soma)tic poetry rituals*. Poet CAConrad. http://somaticpoetryexercises .blogspot.com/

Cage, J. [jdavidm]. (2007, July 14). John Cage about silence [Video]. *YouTube*. https://www .youtube.com/watch?v=pcHnL7aS64Y (Original work published 1952).

Chavez, F.R. (2021). *The Anti-Racist writing workshop: How to decolonize the creative classroom*. Haymarket Books.

Chu, D. (2021). *Cemetery picnic*. Bennington Review. https://www.benningtonreview.org/issue -nine-chu

Clifton, L. (1993). Won't you come celebrate with me. *Book of light*. Copper Canyon Press.

Codjoe, A. (2020). *Blood of the air*. Northwestern University Press.

Codjoe, A. (2020). *Bluest nude*. Milkweed Press.

Codjoe, A. (2021). *Anything with eyes*. Unpublished manuscript.

Collins, B. (1988). Introduction to poetry. In *The apple that astonished paris: Poems* (p. 58). University of Arkansas Press.

Collins, B. (1996). Marginalia. *Poetry*, *167*(5), 249–251. Retrieved July 26, 2021, from http://www .jstor.org/stable/20604700

Collins, B. (2002, September 6). *The names*. The New York Times. https://www.nytimes.com /2002/09/06/opinion/the-names.html

Croggon, A. (2002). Silence broke my mouth. *Attempts at being*. Salt Publishing.

Cruz, V.H. (2001). El poema de lo reverso. *New and selected poems 1966–2000*. Coffee House Press.

Cummings, E.E. (2002). Silence. *95 poems*. Liveright.

Davis, M. (2020). *Singularity*. Poets.Org. https://poets.org/poem/singularity-0

Dawes, K. (2007). *And What of the Haiku?* Poetry Foundation. https://www.poetryfoundation .org/harriet-books/2007/03/and-what-of-the-haiku

Dawes, K. & Kinsella, J. (2020) *From "a coda to history."* Poems. https://poets.org/poem/coda -history

Deleuze, G. (1990). *The Logic of Sense* (C.V. Boundas, Ed.) (M. Lester, Trans.). Columbia University Press.

Deleuze, G. (1998). *Spinoza: Practical Philosophy*. City Lights Books.

Deleuze, G. & Guattari, F. (1987). *A thousand plateaus: Capitalism and schizophrenia* (B. Massumi, Trans.). University of Minnesota Press.

Diaz, N. (2020). From the desire field. *Postcolonial love poem*. Graywolf Press.

Dickinson, E. (1958). Letter 459a. In T. H. Johnson (Ed.), *Emily Dickinson: Selected letters*. Harvard University Press. (Original work published 1876).

Dickinson, E. (1998). Much madness is divinest sense - (620). In *The Poems of Emily Dickinson: Variorum Edition*. Harvard University Press. (Original work published 1862).

Dickinson, E. (1998). I heard a fly buzz - when I died -. In R.W. Franklin (Ed.), *The poems of Emily Dickinson: Reading edition*. Harvard University Press. (Original work published 1896).

Dickinson, E. (1999). 'Hope' is the thing with feathers. *The Poems of Emily Dickinson* (R.W. Franklin, Ed.). Harvard University Press. (Original work published 1891).

Dickinson, E. (2016). *Envelope poems*. (J. Bervin & M. Werner, Ed.). New Directions.

Diggs, L. N. (2013). *The originator*. Poetry Foundation. https://www.poetryfoundation.org/ poems/56494/the-originator

Dove, R. (1980). Adolescence II. *Yellow house on the corner*. Carnegie Mellon University Press.

Drummond de Andrade, C. (2015). The elephant. *Multitudinous heart* (R. Zenith, Trans.). Farrar, Straux and Giroux.

Ellams, I. (2020, May). Fuck time. *POETRY*, 121.

Fiebelkorn, I.C., Pinsk, M. A. & Kastner, S. (2018). A dynamic interplay within the frontoparietal network underlies rhythmic spatial attention. *Neuron*, *99*(4), 842–853.e8. https://doi.org/10 .1016/j.neuron.2018.07.038

Forché, C. (1993). *Against forgetting: Twentieth-century poetry of witness*. W.W. Norton.

Francisco, R. (2017). Silence. *helium*. Button Poetry.

Frost, R. (1920, December) Fire and ice. *Harper's Magazine*. https://harpers.org/archive/1920/12/fire-and-ice/

Frost, R. (1972). The figure a poem makes. In E. Lathem & L. Thompson (Eds.), *Robert Frost: Poetry and prose* (pp. 394–395). Holt, Rinehart and Winston.

Gallagher, T. (1986). Sing it rough. In *A concert of tenses: Essays on poetry* (p. 83). University of Michigan Press.

Gallas, J. (2014, July 15). *Translation Tuesday: Selections from Anna Akhmatova's "requiem."* Asymptote. https://www.asymptotejournal.com/blog/2014/07/15/translation-tuesday-selections-from-anna-akhmatovas-requiem/

Gardinier, S. (2008). *Today: 101 ghazals*. Sheep Meadow Press.

Gardinier, S. (2011). *Iridium & selected poems 1986–2009*. Sheep Meadow Press.

Gardinier, S. (2021) *Some Manhattan rivers*. Unpublished manuscript.

Gay, R. (2013). Ode to drinking water from my hands. *Exit, 7*(2).

Gay, R. (2015, April 30). *A small needful fact*. Split This Rock. https://www.splitthisrock.org/poetry-database/poem/a-small-needful-fact

Girmay, A. (2007). *Teeth*. Curbstone Books.

Girmay, A. (2011). *Kingdom animalia*. BOA Editions, Ltd.

Girmay, A. (2011). Ode to the little "r." *Gulf Coast: A Journal of Literature and Fine Arts, 23*(2).

Girmay, A. (2011). *The black maria*. BOA Editions, Ltd.

Girmay, A. (2017). *You are who I love*. Split This Rock. https://www.splitthisrock.org/poetry-database/poem/you-are-who-i-love

Goodreaux, M.M. (2019). The appetizers that ate us. *Black jelly*. Fly by Night Press.

goodrum, m. (2013). *definitions uprising*. NYQ Books.

goodrum, m. (2015). *Lament for a son of the Oyate*. Unpublished manuscript.

goodrum, m. (2019). *Something sweet & filled with blood*. Great Weather for Media, LLC.

Griffiths, R.E. (2019). *Elegy, surrounded by seven trees*. Poets.Org. https://poets.org/poem/elegy-surrounded-seven-trees

Griffiths, R.E. (2020). *Seeing the body*. W.W. Norton & Company.

Guerra, Y. (2021). *Mushroom Haiku*. Unpublished manuscript. https://yeseniaguerra.com/

Hahn, K. (2012, May). *The dream of a lacquer box*. Poetry. https://www.poetryfoundation.org/poetrymagazine/poems/55546/the-dream-of-a-lacquer-box

Hanh, T. N. *Cloud in each paper*. Awakin. https://www.awakin.org/read/view.php?tid=222

Haraway, D. (1988). Situated knowledges: The science question in feminism and the privilege of partial perspective. *Feminist Studies, 14*(3), 575–599. https://doi.org/10.2307/3178066

Haraway, D. (2016). *Staying with the trouble: Making kin in the chthulucene*. Duke University Press Books.

Hartig, J. (2021). *Toward midnight*. Unpublished manuscript.

Hartman, C. (2015). The pianos. *Verse: An introduction to prosody*. Wiley-Blackwell.

Hartman, C. (2021). *Same*. Unpublished manuscript.

Hayes, T. (2018). *American sonnets for my past and future assassin*. Penguin Books.

Heaney, S. (1999). Blackberry-Picking. *Opened ground: Selected poems 1966–1996*. Farrar, Straus, and Giroux.

Heijinian, L. (2000). Materials (for Dubravka Djuric). In *The language of inquiry* (pp. 161–176). University of California Press.

Higginson, T. W. (1891, October). Emily Dickinson's letters. *The Atlantic*. https://www.theatlantic.com/magazine/archive/1891/10/emily-dickinsons-letters/306524/

Hiss, T. (2010, September 1). *Wonderlust*. The American Scholar. https://theamericanscholar.org/wonderlust/

References

Hoagland, T. (2013, April 11). Twenty little poems that could save America. *Harper's Magazine.* https://harpers.org/2013/04/twenty-little-poems-that-could-save-america/

Hong, C.P. (2006, July 31). *How words fail.* Poetry Foundation. https://www.poetryfoundation .org/articles/68629/how-words-fail

Hong, C.P. (2020). *Minor feelings: An Asian American reckoning.* One World.

Hong, M.P. (2002). *To be the poet.* Harvard University Press.

Houston, J. (2015). Light on sound [Exhibition]. Latimer House Museum, New York, NY.

Houston, J. (2019). Letter to the future [Exhibition]. Occurrence Gallery, Montréal, Canada.

Houston, J. (2021). News. *Jessica Houston.* https://www.jessicahouston.net/news

Howe, F. (1998). *Lecture on Bewilderment.* Personal Collection of F. Howe, Small Press Traffic at New College, San Francisco, CA.

Howe, F. (2003). *The wedding dress: Meditations on word and life.* ProQuest Ebook Central. https://ebookcentral-proquest-com.tc.idm.oclc.org

Howe, M. (2019). *Singularity.* Poets.Org. https://poets.org/poem/singularity

Hugo, R. (1979). *The triggering town: Lectures and essays on poetry and writing.* W.W. Norton & Company.

Ives, L. (2013). Early poem. *Orange roses.* Ahsahta Press.

Jones, S. (2015, January 19). *A poet's boyhood at the burning crossroads.* The New York Times. https://opinionator.blogs.nytimes.com/2015/01/19/a-poets-boyhood-at-the-burning -crossroads/

Kant, I. (1987). *Critique of judgement* (W. Pluhar, Trans.). Hackett Publishing Company. (Original work published 1790).

Keats, J. (1958). Ode to a Grecian urn. In H. W. Garrod (Ed.), *The poetical works of John Keats* (2nd ed.). Clarendon P. (Original work published 1820).

Keith, R. (2021). *Miss dishes' dementia goes shopping.* Unpublished manuscript.

Keith, R. (2021). *Voyager 2.* Unpublished manuscript.

Kentridge, W. (n.d.). The centre for the less good idea. *The centre for the less good idea is an interdisciplinary incubator space for the arts based in Maboneng.* Johannesburg. https:// lessgoodidea.com/about

Kingston, M.H. (2002). *To be the poet.* Harvard University Press.

Knight, E. (1986). *The essential Etheridge Knight.* University of Pittsburgh Press.

Komunyakaa, Y. & McClung, L. (2020). *From "trading riffs to slay monsters."* Poems. https://poets .org/poem/trading-riffs-slay-monsters

Laing, O. (2011). *To the river: A journey beneath the surface.* Canongate Books.

Le Guin, U. (2001). Coming back from the silence. In C. Freedman (Ed.), *Conversations with Ursula K. Le Guin* (pp. 92–103). University of Mississippi Press.

Lewis, R.C. (2016, February 25). *The race within erasure.* [Lecture]. Literary Arts. https://literary -arts.org/archive/robin-coste-lewis-2/

Liebegott, A. (2019, March 19). *Road trip: Marie Howe.* The Believer. https://believermag.com/ logger/road-trip-marie-howe/

Lorca, F.G. (2007). Theory and play of the duende. *Poetry in translation* (A.S. Kline, Trans.). https://www.poetryintranslation.com/PITBR/Spanish/LorcaDuende.php

Lorde, A. (2000). Poetry is not a luxury. In M. McQuade (Ed.), *By herself: Women reclaim poetry* (pp. 364–367). Graywolf Press.

Lund, C. (2016, May). *Laurie Anderson: Advice to the young.* Louisiana Channel. https://channel .louisiana.dk/video/laurie-anderson-advice-young

Massumi, B. (2002). *Parables for the virtual: Movement, affect, sensation.* Duke University Press.

McKittrick, K. (2021). *Dear science and other stories.* Duke University Press Books.

Merwin, W. S. (1993) Separation. In *The Second Four Books of Poems* (p. 15). Copper Canyon Press.

Miller, C. (2021). *His short story*. Unpublished manuscript.

Miller, C. (2021). *Viable*. Lily Poetry Review.

Moon, K. A. (2014, February 3). *Imagine*. Poem-a-Day. https://poets.org/poem/imagine

Mullen, H. (2002). Dim lady. *Sleeping with the dictionary*. University of California Press.

Museum for Preventative Imagination [MACRO - Museo per l'Immaginazione Preventiva]. (2020, October 30). *TIMOTHY MORTON, lockdown is reopening, reopening is lockdown* [Video]. Streaming Service. https://www.youtube.com/watch?v=0WFqp09mikk&ab_channel=MACRO-Museoperl%27ImmaginazionePreventiva

Myers, C. (1974). *Wings*. Scholastic Press.

Neruda, P. (1990). *Selected Odes of Pablo Neruda*. (M.S. Peden, Trans.). University of California Press. (Original work published 1904–1973).

Neruda, P. (1994). Ode to Things. *Odes to Common Things* (K. Krabbenhoft, Trans.) (p. 11). University of California Press.

Neruda, P. (2001). *The book of questions* (W. O'Daly, Trans.). Copper Canyon Press.

Neruda, P. (2009) Ode to the onion. *Full woman, fleshly apple, hot moon*. Harper Perennial Modern Classics.

Neruda, P. (2017). *All the odes: A bilingual edition*. Farrar, Straus and Giroux.

Nezhukumatathil, A. (2003). Red ghazal. *Miracle fruit*. Tupelo Press.

Niccolini, A.D., & Pindyck, M. (2015). Classroom acts: New materialisms and haptic encounters in an urban classroom. *Reconceptualizing Educational Research Methodology*, 6(2). https://doi.org/10.7577/rerm.1558

Olds, S. (2016). *Odes*. Knopf.

Oliver, M. (1994). *A poetry handbook*. Mariner Books.

Ovid. (2004). *Metamorphosis* (D. Raeburn, Trans.). Penguin Classics.

Paglia, C. (2006). *Break, blow, burn*. Pantheon Books.

Panchy, J. (2021). *Erasure*. Unpublished manuscript.

Pancy, J. (2021). *Spring*. Unpublished manuscript.

Pandemic Poems Project. (2020). *Pandemic poems x PSNY collaboration*. Pandemic Poems. https://www.pandemicpoems.org/pandemic-poems-x-psny

Paz, O. (1979). Wind, Water, Stone. *The collected poems of Octavio Paz, 1957–1987*. New Directions Publishing Corporation.

People's Poetry Poetry Gathering - Poem Towers. (2001). *People's poetry poetry gathering - poem towers*. https://web.archive.org/web/20120306144919/http://www.peoplespoetry.org/pg_spotlighttwr.html

Phillips, T. (1973). *Humument*. Tom Phillips. https://www.tomphillips.co.uk/humument

Pindyck, M. (2017). Teaching literacy as and through erasure. *The English Journal*, 106(5), 58–63.

Pindyck, M. (2020, May). Ode to the subway door's scratches. *Seneca Review*, 50(1), 70.

Plath, S. (2013). *The bell jar*. Harper Perennial Modern Classics. (Original work published 1963).

Poetry Foundation. (2021). *Ghazal*. Poetry Foundation. https://www.poetryfoundation.org/learn/glossary-terms/ghazal

Poetry in Translation. (n.d.). *Sappho: Selected poems and fragments*. https://www.poetryintranslation.com/PITBR/Greek/Sappho.php

Poetry Society of America. (2021). *Stopping by with Maggie Smith*. Poetry Society of America. https://poetrysociety.org/features/stopping-by/stopping-by-with-maggie-smith

Potebnya, A. (1905). *Notes on the theory of language*. Kharkov.

Pound, E. (1926). In a station of the metro. *Personae*. New Directions Publishing Corporation. (Original work published 1916).

Pound, E. (1960). Vorticism. *Gaudier-Brzeska: A memoir*. New Directions Books. (Original work published in 1916).

References

Proctor, A. (Host). (2016, February 25). Robin Coste Lewis (Rebroadcast). [Audio podcast episode]. In Literary Arts. Literary Arts. https://literary-arts.org/archive/robin-coste-lewis -rebroadcast/

Ramazani, J. (2009). *A transnational poetics*. University of Chicago Press.

Rancière, J. (2004). *The politics of aesthetics: The distribution of the sensible* (G. Rockhill, Trans.). Continuum International Publishing Group.

Rancière, J. (2010). *Dissensus: On politics and aesthetics* (S. Corcoran, Trans.). Bloomsbury Academic.

Ratzabi, H. (2009). *The apparatus of visible things*. Finishing Line Press.

Ratzabi, H. (2014, July). Of the veritable ocean. *About Place Journal, 3*(1). Retrieved August 30, 2021 from https://aboutplacejournal.org/issues/enlightened-visions/water-blood-being/hila -ratzabi/

Restler, V. (2020). *Poem for seventeen humans and the space we built together during a time we never could have imagined*. Unpublished manuscript.

Retallack, J. (2004). *Poethical wager* (1st ed.). University of California Press.

Rich, A. (1995). *What is found there: Notebooks on poetry and politics*. Virago.

Rich, A. (2009). *A human eye: Essays on art in society, 1997–2008*. W. W. Norton & Company.

Riggs, S. (2010). *60 textos*. Ugly Duckling Presse.

Riggs, S. (2019). *From the nerve epistle by Sarah Riggs*. The Poetry Project. https://www.2009 -2019.poetryproject.org/from-the-the-nerve-epistle-by-sarah-riggs/

Riggs, S. (2021). *The nerve epistle*. Roof Books.

Rilke, R.M. (1954). *Letters to a young poet* (M.D.H. Norton, Trans.) (Rev. ed.). Norton.

Rilke, R.M. (1982) Turning point. In S. Mitchell (Ed.), *The selected poetry of Rainer Maria Rilke* (S. Mitchell, Trans.) (pp. 133–135). Random House. (Original work published 1912).

Rilke, R. M. (1995). The archaic torso of Apollo. In S. Mitchell (Ed.), *Ahead of all parting: The selected poetry and prose of Rainer Maria Rilke* (S. Mitchell, Trans.) (pp. 67–68). Random House, Inc.

Ritchie, H. & Roser, M. (2021). *Extinctions*. Our World in Data. https://ourworldindata.org/ extinctions

Rosenblatt, L. (1964). The poem as event. *College English, 26*(2), 123–128. https://doi.org/10.2307 /373663

Ruefle, M. (n.d.) On Erasure. *Quarter After Eight, Volume 16*. https://www.ohio.edu/cas/quarter -after-eight/table-contents

Scarry, E. (2000). *On beauty and being just*. Princeton University Press.

Scott, J. (2020, October 22). Florida could see a sea turtle baby boom—thanks to pandemic. *National Geographic News*. https://www.nationalgeographic.com/travel/article/florida-could -see-a-sea-turtle-baby-boom-thanks-to-pandemic

Sealey, N. (2021). 'Pages 1–4,' an excerpt from *The Ferguson Report: An erasure*'. Poem-a-Day. https://poets.org/poem/pages-1-4-excerpt-ferguson-report-erasure

Shakespeare, W. (1609). *My mistress' eyes are nothing like the sun (Sonnet 130)*. Poets.org. https:// poets.org/poem/my-mistress-eyes-are-nothing-sun-sonnet-130

Shihab-Nye, N. (1995). *Words under the words: Selected poems*. Eighth Mountain Press.

Silverman, T. (2009). *Houses are fields*. Louisiana State University Press.

Silverman, T. (2021). *Orphan letter*. Unpublished manuscript.

Silverman, T. (2021). *Season's ghazal*. Unpublished manuscript.

Simic, C. (1971). Stone. *Dismantling the silence* (p. 59). G. Braziller.

Simon, R. (2009). *Marginal road*. Hollyridge Press.

Simon, R. (2021). *Explaining the offsides rule*. Unpublished manuscript.

Simon, R. (2021). *In praise of queer coaches*. Unpublished manuscript.

Skinner, J. (2001). *Ecopoetics no. 1: Winter 2001*. Periplum Editions.

Smith, D. (2019, December 18). *Two poems*. The Offing. https://theoffingmag.com/poetry/two
-poems-4/

Smith, D. (2017). Little prayer. *Don't call us dead*. Graywolf Press.

Smith, T.K. (2018). Declaration. *Wade in the water*. Graywolf Press.

Snaza, N. (2019). *Animate literacies: Literature, affect, and the politics of humanism*. Duke
University Press Books.

Snyder, G. (2021). *A dent in a bucket*. Unpublished manuscript.

Spahr, J. (2011). *Well then there now*. Black Sparrow Press.

Stafford, W. (1962, March). Vocation. *Poetry, 99*(6). Retrieved August 30, 2021 from https://www
.poetryfoundation.org/poetrymagazine/browse?contentId=28963

Stafford, W. (1998). *Crossing unmarked snow: Further views on the writer's vocation* (P. Merchan,
& V. Wixon, Ed.) University of Michigan Press.

Stein, G. (2012). *Stanzas in meditation: The corrected edition* (S. Hollister & E. Setina, Eds.).Yale
University Press.

Stevens, W. (1923). Tea at the Palaz of Hoon. In *Harmonium* (p. 111). A.A. Knopf.

Stevens, W. (1942). Of modern poetry. In *Parts of a world* (pp. 105–106). A.A. Knopf.

Stevens, W. (1954) Man carrying thing. In *The collected poems of Wallace Stevens* (p. 350). Alfred
A. Knopf.

Stevens, W. (1954). Thirteen ways of looking at a blackbird. *The collected poems of Wallace
Stevens*. Alfred A. Knopf. (Original work published 1928).

Stevens, W. (1965). *The necessary angel: Essays on reality and the imagination*. Vintage.

Stevens, W. (1982). Notes toward a supreme fiction. In *The collected poems* (pp. 403–404).
Vintage Books Random House.

Stevens, W. (1996). 279 - To L. W. Payne, Jr. In H. Stevens (Ed.), *Letters of Wallace Stevens* (pp.
250–252). University of California Press. (Original work published 1928).

Stevens, W. (1996). 396 - To Hi Simons. In H. Stevens (Ed.), *Letters of Wallace Stevens* (pp.
346–350). University of California Press. (Original work published 1940).

Sutton, R. (2014). Toni Morrison: Write, erase, do it over [Interview]. *American Artscape
Magazine*. https://www.arts.gov/stories/magazine/2014/4/art-failure-importance-risk-and
-experimentation/toni-morrison

Svalina, M. (2010). *Destruction myth: Poems*. Cleveland State University Poetry Center.

Tippett, K. (Host). (2016, July 28). Before you know kindness as the deepest thing inside...
[Audio podcast episode]. In *On being: The on being project*. https://onbeing.org/programs/
naomi-shihab-nye-before-you-know-kindness-as-the-deepest-thing-inside/

Tippett, K. (Host). (2020, June 25). Jason Reynolds: Imagination and fortitude. [Audio podcast
episode]. In *On being: The on being project*. https://onbeing.org/programs/jason-reynolds
-imagination-and-fortitude/

Toomer, J. (1923). *Storm ending*. Poetry Foundation. https://www.poetryfoundation.org/poems
/53986/storm-ending

Toomer, J. (2011). *Cane*. Liveright New York. (Original work published 1923).

Trethewey, N. (2000). History lesson. *Domestic work*. Graywolf Press.

Valentine, J. (2007). Mare and newborn foal. *Door in the mountain: New and collected poems,
1965–2003* (p. 250). Wesleyan University Press.

Vinz, R. (2021). *As spiders make webs: Constructing sites for multidisciplinary learning*.
Unpublished manuscript.

Vuong, O. (2016, May 30). *Surrendering*. The New Yorker. https://www.newyorker.com/magazine
/2016/06/06/ocean-vuong-immigrating-into-english

Watson, G. (2014). *A philosophy of emptiness*. Reaktion Books.

Weiss, J. (2008). Personal reflection: Finding theory. In J. Anyon (Ed.), *Theory and education
research: Toward critical social explanation* (pp. 75–80). Routledge.

References

Whitman, W. (1892). Songs of Myself. *Leaves of grass*. David McKay Philadelphia.

Wordsworth, W. (1995). The world is too much with us. *Wordsworth poems*. Alfred A. Knopf. (Original work published 1807).

Wright, J. (1992). The jewel. *Above the river: The complete poems* (Reprint Ed.) (p. 122). Farrar, Straus, and Giroux.

Yeats, W. B. (1989). The second coming. In R.J. Finneran (Ed.), *The collected poems of W.B. Yeats*. Scribner Paper Fiction. (Original work published 1920).

Young, M. (2008). *Sidewalk poetry*. Public Art Saint Paul. https://publicartstpaul.org/project/poetry/#about_the_project

Yuhas, D. (2021, March 9). Year of the pandemic: How have birds and other wildlife responded? *Audubon*. https://www.audubon.org/news/a-year-pandemic-how-have-birds-and-other-wildlife-responded

INDEX

Index

Index

Index